"Homesteading" today can be anything from fixing up an inner city townhouse to starting in the middle of nowhere with just a piece of newly acquired land. The author did it the latter way, but much of what appears here can be used by anyone, any age, in any similar situation, anywhere.

THE LAND (freely translated to mean any piece of real estate), how to find it, best places to look, dealing with the owner, loans and mortgages, how to get the most with almost no out-of-pocket cash is logically covered in minute detail first.

RECYCLING AN OLD HOUSE from the foundation and underpinnings to the roof, including siding, windows, doors, plumbing, wiring, and insulation helps get any kind of building in shape fast.

BUILDING WITH NATURAL MATERIALS shows how to create a log cabin, stone or sod hut, adobe shelter, or semi-permanent tepe whether for year 'round living or as a get-away-to place.

GARDENING AND FARMING indoors or outdoors, the Churchill way, with helpful tips on the organic method brings forth the freshest vegetables, fruits, and the nicest decorative plants to brighten tastes or views.

All this, and more, in 17 sod-busting, door-opening chapters detailing:

TOOLS AND HOW TO USE THEM-including care under varying conditions and sharpening tips

THE WATER STORY-finding drinking water, purification techniques, important things to know about sanitation

MAKING SUGAR-alternatives from nature's own resources

MEAT, MILK, AND EGG PRODUCERS-raising all you need, or more

BUTCHERING-ways to get the most from everything

WILD EDIBLES AND FISH PONDS-using nature's bounty and home-grown fish to supplement other foods

STORING AND PRESERVING FOODS-especially without refrigeration

SPINNING, WEAVING, AND KNITTING-a little time and much of wear needs can be filled

MAKING SOAP and other useful things-from yogurt to sourdough

ANIMALS AND FARMING-how to use the horse, and care for it properly

GOVERNMENT HELP-complete rundown on what is available at little or no cost

Author Churchill, who writes frequently for **The Mother Earth News** and other related publications, had his family to help, but says anyone can do it, and easier now, with THE HOMESTEADER'S HANDBOOK.

He's the proof.

the
Homesteader's
Handbook

the
Homesteader's
Handbook

JAMES E. CHURCHILL

Illustrations by Bradford Arneson

Stackpole Books

THE HOMESTEADER'S HANDBOOK

Copyright ©1974 by
James E. Churchill

Published by
STACKPOLE BOOKS
Cameron and Kelker Streets
Harrisburg, Pa. 17105

Printed in the U.S.A.

Library of Congress Cataloging in Publication Data

Churchill, James E   1934-
    The homesteader's handbook.

    Includes bibliographical references.
    1. Agriculture--Handbooks, manuals, etc. 2. Agriculture--United States. 3. Home economics, Rural--Handbooks, manuals, etc. I. Title.
S501.C47   630'.2'02   74-1333
ISBN 0-8117-0815-2

This book is dedicated
to Joan, whose patience,
loyalty and devotion
made it all come true.

Contents

1 **Finding a Piece of Land   11**

Acquiring Federal Land   Searching for Privately Owned Land   The Land
Purchase   Hawaii   Alaska   Canada   Mortgages and Loans   Where to Write
to Find Federal Lands . . . Land in Alaska . . . Land in Hawaii . . . Land in
Canada   Where to Write About Special Land Financing Programs   Where to
Get Maps and Weather Data

2 **Tools and How to Use Them   26**

Hammers, Mallets, Sledges   Saws   Axes and Cutting Tools   Hole Boring Tools
Screwdrivers   Miscellaneous Items

3 **Recycling An Old House   35**

Foundations and Underpinnings   Siding, Windows and Doors   The Roof
Ceilings and Floors   Plumbing, Wiring and Insulation

4 **Building With Natural Materials   48**

Your Own Log Cabin   Building a Stone Cabin   The Sod House   The Adobe
House   The Tepee

5 The Water Story   69

Don't Overlook Rainwater   Water Purification   Spring Water   Your Own Well
Cleaning an Old Well   Waste Disposal

6 Organic Gardening and Farming   83

Locating a Garden   Tilling a Garden   Planting   Making Compost   Mulching
and Weed Control   Earthworms   Insect Control   What to Plant

7 Growing an Indoor Garden   95

Building a Green Box   Lighting the Mini-garden   Necessary—The Right Soil
Automatic Watering   Starting and Transplanting Plants

8 Making Your Own Sugar   101

Honey and Beekeeping   Maple Syrup and Sugar   Sweets From Fruits and
Berries   Sorghum Molasses

9 Meat, Milk and Egg Producers   113

Goats   Rabbits   The Family Cow   Sheep   Pigs   Chickens   Ducks and Geese

10 How to Do Your Own Butchering   130

Hogs   Beef Cattle   Sheep   Goats   Game Animals   Rabbits   Poultry

11 Food Without Farming   141

January and February   March and April   May and June   July and August
September and October   November and December   Your Own Fish Pond

12 Preserving Foods   156

Outside Winter Vegetable Storage   Cabin Storage Bin   Cellar Storage
Pickling Vegetables   Canning and How to Do It   Smoking Meats   Pickling
Meats   Your Own Ice House   Some Recipes

13 Spinning, Weaving and Knitting   170

Fleece Cleaning   Carding   Spinning   Wool Dyeing   The Navajo Loom   Using
the Navajo Loom   Knitting

14 Soapmaking and Miscellaneous Matters 187

Lye Making   Selecting Lard and Tallow   Making Soap   To Make Butter   To Make Yogurt   To Make Sourdough   Homemade Breakfast Food   Tips From Experience

15 Farming With Horses 195

Care of the Draft Horse   Harnessing Up   Plowing With Team and Walking Plow   The Horse's Foot Ailments   Horseshoeing

16 First Aid and Health Problems 205

Controlling Bleeding   Closing a Cut   Fractures   Childbirth   Tooth Problems Eye Problems   Useful Herbs

17 Big Brother Will Help 218

Index 222

1

FINDING
A PIECE OF LAND

IN THE PAST years we have explored dozens of methods of obtaining land and are confident that anyone with desire and determination can acquire land somewhere in the United States or Canada which is, or can be developed into a self-sufficient homestead. This chapter will endeavor to point the way.

ACQUIRING FEDERAL LAND

The biggest landholder in the United States is the Federal Government. The government has approximately 460 million acres of public domain land. About 290 million acres of this public land is found in Alaska and most of the remaining 170 million acres found in Arizona, Montana, Wyoming, Colorado, New Mexico, Oregon, Nevada, Idaho, California and Washington with small amounts in Alabama, Arkansas, Florida, Louisiana, Michigan, Minnesota, Mississippi and Wisconsin.

Confronted with these figures a prospective homesteader might logically assume that the best and cheapest way to get land would be to relieve "Big Brother" of some of his. Tis and 'tain't.

On the positive side, the Homesteading Act of 1862 is still in effect.

11

This means that most all public domain land could theoretically be filed on for homesteading. The catch here is that almost all, if not all land suitable for homesteading has been taken up years ago. In fact, most states haven't had a homestead patent filed in the last twenty years. This is a result of the quality of the available land, economic conditions and the requirements of the Homestead law. The Federal government does not discourage anyone from applying for a homestead patent though, if one can find a parcel of public domain land that is suitable.

The procedure for filing for a homestead patent is to first locate the land and then by searching county records and maps determine if it is public domain land. No maps exist for the purpose of locating lands suitable for homesteading. Nevertheless, when you have determined that the land *is* available for homesteading, contact the applicable land office of The Bureau Of Land Management and ask for the proper forms and information for filing. The Bureau Of Land Management cautions against starting any activity on the parcel until the patent has been allowed.

Besides homesteading land The Bureau Of Land Management has thousands of other acres for sale. These sales are by public auction, either oral or written sealed bids. They are held at the land office which has jurisdiction over the parcel offered. (A list of land offices and their addresses appear at the end of this chapter.) These lands are mainly nonagriculture, nonrecreational lands as they are listed. Any improvements would have to be done by the buyer. In addition there are preference rights for adjoining landowners. This specifically means that an adjoining landowner has the right to buy the land by paying three times the appraised price or by matching the highest bid, whichever is less.

A prospective homesteader can find out what parcels are for sale by writing to The Bureau Of Land Management land office for the states which have public land offices and to Silver Spring, Maryland for the states which have public lands but no land office. Many of these parcels are advertised as having no access which means that they are completely surrounded by private lands and the government will not guarantee access. Thus it might be necessary to develop an agreement with a neighbor to be able to enter onto your purchase. In addition there is generally no water and a well would have to be drilled.

However, with dedication and luck a homesteader can latch onto a parcel such as one listed in the federal magazine "Our Public Lands" for Oregon, identified as OR 8587-39, 60 acres, appraised value $1750.00, approximately ten acres, suitable for the production of alfalfa and small grains, the rest covered with grass. In addition access is guaranteed by a county road forming the eastern boundary of the tract. The right family might latch onto this parcel and develop it into a farm.

For this and most other parcels of land dispensed by The Bureau Of Land Management the land is appraised and sold at a fair market price. Do not be deceived by pie-in-the-sky promoters who advertise free public lands; there are none.

The procedure most people follow for actually procuring a parcel of public land is to first subscribe to *"Our Public Lands,"* a magazine printed by the United States Government Printing Office, Public Documents Department, Washington, D.C. 20402. It is published quarterly and costs $2.70 per year. Near the back of this magazine is a "Public Sale Bulletin Board" section which lists the parcels of public lands which will be sold all over the United States in coming months. When they see a parcel which interests them they write to the land office in the state where the parcel is located and ask for a bid form and further particulars. Then when they have further information, if the parcel is still to their liking they make a trip to physically inspect the property. Next they either bid by going to the auction or sending a sealed bid to the auction. A sealed bid is fixed, of course, and has the disadvantage of possibly overbidding what you would have had to pay or losing by a slim margin to another oral bidder. Being present at the bidding or having a representative present is by far the best way to buy land at public land auctions. Besides the public auction The Bureau Of Land Management has some land that is sold at "continuing sale" or to the first buyer who comes along. Sometimes this land is overpriced or has other drawbacks which make its disposal difficult for the government.

In addition to large parcels the Federal Government has a Small Tracts Law whereby small tracts of land can be leased or purchased (under five acres) upon which to build a home or cabin or establish a mineral claim.

SEARCHING FOR PRIVATELY OWNED LAND

In addition to the public lands there are thousands upon thousands of privately owned parcels of land which change hands every year and this is probably the way most homesteaders will acquire their farm. Many people start searching for their private lands by deciding what climate they are compatible with.

A very useful tool for pinpointing climatic conditions are the climate maps published by the Government Printing Office or the Annual Report Of Climatological Data for the state you are interested in. Each state weather bureau also issues monthly and annual reports of the records of its observations. They can be obtained by writing to the state meteorologist.

Once you have decided the state or states you are interested in you can zero in by studying maps of the area. Most useful are the topographical maps which can be obtained from the U. S. Geological Survey. First however you will need a state index map which will give a name or a number for the topographical map which covers the area you are interested in. This index map is free from the U. S. Geological Survey.

Once you have decided on an area a preliminary idea of what kind of farms or land is available can be obtained by consulting the local real estate brokers. A list of the accredited ones can be found by writing to The National Institute Of Farm and Land Brokers, 155 East Superior Street, Chicago, Illinois 60611. Two nationwide real estate agencies which handle many small farm and rural land parcels are Strout Realty, P. O. Box 2757, Springfield, Missouri 65803 and United Farm Agency, 612 West 47th, Kansas City, Missouri 64112. They will send a free catalog to anyone writing to request one and in addition, if you fill out the form that they send along, they will forward your name to the brokers in the area you select. The brokers will send listings from their immediate area.

The next step might be to subscribe to the local paper. A wealth of information can be obtained from their classified ads such as land prices, food prices, wages, how much off-farm work can be had, etc.

Next it would be wise to plan to visit the area. Take along all the road maps and topographical maps you will need to stay oriented. Plan to go on a weekday so the county courthouse will be open. Talk to the county clerk about land prospects. He has intimate knowledge of transactions and negotiations going on in his tax district and he may even know of county land that is for sale.

The local Chamber Of Commerce, friendly folk that they are, cannot be relied upon to give unbiased information. Their job is to "sell" their area but they are useful for locating such contacts as lawyers, doctors, dentists, real estate brokers, private parties with land to sell, etc.

After three or four trips to the area and still finding yourself without a location, try finding a parcel of real estate on your own. This can be done by telling everyone you meet that you are looking for land and, more aptly, by advertising in the papers. Every community has a publication that is read by most of the locality's rural people. Find out what this is and advertise in it. We found our homestead with this ad: "Wanted To Buy. Rural land suitable for residence and garden. Some water." That's all the ad said but it brought us around 50 replies. We finally bought a forty-acre parcel with a log cabin, much good timber and a large pond for $2100.00. Comparable sites in that area were selling for three times that amount through brokers.

THE LAND PURCHASE

Naturally when you buy land "on your own" you will want to consult a lawyer to check the transaction. Try not to accept a quit claim deed, always demand a warranty deed from a private owner.

It is prudent to pay for an appraisal on a parcel of expensive real estate which you purchase yourself. This usually costs less than $100.00 and might save one much more. An accredited appraiser can be located through the local banks. Of course if you are going to borrow money to buy the parcel an interested bank will probably want to send out their own appraiser.

It is very prudent to stay on friendly terms with the present owners all through the negotiations and after. They can answer questions and volunteer information which would take you months or years to discover. This can be something simple, "Dick Crosby down the road has a daughter about your daughter's age," or it can be something more complicated like, "Don't try to raise chickens in the north end of the barn, there is a hole somewhere in the foundation and every weasel in the country will use it to carry off your baby chickens." The former owner probably knows exactly where the septic tank is if you have trouble finding it and so on. If you drive too hard a bargain and make him resentful of course he might not feel like helping you. This is not to say, however, that you should take as gospel any idea he offers.

Most, if not all owners, will ask a higher price than they will settle for. Try to negotiate, offering a price lower than you are willing to pay. You can always "up" the offer. Usually if the seller and buyer are both of good will they will be able to strike an agreement. Take all the time to "think it over" that you want, realizing of course that there is some slight risk that you might lose the parcel to another buyer. While you are "thinking it over" be sure the seller knows how to contact you if he suddenly decides to take your offer. This simple fact alone has closed many a real estate transaction.

Go to a real estate dealer only after you have exhausted every opportunity to buy land on your own. A very good one can do you a lot of good but these sometimes are hard to find. Most real estate people are opportunists and tend to tell you most anything to get your name on an offer.

If you do go to a broker try to avoid signing any offer to purchase incidental to which you have to make a deposit. The circumstances of the offer and the law might be such that he could legally keep this money whether you buy the farm or not. If it is necessary to put up earnest money, pay by check, write "earnest money" on the check and make sure it is paid into escrow or to your lawyer so that if the deal falls through you will still get the money back.

Many alert folks have purchased farms less the broker's discount by going back to the desired place at a much later date without the broker and advising the owner to take it out of the broker's hands and then they will make an offer. This can save enough money to buy a flock of chickens and a few goats even if you and the owner split the broker's commission. The broker's listing, however, is a legal contract and many sellers would be leery of trying to circumvent it for, depending on the state and the court, once the buyer has been shown the property by the agent or broker, he could probably successfully sue the seller to recover his commission.

On the positive side, however, the broker can sometimes arrange financing for a borderline case, find parcels which would be very hard to locate by yourself and act as an intermediary between an unfriendly seller and buyer.

Now if you are very short of "bread" there are still ways to acquire a modest amount of land. In some areas it is possible to locate odd parcels of county land, of a few acres each, which are for sale for very little. Since the county doesn't value the land much they don't inspect it either. One young couple acquired their homestead on such county land by hiring a nearby farmer to plow an acre parcel. When it was disked and harrowed they went to a local cucumber buyer and took out a contract to raise cucumbers. Since the seed went with the contract and the rich ground didn't need any fertilizer they just planted their crop, picked the cucumbers when they were ready and sold them via the contract with the company. It was hard work but they made enough from the acre of cucumbers to buy the land from the county ($25.00), build a modest temporary house ($350.00) and buy enough staple food to last the winter. Unusual, yes, but it indicates what can be done, with luck. One could say, of course, that from the ethical standpoint, they should have tried to first rent or get permission to plant the parcel from the county officials. Who knows, it might have been easily enough obtained.

In several places where there is timber land, title can sometimes be acquired by placing a down payment against purchase of the land and cutting the timber to pay off the mortgage. This works best in isolated areas of poor roads. This is hard work also but it is a way of getting the land right now instead of waiting a long time for it.

Many farms are for rent also and if you have some farming knowledge you might be able to rent a farm and acquire the experience of running the farm before paying for it. Renting has other advantages, not the least of which is if things don't "work out" you can move without going to the trouble of finding a buyer. Rents of small old houses and a few acres of land can be as low as $20.00 a month in some areas.

At the chapter end is a list of the states with the average price of farmland for each state. This is an up-to-date record for working farmland. Farms close to cities and farms bought for speculation will be higher. Remote and rundown farms will be lower.

HAWAII

On the more exotic side, a homesteader who desires to live from the land with only minimal property responsibilities could find one of the eight islands of Hawaii a veritable paradise. Fruit, vegetable plants and seafood abound and no one will ever starve in this state. Our contacts insisted that the island of Molokai was the ideal location because of the sparse population and abundance of wild natural food.

Some state land is available on the Islands and realtors do a brisk business in all kinds of property. Prospective farmers with some investment potential could probably find an agricultural situation which would meet their needs.

ALASKA

Far to the north of Hawaii, the huge State of Alaska with unlimited opportunities for the homesteader lies waiting. More public domain land lies within the boundaries of Alaska than in all the other states combined.

At this writing no Federal homestead lands are available because of native land claims but this hardly matters since the State of Alaska long ago claimed much of the good farm land.

Far from clutching this land to their bosom, the state is doing a brisk business in passing this land on to private citizens. They do this by selecting a tract, inspecting it for its suitability for farming, setting a minimum price and then offering it at public sale. The eligible bidder must be a citizen of The United States and at least 19 years old. But a bidder need not be a citizen of Alaska.

Since it is the responsibility of a prospective farmer to evaluate a homestead before he bids he should consider a few basic points. First, never select a homestead under snow, always look at it in the summer since what looks like a flat valley in winter could be a swamp, etc. Also note the existent vegetation on the land. If it isn't good healthy large trees such as birch and spruce or vigorous native grass it probably won't raise good crops either. Also take time to dig down in the soil. The soil should be at least deep enough to plow before a homestead should be considered. Very shallow soils underlain with heavy clay might not drain very well while gravelly and sandy soils might be too dry. Take all the time necessary to determine the suitability of the soil for farming before you commit yourself. No farmland should be selected where permafrost underlies the area.

A shortage of adequate drinking water exists in some parts of Alaska with settlers sometimes having to travel for miles to find water to haul to their homesite. Many, many homesites have been abandoned because of inadequate water supplies. Usually the adequacy of water supply can be determined by consulting natives or the appropriate government agency.

Naturally, heavily wooded homesteads will have to be cleared before farming can commence. Land clearing can be done by hand; in fact, in terms of conserving the topsoil it is the best way but it yields a poor return for the time spent. Some people with dense stands of trees have spent an entire year of their spare time just trying to clear an acre. Hiring land cleared can be fast but expensive. These factors should be taken into consideration when selecting a homesite.

In addition to the large homestead, provisions are made for small tracts of land for cabin building. These are almost invariably located in remote areas but if isolation is your thing many, many beautiful cabin sites exist where a garden can be cleared and a supply of wild meat and plants obtained. In fact, many areas exist where no formal procedure is necessary at all to procure a cabin site or to move into an abandoned cabin in our largest state.

CANADA

South of Alaska but north of the lower 48 lies our friendly neighbor, Canada. Canada, with its rich resources, peaceful political climate and sparse population, offers many opportunities for homesteaders.

Generally speaking, the coastal province of British Columbia has the mildest climate; in fact, many people say British Columbia has "everything", pointing out the opportunities in farming, industry, logging and several other enterprises. For persons desiring to live simply on their own land with self-sufficiency their goal, there are many locations along the Coast which are almost ideal. No Crown land is sold to nonresidents however and a person must have a landed immigrant status before he can purchase provincial land. This is hardly shattering information though because good farmland is to be had there from private sources from $35.00 an acre and up. Also many remote locations offer opportunities for temporary homesteading without outlay of capital—as long as you don't run afoul of the local constabulary.

Bordering British Columbia is the prairie province of Alberta. Alberta, while not actively encouraging homesteading, does have some land which can be used for this purpose. In addition there are many other ways such as grazing or cultivation leases by which land can be obtained. From time to time they have cottage development sites on public land and of course almost any type of farm can be obtained from private sales. In Alberta as in all Canadian provinces no homesteads are available to aliens.

The province of Saskatchewan has no Crown land for sale but private farmland is readily available from $10.00 an acre and up, likewise in Manitoba. Ontario encourages agriculture and will offer the facilities of a very good agricultural research and development board to assist the struggling farmer. They have agricultural lands which can be leased with an option to acquire. To qualify for these leases you must have a designated amount of capital and farming experience. Quebec and the Maritime provinces too look with favor upon agricultural pursuits and offer help and encouragement. However, generally speaking, they have only private and tax-forfeited lands for sale. All Canadian provinces have tax sales which are sometimes good places to obtain farmland.

MORTGAGES AND LOANS

Since many of us will be attempting to buy our land by paying only part of the cost we will of necessity be borrowing money someplace. There is nothing disgraceful or unwise about buying real estate on "time". Interest rates are usually about the same as the dollar shrinkage so the interest you have to pay will in many instances be offset by the cheaper dollars that you pay out in the long run. In fact, many experts say that paying off a mortgage ahead of time or paying cash for real estate does not make sense unless that's the only way you can get it.

The most widely available and easily researched loan is the conventional mortgage. All a prospective borrower has to do is have about 20% of the purchase price for a down payment, make an offer to purchase from the seller and go to the bank and ask to see a loan officer and explain the proposition to him. After your meeting he will probably cause the bank's appraiser to go out and appraise the property. If it is priced right according to their appraisal the bank can issue the mortgage. Whether they do or not will depend in large part on whether they think you have the means to pay the loan off. Contrary to public opinion banks are not in business to foreclose on mortgages. They avoid this if at all possible.

When you go to apply for a loan remember that you are going to be judged by a loan officer according to his parameters. This means he will probably look for well kept hair, trimmed moustache, clean clothes and shoes. By all means wear a business suit if you can. If you are still working at a straight job this will go a long ways towards making the loan a fact. He will ask you where you are working, but not how long you expect to continue to work at the job. Your banker might love factory workers but he might not love would-be farmers who do not have any experience. A conventional mortgage, incidentally, is usually not issued for land without habitable buildings.

Savings and Loans associations put up much of the money for purchasing homes or homes with small acreage, thus that little house with two acres in the quaint village might be just the set of circumstances to gladden a loan officer's heart. Savings and Loans will go up to 90% of the appraised value too so if you can find a place which sells for less than the appraised value you may be able to buy it with just a few dollars for legal fees or closing costs.

Also it seems to us that Savings and Loans are a little less "stuffy" when it comes to dealing with people. Savings and Loans might be just what the prospective homesteader needs to make his plan complete.

There is another way that a seller can pass his property on to a buyer known as the purchase money mortgage. This is quite simply the same as a conventional mortgage but instead of the bank or other institution supplying the money the seller agrees to accept payment in equal increments over a specified period of time.

The Land Contract, too, is a way that ownership is passed on to a buyer. Most land contracts are written to favor the seller and most specify that if a payment is defaulted, even the last one, all the preceding payments are lost and the property reverts to the seller. This is about the worst way to buy except that it will allow a prospective homesteader to move on to the property and start making a home. After the place becomes more valuable a conventional mortgage might be arranged and the land contract could then be satisfied and retired. If one must buy on a land contract it is wise to consult an attorney before signing up.

The greatest financier of farm property might be the U.S. Government, especially for people who can't find financing elsewhere. At this writing, loans for 40 years at 5% interest are available through The Farmers Home Administration. These rates may now be a little higher. To qualify here you must be able to report some farming experience.

"Big Brother" has compassion for folks who have no farming experience too. Through The Federal Land Banks which have over seven hundred local offices distributed throughout the country a loan can be obtained which will allow the purchase of a farm by folks who have never planted a seed, but intend to.

Further, if that prospective homestead you'd like to have won't qualify as a farm under the rules for Federal loans it might qualify under a recreational loan, a conservation loan, a forestry loan, an opportunity loan, rural housing loan, a watershed loan or even an emergency loan. In fact, there are so many ways to obtain a farm loan from the U.S. Government that it would take considerable space just to detail all the ways. A few examples are: booklet PA-977, Home Ownership. This booklet details the methods of obtaining loans in rural areas for building, repairing, or buying a rural homesite. Terms are 1% for low-income families with 33 years to pay it back. Another example is booklet #62, Program Aid-62 Farm Ownership. Loans can be obtained for almost any reason pertaining to farming and can have a maximum value of $100,000. Consult the chapter "Big Brother Will Help" and references at the end of this chapter for more booklet listings and addresses.

State	Average Value Per Acre Of Farmland	Increase In Past Year	Increase In Past 5 Years
Alabama	$ 250	7%	54%
Arizona	$ 74	9%	15%
Arkansas	$ 314	9%	48%
California	$ 504	3%	18%
Colorado	$ 111	11%	30%
Connecticut	$1,200	11%	57%
Delaware	$ 613	9%	47%
Florida	$ 399	6%	37%
Georgia	$ 323	21%	91%
Idaho	$ 205	9%	30%
Illinois	$ 543	12%	22%
Indiana	$ 460	6%	16%
Iowa	$ 433	12%	33%
Kansas	$ 174	17%	23%
Kentucky	$ 316	14%	40%
Louisiana	$ 409	13%	47%
Maine	$ 201	12%	59%
Maryland	$ 742	3%	51%
Massachusetts	$ 711	11%	47%
Michigan	$ 402	14%	47%
Minnesota	$ 257	9%	37%
Mississippi	$ 274	5%	52%
Missouri	$ 284	15%	53%
Montana	$ 67	8%	30%
Nebraska	$ 184	14%	37%
Nevada	$ 66	18%	32%
New Hampshire	$ 310	15%	64%
New Jersey	$1,409	13%	67%
New Mexico	$ 48	8%	26%
New York	$ 344	11%	57%
North Carolina	$ 427	8%	35%
North Dakota	$ 105	7%	32%
Ohio	$ 476	11%	34%
Oklahoma	$ 205	8%	42%
Oregon	$ 174	11%	33%
Pennsylvania	$ 453	6%	67%

State	Average Value Per Acre Of Farmland	Increase In Past Year	Increase In Past 5 Years
Rhode Island	$ 918	11%	48%
South Carolina	$ 346	20%	71%
South Dakota	$ 91	4%	16%
Tennessee	$ 345	19%	55%
Texas	$ 175	10%	43%
Utah	$ 105	9%	24%
Vermont	$ 287	14%	72%
Virginia	$ 365	14%	52%
Washington	$ 239	5%	30%
West Virginia	$ 173	17%	59%
Wisconsin	$ 301	14%	62%
Wyoming	$ 48	5%	27%
U.S. Average	$ 230	10%	37%

Note: Official figures not collected for Alaska or Hawaii. Source: U.S. Dept. of Agriculture.

WHERE TO WRITE TO FIND FEDERAL LANDS

Bureau Of Land Management
555 Cordova Street
Anchorage, Alaska 99501

Bureau Of Land Management
Federal Building
Room 3022
Phoenix, Arizona 85025

Bureau Of Land Management
Federal Building, Room E 2841
2800 Cottage Way
Sacramento, California 95825

Bureau Of Land Management
Federal Building, Room 14023
1961 Stout Street
Denver, Colorado 80202

Bureau Of Land Management
Room 334, Federal Building
550 W. Fort Street
Boise, Idaho 83702

Bureau Of Land Management
Federal Building
316 M 26th Street
Billings, Montana 59101

Bureau Of Land Management
Federal Building, Room 3008
300 Booth Street
Reno, Nevada 89502

Bureau Of Land Management
U.S. Post Office and Federal Building
South Federal Place
P. O. Box 1449
Santa Fe, New Mexico 87501

Bureau Of Land Management
729 Northeast Oregon Street
P. O. Box 2965
Portland, Oregon 97208

Bureau Of Land Management
8217 Federal Building
P. O. Box 11505
125 South State
Salt Lake City, Utah 84111

Bureau Of Land Management
U.S. Post Office and Court Building
2120 Capitol Avenue
P. O. Box 1828
Cheyenne, Wyoming 82001

Bureau Of Land Management
7981 Eastern Avenue
Silver Spring, Maryland 20910

WHERE TO WRITE TO FIND LAND IN ALASKA

Agricultural Stabilization and
  Conservation Service
Room 413, 516 Second Avenue
Fairbanks, Alaska 99701

Farmers Home Administration
Arctic Bowl Building
954 Cowles
Fairbanks, Alaska 99701

Soil Conservation Service
Severns Building
P. O. Box F
Palmer, Alaska 99645

U.S. Forest Service
Regional Office, P.O. Box 1631
Juneau, Alaska 99801

William Poe, Realtor
337 W. 5th Avenue
Anchorage, Alaska 99501

Gates & Company Realty
2405 C Street
Anchorage, Alaska 99503

Nielson Real Estate
606 W. Northern Lites
Anchorage, Alaska 99503

State Division Of Lands
344 Sixth Avenue
Anchorage, Alaska 99501

University Of Alaska Experiment
  Station
Box AE
Palmer, Alaska 99645

University Of Alaska Cooperative
  Extension Service
University Of Alaska
College, Alaska 99701

WHERE TO WRITE TO FIND LAND IN HAWAII

Realtor Peter Hayashi
190 Keawe Street
Hilo, Hawaii 96720

Molokai Chamber Of Commerce
Kaunakakai
Molokai, Hawaii 96748

Hawaii Board Of Agriculture and
  Forestry
King and Keeamoku Street
Honolulu, Hawaii 96813

WHERE TO WRITE TO FIND LAND IN CANADA

British Columbia

Director Of Lands
British Columbia Lands Service
Parliament Buildings
Victoria, British Columbia

I. K. Ross
Dawson Agencies Ltd.
1262-3rd Avenue
Prince George, British Columbia

Stan R. Parker
H. G. Helgerson Ltd.
612 W. 3rd Avenue
Prince Rupert, British Columbia

M. C. Johnston R.I. (B.C.)
Johnston and Swain Realty Ltd.
2372 West 4th Avenue
Vancouver 9, British Columbia

Nova Scotia

Nova Scotia Farm Loan Board
Department Of Agriculture
Truro, Nova Scotia

Halifax-Dartmouth Real Estate
   Board Ltd.
Granville Street
Halifax, Nova Scotia

Registrar Of Crown Lands
Department Of Lands And Forests
Halifax, Nova Scotia

Yukon Territory

Land Office, Yukon Territorial
   Government
Whitehorse, Yukon

Dumas Realty Ltd.
210 Main Street
Whitehorse, Yukon

Saskatchewan

Saskatchewan Industry Development
7th Floor, Power Building
Regina, Saskatchewan

Regina Real Estate Board
1805 Rae Street
Regina, Saskatchewan

Saskatoon Real Estate Board
1149 8th Street East
Saskatoon, Saskatchewan

Ontario

Ministry Of Agriculture And Food
Parliament Buildings
Queen Park
Toronto, Ontario

Manitoba

Province Of Manitoba
Department Of Lands, Resources and
   Environmental Management
810 Norquay Building
Winnipeg, Manitoba

Manitoba Real Estate Association
1315 Portage Avenue
Winnipeg, Manitoba

Alberta

Government Of The Province Of
   Alberta
Department Of Lands And Forests
Natural Resources Building
109th Street and 99th Avenue
Edmonton 6, Alberta

Quebec

Chief Of Lands Service
Department Of Lands And Forests
Quebec, Quebec

New Brunswick

Director Of Lands
Department Of Natural Resources
Fredericton, New Brunswick

Newfoundland

Director Of Crown Lands And
   Surveys
Department Of Mines, Agriculture
   And Resources
St. Johns, Newfoundland

Questions which can't be answered directly by these agencies will be referred to other sources. There is hardly a question about Canada that can't be satisfied by one or another of these agencies or affiliations.

MONEY FOR YOUR LAND

GOVERNMENT PAMPHLETS:

Write to The Superintendent Of Documents
Government Printing Office
Washington, D.C. 20402

This Is FHA #PA6973
Farm Ownership Loans #PA62
Farm Operating Loans #PA61002
Increasing Farm And Ranch Income Through Grazing Associations
    #PA773
Home Ownership #PA6977
Emergency Loans #PA490
Farm Labor Housing #PA521
Watershed Loans #PA406
Loans For Resource Conservation And Development #PA799

WHERE TO GET MAPS:

United States
(For states east of the Mississippi River)

Distribution Section
U. S. Geological Survey
1200 South Eads Street
Arlington, Virginia 22202

(For states west of the Mississippi River)

Distribution Section
U. S. Geological Survey
Federal Center
Denver, Colorado 80225

Canada

Department Energy, Mines and Resources
Surveys and Mapping Branch
615 Booth Street
Ottawa, Ontario

WHERE TO GET WEATHER RECORDS:

National Climatic Center
NOAA Environmental Service
Federal Building
Asheville, North Carolina 28801

Environmental Data Service
Environmental Science
  Services Administration
Rockville, Maryland 20852

2

TOOLS AND
HOW TO USE THEM

A HOMESTEADER'S SUCCESS in living and carving a home out of rural or remote areas might depend to a great extent on his ability to use tools. Tools can be roughly divided into four classes: pounding tools, cutting tools, gripping tools and digging tools. Pounding tools can include the carpenter's hammer, ball-peen hammer, the mallet and the sledge.

HAMMERS, MALLETS, SLEDGES

The carpenter's hammer or claw hammer consists of a hammer head with a face for pounding nails opposite a set of claws for pulling them. The handle is set through the head at the "eye", and the "neck", which is an extension of the eye, extends down onto the handle to support it more fully. The handle, usually of hickory or other tough wood, is held in the head by small wedges.

Carpenters' hammers need very little care if they are used on nails only. If the hammering face should become damaged it can be filed with a flat file back to its original shape. Before filing the hammer head, try to ascertain which way the head was originally. Some carpenters' hammers are flat across the face and some are bell-shaped. Naturally if the head has deep grooves or is badly damaged it probably can never be brought back to its original shape.

Replacing the handle of a hammer will be a common occurrence. A hammer handle can be made from a piece of well-seasoned hardwood or it can be purchased. If the handle is to be homemade, select trunk wood that has been lying in some cool dry place such as a woodshed for at least a year, so that it doesn't warp when it is used. Better yet, watch for a piece of very clean grained hickory trunk and store it especially for making axe and hammer handles. The handle can be made according to the directions shown in accompanying illustration.

The end of the handle to be inserted into the eye of the hammer head has to be carefully shaped. This is usually done with a wood rasp. However, a coarse file or a knife will work also. When the handle starts to take on the dimensions of the eye keep trying to fit it in, removing and replacing it until it is as tight a fit as possible. Once the handle is in place it should be checked for plumb—that is, it should be perpendicular to the head. Enough wedges should be driven into the handle to make it super tight. Purchased handles will have new wedges as part of the package. If you make your own handles, of course, you are going to have to make your own wedges, but a wooden wedge works well and one can be whittled out of the same piece of hickory from which the handle was made. Sometimes the wedges from the old handles will still be usable and transferable. A properly hung hammer will be absolutely tight and will strike true from the handle.

The other types of hammers useful to the homesteader, the sledge, the ball-peen hammer and the wooden mallet, are all repaired and rehung in a like manner.

The novice carpenter will quickly learn that the nail must be struck squarely or else it will bend. Thus, grip the hammer at about the same level as the nail and strike squarely down on it. Bent nails are pulled out easily enough, usually, with the claws. To pull deeply embedded nails, it is helpful to place a wooden block under the hammer head for more leverage.

Sledges are the thing for pounding fence posts, driving stakes, breaking rocks and other miscellaneous chores where a heavier-than-usual hammer is needed. Wooden mallets, which can be home-manufactured handily enough from hardwood, also can be used for driving fence posts, wood chisels and gouges.

The ball-peen hammer, which is something like a carpenter's hammer without the claws, can be used for flattening or peening rivets, forming metal and driving a cold chisel. (The latter is something every homesteader needs.) Anyway, wherever you look on the homestead, you are apt to see something that needs pounding.

SAWS

Saws are very important for the homesteader. Saws will enable him to cut wood, build a cabin, saw lumber and logs for tables, chairs, benches

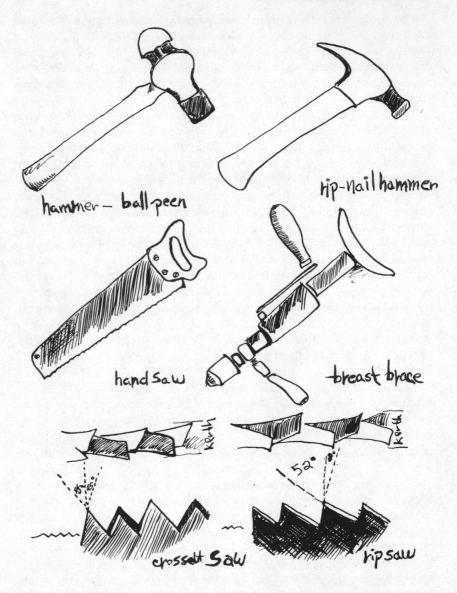

hammer – ball peen

rip-nail hammer

hand saw

breast brace

crosscut saw

ripsaw

and stands. Saws also can cut metal, meat, frozen fish and have a lot of uses.

Wood saws are divided into two categories. The first category is the cross-cut saw. This saw, depending on how big the teeth are, can be used for sawing a silo-sized Douglas fir or a fractional-inch slice of rare board for making a jewelry box.

The teeth in a cross-cut saw are sharpened to a bevel edge so that they cut across the grain of the wood like tiny knives. Since the saw has a "set" or a kerf, the teeth actually form two cutting lines and the wood between the two cuts is forced out by the teeth sliding back and forth. This wide cut keeps the saw from binding or sticking since it is actually wider than the thickness of the saw blade above the teeth. The number of teeth per inch is what determines the saw's best use. For general work a cross-cut saw with eight or nine points to the inch will be most useful. This many points will saw most lumber. Wet or green wood can best be cut with a saw having six or seven points to the inch while very hard dry wood will cut easiest with ten points to the inch.

Ripsaws are coarse-tooth saws used for ripping or cutting in the same direction as the grain of the wood. Ripsaws usually have five or six points to the inch although they can be obtained with only two teeth to the inch. Ripsaws can also be used for cutting across the grain of a board when the board is wet or green. The kerf is wide with a ripsaw; therefore it is not too satisfactory for fine work.

Both ripsaws and cross-cut saws can be sharpened by the homesteader and since a sharp hand saw will cut with ease and a dull one will hardly cut at all the sharpening skill is well worth developing. The tools needed for sharpening a saw are a vise or device for holding the saw sturdily in a vertical position, teeth up, a three-cornered file and a saw set or punch and hammer.

The first step in sharpening a saw is to clean the blade of rust. This can be done with sand and kerosene or steel wool and kerosene, or with penetrating oil and an abrasive if you happen to have some. Many people do not realize what a real good abrasive a handful of sand and a dash of kerosene make or, for that matter, a handful of sand and water. Rub the abrasive on the rust and wash off the loosened material, rub some more and wash some more until the rust is mostly gone. After it is clean rub the blade with an oiled rag to prevent its rusting again.

When the blade is clean clamp the saw firmly in the vise with the teeth up and examine the teeth very carefully. Usually, if the saw is dull, the teeth will be blunted or turned over on the points unless it is very bad, though the bevel of the teeth will still be visible. Take the triangular file—ideally a seven-inch slim taper triangle—and by following the taper or bevel of the teeth resharpen the points. If done carefully, one should be able to rebuild the teeth to almost their original dimensions. This requires only a few light strokes. As will be noticed, alternate teeth on a saw are beveled in opposite places, so the saw will cut on both the forward and rearward strokes. In sharpening, it is necessary to sharpen or rebevel the teeth which are beveled to the right from one side and then turn the saw around or stand on the other side of the saw to bevel them the other way.

There is a significant difference in the teeth on a ripsaw or a cross-cut saw when it comes to sharpening them. A ripsaw is filed 90° to the blade in all directions while a cross-cut saw is filed 45° to the line of teeth and 15° below the bevel. As mentioned, the teeth themselves will indicate how they should be refiled when examined closely.

After the teeth are sharpened or rebeveled, the saw probably should be reset. Reset means to bend the teeth away from each other so that they form a kerf wider than the saw blade. A device (saw set) can be purchased for about $3.00 that does this very speedily and accurately or it can be done with a block of wood, a small punch and a hammer.

Setting the saw with a block involves selecting a piece of milled lumber, the harder the wood, the better, and beveling one edge for the desired degree of tooth set. Then clamp the saw blade to the wide surface with the teeth protruding above the bevel to their full height. It is important to clamp the saw blade all along the edge of the board so that it doesn't "give". Then take the small punch and hammer and bend the teeth over to the bevel. Cross-cut saws are bent so the angle of the teeth or the sharpened edges are towards the center. As with the sharpening, the setting must be done for half the teeth from one side and the other half from the other side.

As mentioned, all saws, from the largest two-man cross-cut saw to a hand saw, can be resharpened and reset with a fair degree of accuracy by anyone who is handy with tools just by studying very carefully the teeth located at the extreme ends of the saw—where they get very little, if any wear. Saw blades which are very far gone probably are not worth repairing since saws can be had at flea markets and farm auctions for as little as a few cents. Like most tools, saws should be stored in a dry place out of harm's way. When they are stored for any length of time they should be first coated with oil or animal fat to minimize rusting.

AXES AND CUTTING TOOLS

The axe is too well known to need any introduction. This tool comes in two different general classifications, the single-bitted axe and the double-bitted axe. The double-bit is the axe for extensive wood cutting. It is generally balanced better and each blade can be sharpened so it can be used longer between sharpenings. When it is used as a woodpile axe it generally has one side sharpened to cut off limbs and chop small logs into firewood and the other side left blunt for splitting chunks. A slightly dull blade splits better than a sharp blade, oddly enough.

The single-bladed axe is most often found on the farm since it is very good for all around use, for chopping and splitting wood, and in an emergency it can be used as a post maul or a stake driver or even for fighting off hungry bears, for that matter.

Axes are also sharpened with a file. For chopping, the blade should be tapered gradually to a fine edge from about 1½ inches back. For splitting, the blade is sharpened to a rather abrupt chisel point, starting back from the edge about one inch.

Axes are very dangerous; the author once spent two consecutive months in a hospital because an overhanging limb deflected an axe blade enough so that it drove into his foot instead of the saw log from which he was chopping limbs. Always make sure the area above the chopper is clear so the axe doesn't catch in a limb or clothesline. Always chop on the side of the log opposite your feet and don't try to split wood that is just casually lying on the ground. Realize if you chop an axe into the ground that you are almost certainly going to dull it significantly. Don't break rocks or pound iron with the back of a single-bitted axe if it can be avoided. This sets up stresses in the metal which will almost certainly cause it to break sooner or later. Keep the axe head tight on the handle and replace the handle when it cracks or gets frayed from splitting wood.

A good axe kept well sharpened will do a whole lot of service for the homesteader but don't waste any money on a hatchet, they aren't useful enough for anyone but campers and trappers. A good all-around axe for the homesteader is a single-bit, four-pound head with a good straight-grained hickory handle. Naturally when the first axe handle goes bad you can make another from ash, hickory or oak.

Besides the axe the tools used for cutting wood and working with logs are the adze, broad axe and drawknife. The adze is a specialized tool for flattening one side of a log. It is highly dangerous in the hands of an amateur and probably it is just as well to avoid its use unless a good doctor is nearby. The broad axe is a short-bladed axe also used for shaping logs. It is single-bladed and can be driven like a chisel to notch and shape logs and lumber, in addition to chopping. The drawknife is a very useful tool which is sharpened on one side of the blade only to produce a shaving edge like a plane.

Now to use an axe, a drawknife and a plane to make a handle for a hammer or an axe: first take a sharp axe and split a handle blank out of a piece of well-seasoned oak, hickory, ash or willow. Other woods will work also. The closer the blank can be made to the desired dimensions of the handle the easier the rest of the job. In fact, good axemen can completely make the handle just with the axe. Now measure the existing axe or hammer-handle and use the drawknife and plane to shape the new one. When it is very close to the right dimensions smooth it down with a piece of glass. Then fit it to the eye of the axe or hammer and wedge it tightly in place. So much for axes and handles.

HOLE-BORING TOOLS

The homesteader will often need to bore holes for fastening things together, taking them apart, building cabins, baby cribs, animal pens and thousands of other cases. Not all the holes he will need to drill will be in wood either; sometimes he will have to drill in metal. The selection and care of drill bits and devices for turning the bits are very important.

Wood augers come in a variety of sizes from the fractional-inch sizes to as much as six inches. The largest augers are made with their own T-handle for turning the bit. Smaller ones have a square shank so they will fit into a "brace." This brace, or bit brace as it is commonly called, is shaped like a crank. The bottom of the brace has a vise or "chuck" for holding the bit and there is a swivel both in the center and at the top. Much leverage can be obtained with this type drill and almost any type of drilling is possible with it except when working in close corners where it can't be turned. In those cases, special bit braces are available or a breast drill can be used. Apart from drilling holes, the bit brace is valuable when used with screwdriver instead of drill bits since the brace gives good additional leverage. Breast drills are equipped with a saddle to place against the chest for feed pressure and a handle like an egg beater for turning the bit. The advantage of this drill is that the bit can be turned faster, therefore it is most useful for drilling holes in metal, especially when the larger sized bits are to be used. A device almost the same as the breast drill but smaller and equipped with a handle at the upper end instead of a saddle is the "hand drill." This kind of drill will usually take only bits up to ¼ inch in diameter.

Wood augers can be sharpened with a file by just simply restoring their cutting edge. This usually only takes a few strokes with a suitably small file. Polishing the cutting edges of the bit to make it sharper yet can be done with a small hard sharpening stone.

Many times metal drills cannot be sharpened with a file; they have to be ground on stone. It takes a long, long time to dull a metal bit using it in a hand drill though.

SCREWDRIVERS

Screwdrivers are very important items and most households will have at least one or two around. Since screws come in a variety of sizes it follows that screwdrivers do also. Fairly good screwdrivers, good enough for all but the professional, are cheap. Some say that you shouldn't use screw-drivers for any other use but on screws. This is not only nonsense, it is against human nature! Keep a few screwdrivers for use on only screws of course, but also have a few for prying up windows, opening paint cans, as emergency chisels or any one of the hundreds of other uses that a screw-driver can fill. Flea markets abound with used screwdrivers so procuring a whole bucketful of them shouldn't upset any budget.

A homesteader who possesses one of the high-speed hand-operated grinders can reshape any screwdriver so it's like new. Also he can restore the temper of a blade that was ground too far back.

Grinding the screwdriver is merely to reshape the flat tapered sides and square off the ends. Naturally the screwdriver should be tapered to the thickness of the screw slot in which it will normally be used. Keep a typical screw at hand when you are touching up a screwdriver blade and grind it until it just fits. The side should retain as much original taper as possible. Many times the screwdriver blade only needs a little filing to bring it back to original shape. If the file or grinding marks can be retained they will help hold the screwdriver in the screw slot. In fact, it has been estimated that the grinding marks on a screwdriver blade hold it in a screw slot at least 20% better.

MISCELLANEOUS ITEMS

Besides the tools already mentioned the homesteader will want to have at least one vise and at least one good pair of pliers. Now ordinary pliers are fair and inexpensive, but a pair of arc joint pliers hold much better. The very best hand-held gripping tool is the lock-joint pliers. Clamps, too, are a very handy thing to have around; if they can be obtained at a farm auction or flea market they are worth picking up. The next most desirable tool would probably be a 12-inch adjustable wrench, but be sure the jaws don't have too much play.

When it comes time to build the cabin or an out building, a few measuring instruments will be handy to have. Try squares are inexpensive and very handy aids for sawing boards straight across or laying out notches in timbers and for squaring up corners. A large carpenter's square is also a very useful tool and when laying out rafters and intricate angles it is al-most a necessity. A level, too, is handy to have and is used when plumbing up cabin walls, setting posts and other structures which should be perpen-dicular to the ground. A steel pocket tape is also almost indispensable when building and is so easily obtained that no one need go without one.

Very often it will be necessary to work with metal and bend or change its shape. The best way to do this is to heat it red or white hot. While a blacksmith's forge is useful and perhaps even ideal for this, a common wood stove stoked with dry hard wood, allowed to burn to coals and then drafted very well will heat almost anything to the point where it can be bent or a hole easily punched in it. I have used my barrel stove, set up outside where the wind would act as a bellows to fan the coals, to heat sheet metal, hexagon stock, screwdriver and axe blades, and car springs for ice chisels. etc. My pounding anvil is a section of railroad rail.

Sooner or later the homesteader is going to want to cut some metal. Fortunately there is an inexpensive, highly efficient hand-operated saw made for just this purpose, the hacksaw. Hacksaws usually consist of an adjustable metal frame with a metal or plastic handle. Hacksaw blades are fitted to the frame by threaded pegs made adjustable by a wing nut. This allows blades to be changed rapidly since they are easily broken items. But blades are inexpensive and a year's supply can be purchased for under a dollar sometimes. Hacksaw blades cannot be sharpened.

When using the hacksaw, three of the teeth should be kept in contact with the work at all times. This avoids too much pressure on one tooth. When sawing bolts, first put the nut on behind the cut so that it can be turned off to straighten out any threads damaged by the saw. Very hard steel pieces such as knife blades or axles, however, cannot be cut with a hacksaw. If a file won't cut it, it can't be sawed either.

Files are so useful few tool chests have enough of them. Files can be used for shaping metal or wood and they are used for sharpening other tools. In addition, when a file gets old and worn out it can be made into a pretty good knife if a grinding wheel is available.

A homesteader's file supply should include at least two three-cornered files and two flat files—one small and one large. Files should have handles. These can speedily be made by driving a corn cob or a section of soft wood on the tang. The way to file is to push the tool away from you across the work and then lift it off the work on the return stroke. File serrations or cutting edges are slanted forward so as to cut on the push stroke. Trying to cut on the return stroke will bend them over and quickly ruin the file.

There are wood files also. A very useful one is the rasp. These usually have several different sizes of teeth. The different sizes are for removing a lot of material or very little. Do not attempt to use a wood rasp on metal; it will quickly be dulled.

Digging tools which the homesteader will use are the spade, short-handled shovel, long-handled shovel, pick, post-hole digger, hoe and a variety of hand cultivators. Digging tools require little care other than keeping them clean and rust free, plus replacing broken handles.

3

RECYCLING AN OLD HOUSE

BEFORE STARTING TO fix up an old house we should know whether it is really worth fixing. Some houses have been neglected to the point where they are just a pile of molding boards and decomposing concrete. Fix the roof on a derelict like this and like as not the joists will break and let the floor fall in. Fix the floor and you will see that the foundation is in danger of collapse, and so on, until you feel like Peter with his finger in the dike. If you bother with one of these cripples at all it should be just to tear it down and use the lumber for another building. A good way to check for rotten boards and concrete is to jab them with an ice pick.

FOUNDATIONS AND UNDERPINNINGS

Some experts size up a building by first examining the foundation. Every house or heavy building has to have a foundation. This sits on a bed of concrete known as footings. Together the footings and the foundation walls hold up the house. The foundation should be straight, level across the top and have no large holes or loose powdery concrete in the joints. Many older houses had foundations of field stone cemented together with lime or cement mortar. This is a very good foundation as long as the cement in the joints still has strength. If it is starting to fail there will be loose stones and the concrete can be scratched quite easily with an ice pick. Inside the basement the walls might be pushed in, in a semicircular pattern at the center of the wall. Usually there will be long cracks, possibly starting

at the top and going to the bottom of the walls. While this is serious
enough, it still can be fixed. Use the extent of damage as an estimate of
how much it will cost in terms of time to fix the wall. Material for such
repairs will usually be only a little concrete.

Hand in hand with cracks in the wall will sometimes be water leaks
which are serious only if they have damaged the furnace or the root cellar
or some other important object permanently fixed in the basement.

Some structures have no basement, only a space under the floor to keep
the wooden members from contacting the ground. This space is crawl
space and it will be necessary to crawl in it to examine the foundation from
the inside. Examine the foundation walls, which are usually of concrete
blocks, for cracking and deterioration.

Some houses have no wall foundations since they just sit on a thick slab
of concrete. Not much you can see here except examine the edges of the
slab for signs of deterioration.

The foundation and the first wooden members called the sills are
usually out of place, sunken or deteriorated when the plaster of the house
is cracked, the doors and windows sticking or the floor uneven. Careful examination should make the damage obvious.

Repairing the foundation, which is a good thing to do first, can amount
to a few hours' or a few weeks' work depending on how bad it is. A good
way to start is to determine how far out of plumb or level the foundation
and sills are. Sometimes the walls are slightly uneven when they are built,
this being compensated for by shimming the sills. Determining proper
level can be done with a line and line level. A line is any length of stout
cord that can be stretched from one corner of the building to the other. It
should be pulled tight and a line level placed upon it. The ends of the line
should be moved up and down to get the level. Once the level is found
stakes can be driven in at the corners of the foundation with the tops of the
stakes at the level found by the string, or level marks can be made on the
stakes. This procedure should be followed all around the building, using
the level of one stake to shoot the level for the next stake. Some surprising
irregularities can be found this way; it is not too uncommon for the foundation of an old house to be several inches out.

Once the foundation's proper level has been established it will be necessary to raise the house with jacks to this level before it can be properly
repaired and the whole structure brought to trim again.

Huge house jacks or jack posts will have to be procured and placed
under the sills to raise the house up from the foundation. This has to be
done very slowly and carefully to avoid damaging the structure. Once it is
resting on the jacks the section of the wall which is free of weight can be
dug out, repaired and brought to level.

To repair a wall dig a trench outside the wall, chip out all loose concrete and remove and clean all loose blocks or stones, and cement them back in place. Make sure this is done thoroughly since repairing the foundation is probably the most important part of renovating the house. After the wall is repaired and brought to the proper level it should be allowed to set for at least four days before the weight of the house is let down upon it.

It is not wise to work on more than one wall at a time nor to start work on the worst wall first. The worst wall, or the one which is the fartherest out of level—especially if it is much higher when it is repaired than the rest of the house—might cause damage to the entire structure before the rest of the foundation is leveled. Therefore always start on the best wall.

Possibly some sills will be found that are rotten when the jacks are put under them. If the sills are soft or dry-rotted they may as well be changed while the house is jacked up. Jacks, of course, will have to be placed under the floor joists or the girders. It will probably also be necessary to remove some siding from around the bottom of the house to get the sill out. Use new treated lumber of the same dimensions as each piece removed. This is a tedious job, but like replacing the foundation walls it has to be done if the existing sills are too rotten to assure strength.

After the foundation is repaired and the building is allowed to rest back on it one can move upward in his appraisal and repair program.

The next item to consider is the floor, consisting of the floor joists, the bridging, girders and the subflooring. The floor joists are the members that extend from the sills across the building to the sills on the other side. They are usually 2 x 8's or 2 x 10's spaced about 16 inches apart.

The girders are heavy wood or steel beams that are placed under the floor joists when the span between sills is too great for the joists alone to support the load. The ends of the girders are usually placed into the foundation walls. Additional support is given the girders by posts placed at regular intervals beneath. These posts are usuaully adjustable or some provision has been made to allow for shimming up the post to level the floor joists.

The bridging consists of X-shaped members nailed between the floor joists to give them rigidity since this helps spread the loading over several members.

Replacing the floor joists isn't too bad a job. Unless the existing one is so rotten as to be a definite hazard it would be well just to leave it in place and nail another joist of the same dimensions right alongside it. The new one can usually be worked into place by sliding it in beside the weak joist with the flat side against the girder and then turning it so the edges are vertical after it is in place. Spike it into place at the ends and nail through it into the existing weak joist. After it is nailed securely in place tie it to the subflooring by toenailing #6d nails at a shallow enough angle to keep the nails from protruding through the finished flooring.

It is definitely possible to replace a weak girder although it is strenuous work. First, provisions will have to be made for jacks or posts to carry the load after the old girder is removed. This can be done by installing a temporary girder beside the one to be removed but it has to be kept far enough away so that it doesn't interfere with the removal. Next, with an electric saw or a very coarse-toothed hand saw, cut the girder into as many pieces as is necessary to remove it. When the old girder is out clean its bed thoroughly of accumulated dirt, sawdust, wasp nests and other debris. Then very carefully measure the length for a new one.

A new girder will either have to be purchased or perhaps hewed from a log at the homestead wood lot. Oak or hickory, peeled and flattened on two sides to fit the floor joists, are probably the strongest girders other than steel. A well-dried timber or post should be used for the girder as green wood can warp. If you have to use green wood it will have to be supported very well until it dries.

Milled lumber is most frequently used to replace the girder. Milled lumber is, of course, the easiest to work with. It should be well dried also. The actual installation is sometimes impossible if the girder is left in one piece. When it can't be slid in one piece into place it will be necessary to cut and splice it. Then the two pieces are slid into the openings in the foundation and the sawed sections are joined to produce a splice. Usually a splice of this type is secured by ½-inch bolts placed through holes drilled in the two sawed sections. The bolts should form a double row placed on 18-inch centers.

Once the girder is in place and spliced the temporary girder can be removed and the floor joists brought to the correct level with wooden shims such as shingles.

If the girder isn't too weak it can be satisfactorily reinforced by nailing 2 x 6's to each of its sides after it has been jacked to its right level.

Installing new bridging can be easily done and requires no explanation.

It often happens that the subflooring, or the layer of flooring directly over the floor joists, has a weak spot. This, too may have to be replaced.

A small weak spot can be repaired by just fitting a section of ¾-inch exterior grade plywood as a patch against the floor where it is weak. This section should be at least six inches larger on all sides than the portion being reinforced. The plywood should be secured to the existing subflooring with threaded flooring nails or screws. In addition, it should

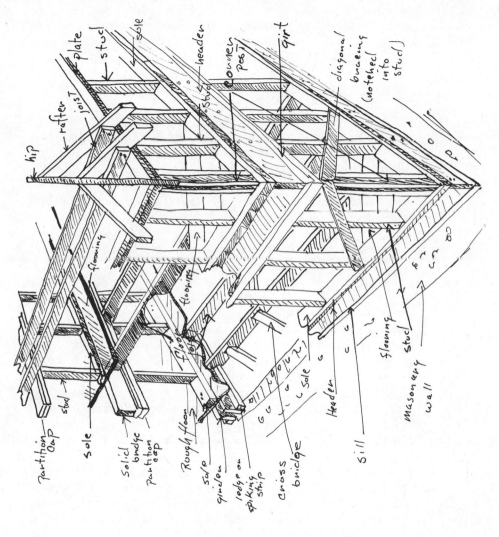

Framing
(house)

be reinforced with sections of 2 x 4's nailed across the patch and between the joists. The reinforcing 2 x 4's should not be more than eight inches apart.

Sometimes all that is necessary is to nail 2 x 4's eight inches apart between the floor joists to correct a weak subfloor or otherwise reinforce it.

SIDING, WINDOWS AND DOORS

Once you have the foundation and the floor secured a likely next step is the exterior. The exterior consists of the siding, windows and doors.

Siding is durable stuff and many kinds don't even have to be painted to withstand the rigors of weather. Some materials typically used for siding are wood shingles, wood siding, plywood, hardboard, asbestos, aluminum, plastic and steel. Of the types mentioned, probably only pine or fir wood siding will ever deteriorate enough to require replacing. It may be necessary with any kind, however, to go over it thoroughly and nail down all loose boards. In fact, most siding jobs on old houses can be restored by renailing and repainting.

If it is necessary to remove the old siding it can be done by sliding a wide blade such as a scoop shovel under the siding and prying loose wide swaths of it.

The most common method of installing new siding is to put it right on over the old. Sometimes the old siding is covered with 30-pound felt paper to make a base for installing the new siding. Sometimes it is necessary to nail furring strips vertically on the side walls as a base for the new siding. The furring strips are nailed to the studding. If the siding is to be applied vertically the furring strips would be applied horizontally.

Furring strips are narrow strips of one-inch boards; every lumberyard has them, but they could be homemade by ripsawing pieces of scrap lumber.

It is possible that one could encounter an old house that just has the siding nailed to the studding without the customary layer of sheathing. In this case, to make the old house weatherproof and warm the old siding could be replaced with ½-inch plywood or the equivalent and then either the old or new siding could be installed. Try to install siding so that the exposed rows come directly at the top and bottom of the windows and doors. Tis makes for a much better job than siding notched out for these openings. When the siding problems have been licked it is time to examine and repair the windows.

There are two basic types of windows, those which can be opened and those which can't. Most old houses have movable windows. The portion of the window that surrounds glass is called the sash. In a double-hung window the bottom sash can move upward and the top one can move down. The window glass or "lights" are usually held in place by putty.

Normally it is desirable to remove and recondition if inspection reveals broken lights, broken sash cord or a window frame needing repair. To remove the sash pry out the thin strips of wood that hold the sash to the frame and both strips of wood that separate the upper and lower sashes.

Once the sash is removed the window can be put on a bench or table for convenient handling. First remove all broken glass and all the putty and metal points that hold the broken glass in place. Next, examine and replace all old broken putty. Then, using paint remover or a scraper, get all the old paint off the frame, then apply at least one layer of a good primer paint. When this dries replace the broken lights and putty them in place. Puttying is usually done by applying a very thin layer of putty to the opening for the lights, then installing the lights and holding them in place with small metal triangles called points. The putty is then applied with a putty knife to form a bead or sloping joint seal. Examine windows already puttied to judge the size of this joint. It should not be so thick that it extends up on the window. Let the putty dry for a day or two and then apply the finish coat of paint. Don't paint the outer edges of the window, however, since this causes sticking when the window is slid up and down.

While the paint is drying examine the window frame. Weather and age may have stripped it bare of paint and made it cracked or rotten. If it needs paint, wire brush off the paint chips and fill in the cracks with plastic wood or caulking compound and then repaint the wood. The parts of the frame that are exposed to the weather and the windowsill should have at least two coats of good oil base paint.

Sometimes the window frame will be so rotten that it needs replacing. Building a new frame takes superior skill and an imposing array of equipment. Usually it will be necessary to purchase a new one from a lumberyard or find a used one in some old building that can be removed without damage. In every large city there is at least one house wrecker that sells window frames complete with sash. These used windows will be much cheaper, of course, then the new ones even if repainting is necessary.

Replacing a window frame involves removing all of the old one. This will leave an opening bordered by 2 x 4's called a rough opening. Carefully clean this rough opening and remove all nails or other roughness that will affect the fit of the new window. Then tack a strip of 3-pound felt around to line the opening where the window frame will fit. Set the window frame in place and use wood shingles or other tapered strips of board to plumb it vertically and horizontally. Nail it solidly in place with 8d nails or larger.

When the windows are all shipshape the doors can be replaced or repaired. Inspection of the doors usually consists of carefully opening and shutting them to see if they swing or are "hung" right. Chances are when you leveled up the floor it affected the way the doors operate. It may be necessary to rehang the door. Before you do, inspect the door-sill; that's the strip of wood directly across the threshold under the door. This hardwood strip probably will be worn out so it may as well be pried up and set aside after the door is removed.

Rehanging a door consists of removing the hinges from either the door or the door frame so the door can be placed correctly for fit and free movement. Set it carefully in place, putting enough shims on the bottom so the door will be ½ inch above the floor, then shim it on the sides so it will be vertically plumb and reattach the hinges. If the hinges were inletted in the door frame before they may have to be reset so they will not interfere with the operation of the door.

When the door is reinstalled and swinging smoothly the doorsill can be replaced. Hardwood sills are available from most lumberyards. Chances are the sill may have to be planed for proper fit at the bottom of the door.

If the door frame needs replacing it can be done by prying off the door trim on the outside of the house and then levering the frame loose. Unlike a window, a door frame can be built easily at the site. Just use lumber of the same approximate specifications and the same exact length of the pieces removed. Replacement doors are one of the things dear to the hearts of salvage dealers everywhere and it's almost a sure thing that you can find a used but good door that will fit your needs from a used lumber dealer.

THE ROOF

Now that the siding, the doors and the windows have been reconditioned, it's time to inspect and repair the roof. Leaky roofs are quite common ailments in older houses. Fortunately this is one of the most easily corrected problems.

Evidence of a leaky roof is usually found by examining the inside of the house. A leaky roof will probably cause the ceiling to be discolored. Of course sooner or later it is going to rain and that will dispel any doubts as to the roof's condition. Rainstorms offer good opportunities for pinpointing the location of leaks.

There are basically two types of roofs; the pitch roof and the flat roof. Naturally flat roofs have to be maintained in the best of condition to shed water but the steepest pitch roofs will shed water until they are in very bad condition. Flat roofs are the easiest to work on, though, so they are the ones most apt to be in good repair.

Roofs can be covered with tin, sheet metal, aluminum, clay, tile, slate, asbestos, asphalt or wood. Of all the materials, asphalt or wood shingles are the ones probably most frequently found in need of replacement.

Flat roofs are usually coated with layers of tar and roll roofing, the final layer being a thick coat of tar containing mineral or gravel granules. Repairing a leak in a flat roof is usually accomplished by just adding another layer of tar.

Many times a roof can be repaired merely by replacing the missing shingles. This is just a matter of sliding the new shingle in and tacking it in place. If the new shingle is asphalt it should also be tarred to the shingle beneath it so wind won't cause it to flap up.

Quite often you will want to replace an entire roof covering. This can sometimes be done by just nailing a new layer of roofing right on over the existing roof. New wood shingles can be put over old wooden ones and new asphalt shingles can be put over either old asphalt or wood shingles but if new wood shingles are to go on a roof formerly asphalt-shingled, the old shingles should first be removed.

When economy is the key word a very good job can be obtained with roll roofing. Roll roofing comes in a variety of patterns and colors and goes on easily and speedily. It is very widely used in some areas.

The nicest looking roof for wooded or rural areas is made of shake shingles. They are very expensive to buy but a clever homesteader can split out his own.

Many leaking roofs are caused by loose flashing around the chimney and stool vents out of place. This can be easily corrected by applying a good thick layer of roofing cement over the leaking area.

Roofing can be a dangerous job, especially on a very steep roof. Some safety precautions are to wear rubber-soled shoes, such as tennis shoes, and use a toe board made up of a length of 2 x 4's spiked to the roof.

With roofing problems corrected, this about takes care of the exterior of the building although the rain gutters and drains should be checked to keep runoff water away from the house. Now move inside and inspect the walls, ceiling, plumbing and wiring.

CEILINGS AND FLOORS

Most ceilings in old houses are made of pressed paper blocks nailed to furring strips, sheets of drywall nailed to furring strips or plaster.

Repairing block ceilings and drywall-covered ceilings almost always consists of removing old material and adding new. Plastered ceilings are usually repaired by cleaning out the chipped areas and adding new plaster. Plaster can be purchased in small amounts from the local hardware store.

Naturally the new plaster will have to be repainted since it probably will not match the old. In extreme cases the old plaster can be removed by pounding on it and the lath washed clean before new plaster is applied. This calls for skilled work and it probably shouldn't be attempted by the amateur. Extensive replastering can be avoided by using plasterboard, which is also available. This plasterboard comes in 4' x 8' sheets and is nailed on.

Some people like to install old fashioned wallpaper to the ceiling to make a different looking room. This of course has to have a secure base but it would be the most economical way of covering a plastered ceiling in bad repair or an unsatisfactory block ceiling.

Happens you don't have any "bread" for recovering the ceiling, you could do what many people did during the Great Depression. They simply pasted newspapers to the walls with paste made of flour. A good thick Sunday edition will almost paper a small room! Paste can be made from white flour by whipping in water until the paste is the consistency of gravy. Add a little salt also. When the paste is ready just apply it to one side of the newspaper and stick it on the wall. Smooth out all the air bubbles. Don't worry about how black it has become from all the moisture. It will soon dry out and turn back to its original sheen. Some folks with an artistic sense use colored sheets of Sunday editions for the ceiling and black and white for the walls. Bright cheerful magazine scenes are welcome for wall covering and some people consign a separate theme to each wall. That is, all dogs on one wall, all horses on another wall and still another wall will have pictures and stories about flowers. It is a chance to design a custom-made wall covering for almost no cost.

Newspaper can be used to make a papier-mâché for filling in cracks and holes in walls before papering them. This is done by soaking newspapers until they become a soggy mass. This is the papier-mâché. Remove it from the water, wring it out and add a little white flour to form a paste. When it is very sticky apply it to the cracks, smooth it well and let it dry. When it is dry it can be sanded smooth and papered or painted over.

Walls can be covered with wood paneling or gypsum drywall or they can be covered with plywood and then painted. Shiplap and tongue and groove lumber can also be used for covering walls.

Once you have the walls covered to your satisfaction you can bring the floor up to standard.

Checking the floors for strength can be done just by jumping up and down on them. If the windows rattle and the furniture shakes there is a good possibility that the joists holding the flooor up are weak. Replace the joists as mentioned before, then proceed to the floor covering or flooring.

Many older houses had just one layer of flooring applied diagonally to the joists. This was hardwood in the better houses and softwood such as fir in the more modest ones. Some very old houses had plank floors made of good white pine. This type of floor is so beautiful it shouldn't ever be covered up; instead, it should be sanded smooth and covered with several layers of floor varnish.

The more standard floor consists of two layers of flooring. The first layer is nailed to the joists and usually consists of ½-inch plywood or one-inch milled lumber, then a layer of building paper and another layer of ⅝ inch smooth plywood or the equivalent.

If your floor is very rough and covered with old linoleum, paint or accumulated grime it might be easiest to just nail another layer of flooring right down on top of it and then apply a soft flooring material such as carpet or tile.

If, however, you have determined that your wood floors are worth saving, clean them up with a rented sander. Carefully follow directions though for using the sander because if you don't you can create a multitude of hills and valleys in an otherwise perfectly good floor.

Those operating on a limited budget who nevertheless want their floors to be topnotch also have recourse to a fine covering known as deck paint. Clean off the existing linoleum, dirt or other additions and then drive all the nail heads down below the surface. Fill in the gouges and cracks with plastic wood or crack filler and then apply several coats of a good deck paint. Sometimes it will take four coats or more to do a topnotch job but deck paint applied over a reasonably smooth surface will transform almost any floor into a thing of beauty.

Another, only slightly more expensive floor covering—if you watch the sales—is indoor-outdoor carpeting. This tough, hard covering can be flopped down over almost any floor and it will cover, beautify and protect it for years. If the underfloor is too rough it is well to use at least one layer of building paper beneath the carpet. If the flooring happens to be concrete and you live in a cold climate cement two layers of 60-pound building felt down over the concrete and then lay the finish carpeting (indoor-outdoor) over them. Assuming the flooring is fixed up satisfactorily, it might be well to next inspect the plumbing and the wiring.

PLUMBING, WIRING AND INSULATION

Those homesteaders operating on a very limited budget probably should take a tip from the robust Amish people and rip out and discard all the plumbing and wiring. Thus the water supply system could be a hand operated pump and the lighting system a kerosene lamp. I have yet to see the electric light that could equal the Aladdin-type lamp for sheer restful light.

Should you want to retain the plumbing in its present form but find that it leaks and has a lot of rusty pipes, probably the best solution is to take out the old cold water pipes and replace them with plastic. Hot water pipes should be replaced with copper tubing if it can be obtained. All kinds of fittings are available for connecting plastic and copper plumbing items to steel pipes.

Electric wiring, aside from replacing wall sockets and light fixtures, is a job for an expert. In addition electrical codes exist in many areas which all but eliminate the amateur from this type of work. Then, too, there are strong safety considerations against "doing it yourself." If you would like to learn how to do your own wiring though there is a wide variety of helpful literature available. See the public library or write for booklets from The Superintendent Of Documents.

Insulation is always used or should always be used in construction whether the house is being built in a warm or a cold climate. In a warm climate the insulated house stays cooler and in the cold climate the insulation makes for a warmer house.

Where and how much insulation will be used is all-important. Ideally the house will have six inches of insulation in the ceiling, four inches in the walls and three inches in the floor if there is no basement. This thickness refers to using the fiberglass-type batting insulation. Foam insulation is usually assumed to be three times as efficient as fiberglass. In addition to the insulation there should be a vapor barrier or reflective surface facing the heated areas of the rooms. Many types of insulation have this reflective surface built in. Two other quite welcome advantages of insulation is that it cuts down noise between rooms, it keeps outside noises out and it cuts down on the heat vaporization, which refers to the thermal ability of a cold object to attract heat. If you sit next to a cold uninsulated wall, the wall will draw heat from your body and make you feel cold even though the air around you is warm. This can be noticed quite readily when in a steel building, an automobile or train.

If you have to insulate an old house place roll or loose insulation in the attic between the ceiling joists, add roll insulation whenever you remove a wall section and blow loose insulation into places you otherwise can't reach.

Books
Whitman, Roger C. *First Aid For The Ailing House*. New York, McGraw-Hill, 1958

Cobb, H. *How To Buy And Remodel The Older House.* New York, Macmillan, 1970

Walkins, A. M. *How To Judge A House.* New York, Hawthorn, 1971

Harmon, A. J. *The Guide To Home Remodeling.* New York, Grosset And Dunlap, 1966

Write for Information on Roofing:

Red Cedar And Handsplit Shake Bureau
5510 White Building
Seattle, Washington 98101

Asphalt Roofing Manufacturing, Assoc.
757 Third Avenue
New York, New York 10017

4

BUILDING WITH NATURAL MATERIALS

I doubt that a single North American has to be told what a log cabin is, and a very high percentage of the population has decided at one time or another in their lives that they would like to build one. There are almost as many ways to construct a log cabin as there are builders and once you get by the "who, me?" stage it isn't bad at all.

YOUR OWN LOG CABIN

First you need the logs. Trees, of course, grow in an endless variety of sizes and lengths and we want only one size for the cabin.

The best trees for log cabins are cedar. They grow straight, they usually have very few large limbs and they almost never rot. Place either white or red cedar on some kind of a support so that it doesn't lie on the damp ground and it might last for three hundred years or more. Scattered about here and there in the Nicolet National Forest in northern Wisconsin are log cabins that were built when pines were first cut in the state. Every bit of milled lumber is rotted away—reduced to dust and wormwood—and only occasionally will any iron object be left, but the solid white cedar logs are still standing almost as good as the day they were installed. If cedar is out, your next choice could be balsam, pine, hemlock, maple, aspen, basswood or whatever tree grows the straightest and closest to the cabin site. Most cabin builders classify logs as follows for their resistance to decay.

Woods that could last a lifetime or more: catalpa, cedar, chestnut, cypress, black locust, walnut. Woods that could last fifty years or more: butternut, honey, locust, white oak, persimmon, sycamore. Woods that could last 25 years or more: white ash, beech, paper birch, yellow birch, white elm, hemlock, sugar maple, red oak, lodgepole pine, Norway pine, spruce. Woods that could last ten years or more: aspen, basswood, cottonwood, balsam fir, black gum, jack pine, poplar, willow.

Not all of these woods are suitable for log cabin building; some will never be found in enough supply of the right dimensions to make a log cabin. Perhaps the most important thing is that the homesteader faced with the possibility or necessity of using a variety of woods could use his longest lasting woods on the lowest logs. Also, if he has to use a short-lived wood, he could treat the logs with a preservative which would greatly prolong their life.

Regardless of the wood used the cabin will be much better built and easier to build and it will keep its shape better if the logs are cut at least six months before they are used. Since all logs should also be peeled before they dry they could be cut in the spring. Spring is when the sap is running and the bark will be loose enough to peel off in long strips. However, less checking and a better quality log results if they are cut in late fall. Fall-cut trees can be peeled with a sharp axe or drawknife. When the logs are cut they should have all the limbs trimmed off as close as possible and they should be cut to the approximate length that will be needed. Then they should be piled at least a foot off the ground on cross logs that won't be used for the building. The logs should be supported in several places and kept separated so the air can circulate between them. Ideally they should also be covered, especially in a fairly wet climate. A shed roof covering can be made of poles and tar paper which will easily last the six months that the logs are to be drying.

If peeling the logs is just too great a task there are at least two alternatives. You can cut a three-inch-wide strip through the bark from one end of the log to the other and then pile the log on the drying platform. After a few months the bark will loosen and can then be peeled off very readily, or you can build the cabin with the bark still on the logs. The problem with leaving the bark on the logs is that it thus peels away very gradually, affecting the appearance and longevity of the cabin and inviting a host of insect pests to set up quarters in the recesses and hiding places formed by the loose bark.

No log should be used that curves very badly in more than one direction. Keep logs as uniform in diameter as possible. If it is necessary to use severely tapered logs they can be cut and spliced by matching the cut ends very closely and spiking them together or by using the short logs placed where there will be windows or doors. If a chain saw is used to cut the logs, you can also make them ready for the cabin with the same tool. Just lay the logs on a support, hold them together with a log dog or nail a piece of lumber across them. Then the chain saw is run between the logs. This does three things. It provides flat surfaces on which the logs can rest while drying, it opens a strip through the bark so that it will peel and it localizes the checking which always occurs in drying logs. Naturally it will be better if all the logs are brought together and each log is assigned a place in the cabin. Use an axe and Roman numerals to mark the logs. Every log except the top and bottom ones will have two mating logs. Thus each log will be sawed with two others. Running the chain saw between the logs once will usually be sufficient but, if it is still rough, reclamp the log dogs and run the saw between them again.

Gathering the logs into one place can be the hardest part of the job. If they are cut along a lake they can be floated in to the site. If they can be cut up a steep hill from the site they can often be slid or dragged down to the site. If a horse can be used it makes short work of skidding the logs. Of course, machinery could also be used. Two strong men skidding on the snow can slide a good-sized log by lashing the butt end on a toboggan.

As mentioned before, the ideal time to do this is immediately after they are cut so they can be assigned a place and scored accordingly with the chain saw.

Lifting the logs into place, unless the logs are really huge, shouldn't be too much of a chore. It can be done with a small block and tackle and a tripod made of poles, or it can usually be done by rolling them up a ramp with "people power." Before you cut a single log, though, check the following items.

1. Carefully check the proposed cabin site for proper drainage, availability of drinking water and hazards such as large trees that could be blown down on the cabin. Also make sure that any nearby creek or lake doesn't rise high enough to flood the site in times of high water.

2. Make sure there are enough logs within a reasonable distance. The following figures are given for a 16 by 22-foot cabin. If yours is a different size the figures can be used as a guide. The extra lengths of logs, if any, are trimmed after they are in place.

Sides: 14 26-foot logs, 11 inches in diameter
Ends: 14 22-foot logs, 11 inches in diameter
Gables: 2 14-foot logs, 11 inches in diameter.
2 12-foot logs
2 10-foot logs
2 8-foot logs
2 6-foot logs

2 4-foot logs
7 26-foot poles, 6 inches in diameter for purlines
26 8-foot poles, 4 inches in diameter for rafters

All figures are for inside cabin measurements. The logs should be kept as uniform inside as is possible to make interior finishing easier.

Now to begin the actual construction. First if the cabin is to be a permanent one it should have a foundation. This foundation can be rocks found in the vicinity or it can be made of concrete blocks. It is well to have the floor about 18 inches above ground to deny access to termites, other pests and rodents. If the supply of rocks or cement blocks is limited a spacing of 12 inches above ground can be used. If rocks are used the very largest ones should be set at the corners of the cabin. Before building the foundation, the area where the cabin is to be placed should be staked off and a string stretched between the stakes so the outline of the cabin is visible to the eye. This will point up some surprising facts. Maybe the doorway will be placed where it won't be convenient, maybe the picture window which you wanted on the south side will be shaded by the old fir tree that you won't want to cut, maybe by moving the cabin a few feet one way or another you can get it on level ground or a dozen other things might become evident that you never would have imagined.

Sometimes it will be desirable to build a cabin in an area where there are no usable rock or cement blocks. Then there is no choice except to use poles for a foundation. One way to do this is to sink large-diameter upright posts down to solid soil or bedrock. These posts should be at least ten inches in diameter and they should be spaced above every six feet. If a preservative is available the posts should be painted heavily with it. At any rate, whatever foundation is used, it should be kept level, but no use knocking yourself out to get it perfectly level because the bottom logs can be shaped to make up for the irregularities.

For the bottom logs, select the largest soundest logs that you have. Roll them onto the foundation and level them up by shaving the bottom surfaces so that they fit very soundly on the foundation. The shaving can be done with a drawshave, an axe, an adze or a broad axe. Whatever tool is used it should be kept very sharp. Proceed with care and caution laying these first two logs and you won't have too much to worry about in laying up the succeeding ones. Once the two longest side logs are in place the end logs can be notched in.

The end logs are the first ones that have to be notched. Might as well use the saddle notch since it is the easiest to make and sheds moisture better than some of the other type notches. First, take the calipers or dividers and measure half the diameter of the bottom log. Then lay the point of the cali-

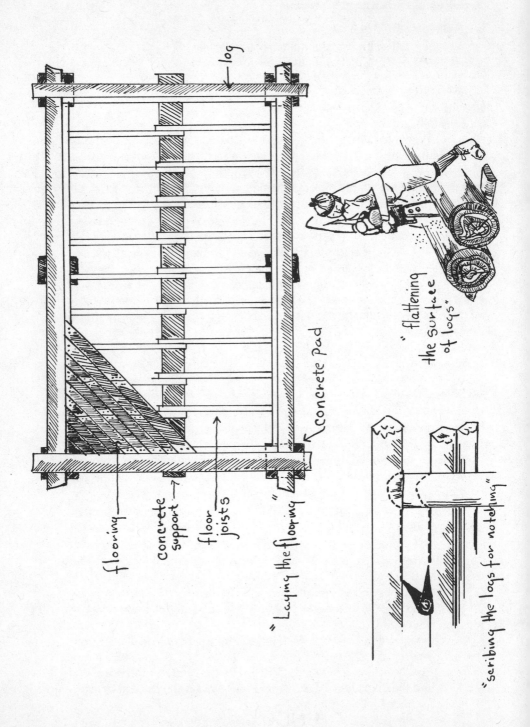

log

"Laying the flooring"

flooring

concrete
support →

floor
joists

Concrete pad

"flattening
the surface
of logs"

"scribing the logs for notching"

pers on the bottom log and scribe a line on the top log. Do this on both sides of the top log. Then very carefully remove the wood inside the half moon marks. Saw perpendicular cuts into the log and gouge out the wood with a gouge chisel if you have one. Ideally the notches will be cupped slightly to make a tighter fit and hold the moisture out. Of course this is going to leave the ends without support. If the end logs are green it might be well to place some support under them until the cabin is done settling. Now the next two logs that you notch into place will be the side logs. The notch for these can be cut exactly as the previous one. Keep going this way building up the sidewalls by notching one log into another until the sidewalls are complete. Make very sure that the walls are going straight up by repeated checking with a plumbline. Once the logs are all in place nail milled lumber, such as a 2 x 4, around the outline of the doors and windows and saw those out. If the openings go up to within one log of the top the top log can be left out until the openings are sawed. All logs should be spiked in place, even when the notching is done satisfactorily. You will notice as you pile the logs one on top of each other that the small and large ends should be alternated. Also notches are just cut in the bottom of the log—never in the top. The log to be notched will always be the one that hasn't yet been placed.

When it is necessary to splice logs, saw the two log ends diagonally. Then drill a ¾-inch hole halfway through the top log and a 7/16-inch hole for the rest of the way. Then place a 12-inch steel spike down in the hole and drive it into the bottom log so that the head of the spike stops against the 7/16-inch hole in the upper log. If no spikes are available wooden pins made from dry spruce or a similar wood can be used. Wooden pins can be made square or hexagon or whatever is easiest as long as they fit tightly in the hole. Holes for the wooden pins can be drilled exactly like the holes for the spikes. At the bottom of each pin a slit can be made and a wedge-shaped chip of wood fitted into the slit. Then when the pin is driven in place the wedge will expand the bottom of the pin and cause it to fit very snugly in the hole. Logs should also be pinned or spiked if they are for a large building over 25 feet and where the opening for the doors and windows are placed. Pinning keeps the logs from springing away from each other as they dry.

Naturally if long spikes are available and you are working with wood that can be nailed without splitting, the easiest method is simply to drive spikes down through the wood every so often.

The roof can and should be made from poles. Nothing is as pleasing to the eye as a peeled pole roof, each log lying side by side in perfect symmetry.

When the wall logs are all in place build the ends of progressively

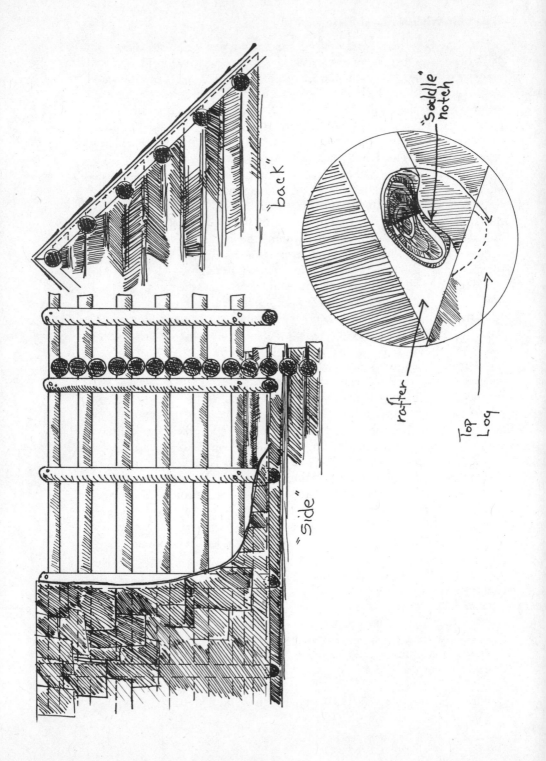

"back"

"Saddle" notch

rafter

Top Log

"side"

shorter logs to form a gable. The gable should be about five feet higher than the walls, especially in heavy snow areas, this so the roof will have the necessary pitch. Each end log will be notched enough so the roof purline or roof poles can be put in place. The ridgepole is placed on top of the topmost gable log. The purlines go the length of the cabin from end wall to end wall. When they are in place the rafters are laid. Notch the rafters so they will "sleep" on the sidewalls, each purline and the ridgepole. Angle-cut the rafters where they fit together at the top and nail them at the ridgepole, sidewalls and at each purline. If you desire a warm roof nail two layers of building felt over the purlines and then fill the space between the rafters with dried cattail leaves and stems, bulrush stems or commercial insulation.

Chinking the logs is easily done by pushing sphagnum moss between the cracks and then holding it in place with the best clay mud in the vicinity. If no good clay is available, sand and cement or lime can be mixed together to form a mud that will harden when it is pushed into the cracks. Nowadays cabin builders use fiberglass insulation, pounding it into place until it fills the cracks tightly and then nailing wooden strips over the cracks to keep it in place.

If your logs are smooth and straight and if you have the time and the patience, permanent chinking can be made from small limbs peeled and nailed in place after pounding fiberglass insulation in the cracks. Incidentally, it will be easier to chink the logs at the time when they are notched in place by placing the insulation on the bottom log. Chink as you go, in other words.

Window and door frames can be made from hewn logs or from milled logs or from milled lumber. Sometimes a sawmill will be close to where you are building and can supply rough-sawn lumber for use. Some of the Old Timers made whip-sawn lumber which you can easily do yourself with a chain saw. Windows, complete with frames, can be obtained from salvage yards. It is well to find the windows though before cutting the openings in the logs so they can be cut to the right size. At first make only a rough opening for the window by nailing two-inch milled lumber around its inside edges. Make the door frame the same way. Doors can be salvaged or made, if necessary, by nailing heavy boards together with building paper sandwiched in between to cut down drafts.

After the windows and doors are in place the floor has to be made. Keep in mind, though, that a floor isn't absolutely essential, especially in warmer climates. A good hard floor may result from normal traffic, depending on kind of soil, especially if it is moistened from time to time. So if time is pressing you can just leave the floor out for the time being and board up the space under the bottom logs, but eventually some better floor will probably be wanted. A floor has to have something to rest on so you will have to spike some sleepers of 2 x 6's or hewn logs to the side logs of the cabin and then place floor joists about one foot apart between them. Cover the joists with tight-fitting milled lumber, cover the milled lumber with heavy paper, and cover the heavy paper with the top layer of flooring. This should result in a draft-free floor.

BUILDING A STONE CABIN

Should there be no logs in the area of your desired cabin or if you would prefer to build a cabin from stone this is possible, too. Volumes upon volumes have been written about building with stone and the super skill of the stone mason, etc., but you will find that if you use a good mixture of stone and cement your walls will proceed up to their designated heights about as well as if you were more experienced. And one advantage of stone is that it can be picked up in varying shapes and sizes and every stone will help fill a form.

Digging in the footings is the first step in building a stone house unless, of course, the ground is stone. The footings can be a trench which should be at least two feet wide and three feet deep. When the trench is complete the hole is filled with stones mixed with enough cement to coat each rock thoroughly.

When ground level is reached forms must be made to hold the stone and cement in place until they "set up." Use strips of plywood about 18 inches wide to build forms for the walls; for good utilization of odd-shaped rocks the walls should be about 18 inches thick also, but thicknesses less than this are satisfactory, too. Nine or ten inches might satisfy some builders. Continue the walls upward by removing the frames after each section of the wall has started to set up, placing them successively on top of the section just finished. Hold them in place with heavy bolts or wire placed across the forms. Using this method the unskilled can build a wall as good as the professional and in doing so he can use a lot poorer material.

Naturally when the window and door areas are reached they will have to be framed in. When the wall is as high as you want it the roof must be built of lumber or logs. Stone houses will generally be the most successful in warmer climates where stone is abundant. Stone houses used in cold climates will have to be lined with some insulating material. They should also be kept well sealed to prevent moisture from freezing between the rocks and splitting the walls. But on the positive side it doesn't require much skill or capital outlay to build a very long-lasting structure wherever you wish to live.

"Stone Cabin"

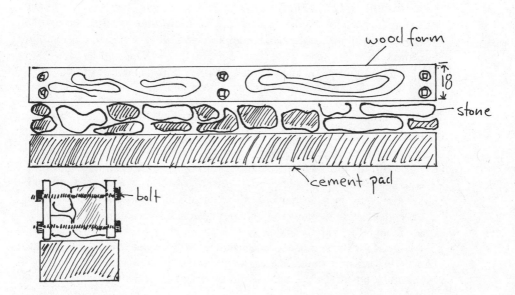

wood form

18

stone

cement pad

bolt

If it is necessary or desirable to build a stone building without forms the rocks have to be selected with great care so they will fit well beside and on top of each other. Some stones will hardly fit anywhere and some, especially hexagonally-shaped or square stones, will fit anywhere. Corner stones are usually the hardest to come by and it might be necessary to shape your own. This can be done with a hammer and cold chisel. The procedure is usually to score the rock along the lines where you want it to break and then hit it very hard, breaking it with the hammer. Skilled stone masons can, by studying the grain of the rock, break a rock into almost any desired size and shape.

One of the best places to find rocks is along a river bed. Other very good places are fence rows and the edges of old fields. Sometimes a single farm will yield enough rocks to build a complete structure. Rocks picked up from stream beds are usually the prettiest but don't be surprised when they lose much of their brilliance upon drying out. If you have to purchase stone it is usually cheaper when picked up at the quarry. Also quarries usually have a pile of scrap or odd stone that is almost free. This type of stone will require a little more work but if time is not pressing it might be the best selection.

THE SOD HOUSE

The sod house or cabin is something else. Not much information has been retained for posterity about the sod house. This is a pity since the properly built sod house in the proper location would shed water and keep its occupants warm in the winter and cool in the summer far better than some of the milled lumber atrocities that the early settlers moved their families into.

Of first importance when planning the sod house is to use great care in its location. Most sod houses will be built on the Plains or in the Far North where timber, especially trees for a wind break, will be scarce. Therefore, it is quite wise to build on the south side of a hill, one at least of enough height to break the winter winds. The site should not be located where water can run down a hill onto the roof or in through the door. Sod houses can be built up from the ground, conventionally, or a hillside can be used as one side of the house. The latter kind of sod houses are called dugouts since they were at least partially dug out of the ground. All of the other usual considerations should be examined such as availability of water, distance from a fuel supply and so on.

Material for the sod house is selected from the oldest toughest grass you can find. Then get someone to plow up several furrows or else cut the sod out with a shovel. The pieces should be about 12 inches wide and two to three feet long. The walls should be at least one foot thick. Alternate one sod on top of the other to form the walls. When the window heights are reached—about three feet from the ground—set in the window frames of planks or other strong material. Continue building up the walls until the desired height is reached. This is usually about six feet six inches. Then taper the end walls in to form gables. Continue the gables up to a maximum height of at least four feet. On top of the gables lay a ridgepole. Pound it down well into the sod, then lay rafters from the side walls to the ridgepole and nail them to the ridgepole. If enough lumber is available the rafters can be spaced about eight inches apart, but if lumber is scarce put the rafters 18 inches apart and cover them with chicken wire. After the rafters are in place cut more sod and lay it on the rafters until the roof is formed. The sod for both the roof and the side walls should be from four to six inches thick. The sod for the roof should be thatched or put on in layers so that each one overlaps the one below. The courses are similar to courses of shingles. The very toughest sod should be laid at the junction of the roof, directly atop the ridgepole.

The door can be made from split poles or it can be a door salvaged from a junk yard. Many of the early settlers simply dispensed with the door and hung a rug or skin in the door opening.

The windows can be salvaged from a junk yard or they can be made from plastic, one sheet for summer, two sheets—one inside and one outside—for winter.

An advantage of the sod house is that with reasonable amounts of rain the grass will keep on growing and the walls and roof will get tighter and tighter.

The floor can be plain dirt. This will be pounded hard enough in time so that the floor can be swept as clean as a board floor. In fact, build it over the right kind of mud and it will be possible to even mop it after awhile. If desired, a wooden floor can also be installed, of course. To do this lay sleepers of timber or logs across the longest dimensions of the sod house. Then spike floor joists of 2 x 6 material on two-foot centers across the sleepers. Cover the floor joists with plywood, hewed poles or boards.

If the ceilings and inside walls of the sod house shed dirt, as they may at first, cover them with old rugs, lumber, wrapping paper stapled to furring strips or sheets of plastic. One house that doesn't shed is adobe.

THE ADOBE HOUSE

The first step in building an adobe house is to check on the availability and supply of building adobe. Good adobe is almost always found at least six inches below the surface of the earth. However, pure adobe soil without any sand is impossible to use without special treatment. Good adobe soil is composed of the proper mixture of soil and sand. Probably the best way to determine if you can use the soil as is, is to test it. Make up a form for molding adobe bricks. This can be made to mold four at a time. The list of materials for making it:

   3 4-foot 1 x 4's
   3 2-foot 1 x 4's
   1 pound of 10d nails
   2 pints of paint

   Paint the inside of the forms so the adobe will not stick. The form, of course, has no top or bottom.

   Now take a posthole digger and dig four different holes at four different locations believed to contain likely soil. Chop up a handful of grass or straw for each brick. Place the sample soil and straw in four different containers, water them thoroughly and let them set overnight. Next morning take the garden hoe and mix the adobe and straw thoroughly. The consistency of this mix should be thick enough that it can be lifted with a manure fork; add more water or soil as necessary.

   Now place the form on a level piece of ground, "flour" the ground with dry dust or with straw chaff to keep the adobe from sticking to the earth beneath the form. Spade the adobe mix into each form, making sure that you know where each sample came from by marking the molds or numbering them. Tamp each brick well and level off the top. If the mix was of the proper consistency the mold can be lifted as soon as it is tamped and the bricks will stay in shape. Now comes a waiting period of from ten days to two weeks to cure the bricks. After the first few days the bricks can be tipped on their side to dry better but otherwise they shouldn't be moved. At the end of this time they can be tested for strength. The usual way is to inspect the brick visually for cracks and to test its strength by attempting to twist it. If it resists breaking it is probably all right. If it crumbles there is too much sand in it and it will have to be mixed with more clay for a better brick. If the brick has shrunk considerably and has large cracks in it there has been too much clay in the mix and this of course can be corrected by adding more sand to the mix. If one of the bricks is just right, take another sample from the same place and place it in a fruit jar full of water, shake it very well, then let it sit and settle for about 24 hours. At the end of this time the layers of sand and clay will be visible since they will settle out away from each other. By holding the jar up to the light you can determine about how much clay to sand you have in your correct mixture. Finding other adobe veins or correcting poor ones is simplified by using this method.

Now when you have the molds made, the site selected and a mixing box constructed you can start molding the bricks. The mixing box can be about one foot deep and about eight feet long and five feet wide. Some adobe builders use a cement mortar box made of boards of about the same dimensions. In all cases the adobe mud should be soaked overnight to destroy the lumps in the soil. After the bricks are molded they should be allowed to set for about two weeks. When they are dry they can be laid on the foundation.

The mud used to stick the adobe to the foundation and to stick the bricks to each other is the same mud that the bricks are made of except no straw is mixed into it. Starting the bricks is just like starting a course of bricks or cement blocks. Square the corners and build up a few courses of brick first. Then stretch a string across to the next corner and lay the bricks between. When the window and door openings are reached some of the bricks will have to be cut and notched. This can be done with a large machete or a hatchet. Also the window and door openings are framed with 2 x 12 or 2 x 8 planks. The door frames are made by spiking the planks together and then nailing a 2 x 4 up and down the outside. The frame is then fitted into the blocks which must be notched to accept the 2 x 4's.

When the top of the windows are reached, a hewed plank of hardwood or steel beam can be used to reinforce the top of the opening. This beam should extend across the window opening and project 12 inches on each side of it. The adobe blocks will have to be trimmed or shaved to bed this beam.

When the next to the top row of blocks is reached the poles to support the roof are added. These poles or "vigas" should be consderable in size—at least 8 inches in diamter, 12 is better. They are laid 4 feet apart extending from one side of the house to the other. Usually a row of blocks is laid around the poles to complete the walls. The roof is then finished by nailing boards or timbers across the vigas and covering them with composition roofing.

The windows and doors are fitted in as in a conventional building and a cone-shaped fireplace called a fogón is built into one corner.

Fogones are a quarter-round cone built into one corner of the room. They are usually small, four to six feet across the base, tapering to the ceiling. A hole is cut in the roof and a steel stovepipe added to extend at least two feet above the roof so the fire will draw well. The fogón is used for cooking as well as heat so it is placed at least 12 inches above the floor. The opening into the fireplace is kept narrow so no reinforcing is needed across the top.

Adobe house floors can be made from adobe blocks or lumber. Naturally adobe is easier to build with than lumber, but some type of floor is a definite asset even in a tent.

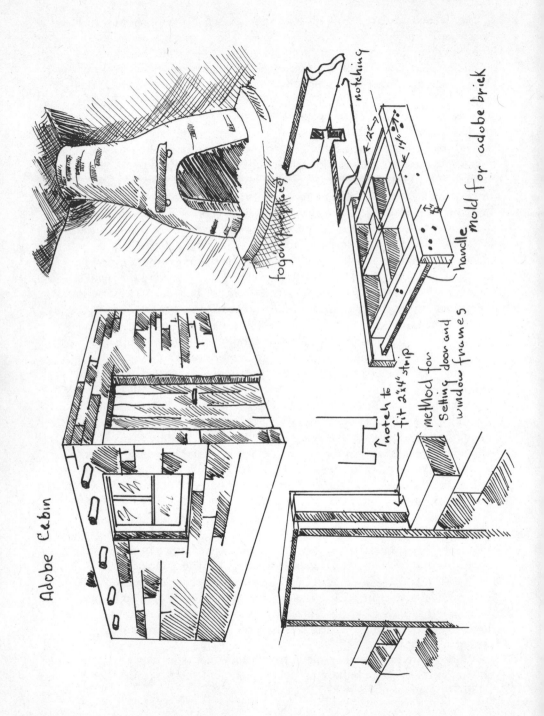

Adobe Cabin

fogon (fireplace)

notching

←12"→ ↑ 14" ↓

mold for adobe brick

handle

notch to fit 2"x4" strip

method for setting door and window frames

THE TEPEE

The undisputed king of tents for nomadic homesteaders has to be the Indian tepee. It can be cooled, heated, ventilated and cleaned easier than most other tents. Probably the two factors which make it outstanding, however, are the feeling of spaciousness and the open fire which can be built in it for heating and cooking.

Anyone with sewing ability or a few dollars for hiring such work can make an Indian tepee. The poles which even the Indians had to purchase at times are best made from red or white cedar but almost any straight pole can be used if peeled and dried. This tepee will require 15 poles, each 24 feet long, about four inches at the butt tapering to two inches at the top.

See the accompanying diagram containing a pattern for making the cover. Covering for the tepee, which can be cotton drill, can be purchased from mail-order houses or stores in most any large city. Since this type of material usually comes in strips 30 or 45 inches wide it has to be sewed together to provide the coverage needed. The finished half circle will have a radius of about 17.5 feet. Don't worry though if your material comes out a few inches one way or another. A radius of approximately 17.5 feet can be formed by sewing five strips of 45-inch material together. Naturally the strips will be progressively shorter, thus the longest one is 38 feet, next 37, 36, 34, 30 and 25.4 feet.

If, after studying the pattern diagram, you jump to the conclusion that the longest piece or strip is going to go around the tepee frame at its bottom and parallel at all points to the ground, you've got it all wrong! The longest strip will actually run diagonally from the ground up toward the top. (See illustration.)

Use a dressmaker's seam to sew the edges together with the longer strip overlapping the lower strip three inches. When the canvas is all sewed together lay it out on a flat surface, take a string and pencil and stretch it out from the center of the longest strip to the center of the shortest strip. Anchor the string to a pivot in the center of the longest strip and draw a radius across the material. If the radius runs out somewhere simply sew another piece of material on to complete it. Then, *without cutting anything,* turn the edges of the material up to the radius and pin to be sewn later. These turned-up edges will double the drill where it touches the ground. A pleasing edge can be made after sewing by trimming the loose edges of the material.

The longest strip has to have half of the entrance hole and the smoke flaps cut into it. Measure down 20 inches from the outer edge of the longest strip and in towards the center 10.4 feet. Do this on both sides and cut out the rectangular pieces. Go to the exact center of the longest

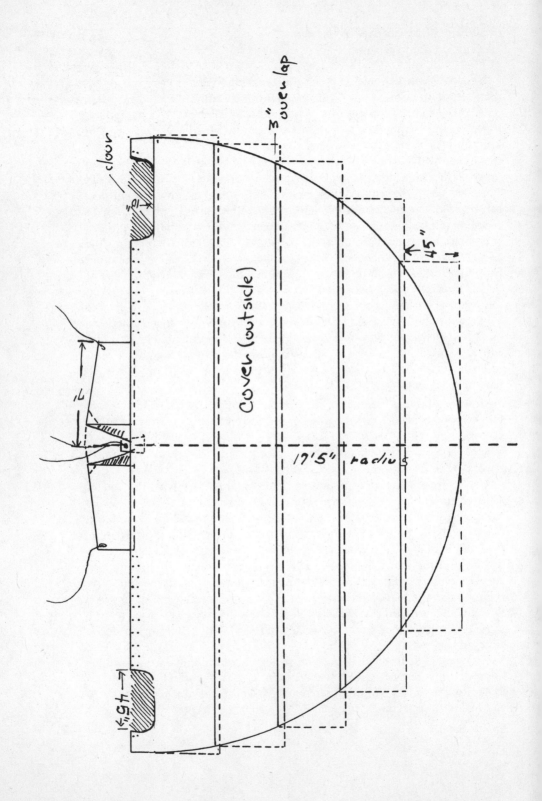

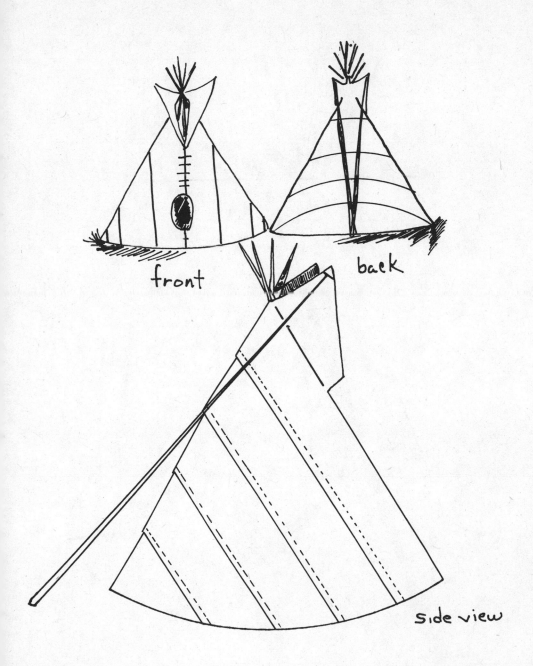

front

back

side view

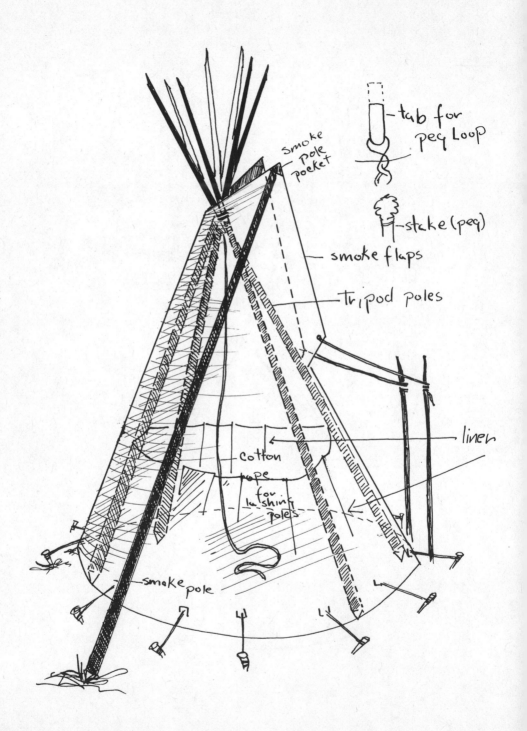

smoke
pole
pocket

tab for
peg loop

stake (peg)

smoke flaps

tripod poles

liner

cotton
rope
for
lashing
poles

smoke pole

strip and cut in approximately 24 inches, this will form the smoke flaps. Now the entrance hole can be cut out or it can be cut out after the two edges of the tepee are brought together. If you cut it out now, cut a half-oval on each side 12 inches in from the outside radius. This oval will be ten inches deep and 45 inches long.

Each outside edge will finally be brought together and fastened. To make this fastening most efficient, holes are punched in both edges of the top strip. These holes are formed by cutting a tiny cross in the material in rows two inches from the outside edge. The crosses are turned back and sewed to form a ⅜-inch hole. These holes will hold the canvas edges together by means of tie pins.

Now make a liner of muslin or similar cloth according to the diagram and set the poles up by first placing four poles directly across from each other tying their tops together and then setting the other poles in place. See the diagram. Notice that the poles are *not set in a perfect circle,* one side is flat for the smoke hole.

If all this sewing and cutting sounds like too much work a complete tepee can be purchased from several different companies or a kit for making a tepee can be purchased from addresses at the end of the chapter.

Books

Rutstrum, Calvin, *The Wilderness Cabin*. New York: Macmillan, 1961
Angier, Bradford and Vena, *How To Build Your Home in the Woods*. 1972
Allen, Edward, *Stone Shelters*. Cambridge, Massachusetts: M.I.T., 1971
Southwick, Marcia, *Building With Adobe*. Chicago: Swallow, 1971
Laubin, Gladys and Laubin, Reginald, *The Indian Tipi—Its History, Construction and Use*. New York: Ballantine, 1971

Booklets

Building a Log House
Cooperative Extension Service
University Of Alaska
Box 1109
Juneau, Alaska

Handbook for Building Homes of Earth
Superintendent Of Documents
Government Printing Office
Washington, D. C. 20402

FHA Pole House Construction
U. S. Department Of Housing And Rural Development
Washington, D. C. 20410

Sources for Indian Tepees

Nomadics
Star Route
Box 41
Cloverdale, Oregon 97112

Goodwin-Cole Company
1315 Alhambra Boulevard
Sacramento, California 95816

5

THE WATER STORY

THERE ARE ONLY three sources of water: rainfall, which must be stored in cisterns or reservoirs; surface water, which is contained in lakes, rivers or streams and subsurface water, which exists in great underground rivers or "veins."

In some areas such as islands in the oceans or mainland locations where little or no surface water exists and a thick layer of rock underlays the soil, catching and storing rainfall is important. Rainfall is usually caught from a roof or a natural slope and channeled into a cistern for storage. Since rainwater is "soft" or mineral-free it is the very best kind for washing clothes, bathing, dyeing cloth, making soap—in fact, for almost everything but drinking.

DON'T OVERLOOK RAINWATER

Modern homesteaders can catch rainwater by sinking a large tile or placing a wooden barrel near one end of the cabin and channeling to it all the roof water by means of rain gutters and downspouts. One can store water this way on whatever scale is desired since it is entirely possible to obtain all the usual water required this way. One-half inch of rain falling on one hundred square feet of roof will produce thirty gallons of water (theoretically). But, actually if you get to use half of this you will be lucky since there are losses from evaporation and so forth. Yet even so, the quantity of water which can be collected this way is tremendous. Of course rainwater should be purified or distilled before drinking.

Another way of obtaining drinking water is to purify surface water. Available surface water could be runoff from a hillside, a creek, a pond, a river or a lake. Very little safe drinking water can be scooped up "free" these days but almost all water can be made safe to drink.

WATER PURIFICATION

The simplest way is to boil it for at least ten minutes. Most people use about a gallon a day so multiply this by the number of drinkers when you calculate the needed supply. Easier than boiling is to construct a simple solar still and let the sun distill the water. Stills can be devised for use in conjunction with woodstoves also and they will deliver safe drinking water whenever the stove is burning. In remote areas melted snow should be safe enough to drink. It takes about ten inches of snow to produce one inch of water in the average household container though.

Clean water can be purified by adding a carefully measured amount of calcium hypochlorite. This chemical is so strong that a tablespoonful will purify one thousand gallons of water. Since you will probably be purifying smaller amounts such as fifty gallons at a time, dissolve the calcium hypochlorite in water and measure out the solution. Example: Dissolve one teaspoonful calcium hypochlorite in one gallon water. Add a scant three cups of this solution to the fifty gallons of water to be purified. Let it work for at least 15 minutes before you use it. Of course there are kits which do all this automatically. They consist of a filter to strain the impurities from the water, a chlorine injector which conveys tiny amounts of chlorine to the water on a continuous basis and another filter to take out the chlorine taste. A source is given at the end of the chapter.

SPRING WATER

Better than artificially purified water is pure sweet water from your very own spring. When a spring is found on the homestead, even though it is a tiny one, it can often be developed to supply both drinking and refrigerator water. To reap these benefits from the spring, dig it out, shore it up, provide a cistern for water storage, then put a building over it to protect it from surface contamination.

Digging out a spring is mostly hand labor. What you are actually trying to do is to open up the "vein" of water so the flow will be as great as its potential. This has to be done with care. Very carefully follow the vein by digging, maybe even with a teaspoon at first until the digging produces an increased flow. Then keep widening and deepening this vein, graduating

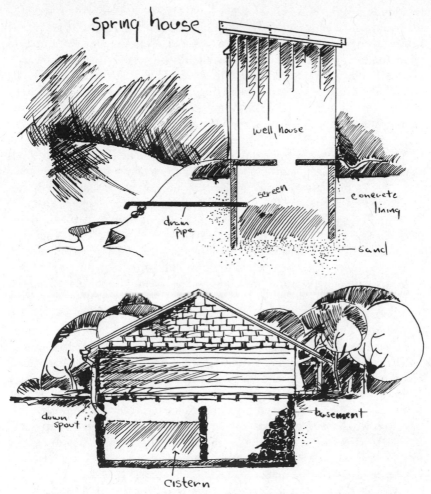

spring house

well house

screen

concrete lining

drain pipe

sand

down spout

basement

cistern

from teaspoon to shovel. When the flow has increased enough to take care of your water needs or when you are apparently getting as much of a flow out of it as it is capable of producing you can start digging for the cistern or supply tank. Naturally this will have to be below the spring so the water will run into it. If the spring is on level ground, the cistern is sunk into the spring and shored up all around with loose (unmortared) rocks which will allow the spring seepage to come in.

YOUR OWN WELL

Man has known of the underground water supply for centuries. The ancient Chinese designed a way to drill wells by dropping a weight attached to a crude drilling head. The weight was lifted by a teeter-totter arrangement and a pole and fulcrum commonly called a spring pole. The Chinese reportedly spent generations drilling a single well but they were able to penetrate hard earth to incredible depths this way.

Most of the early wells were dug wells. That is, the well digger just started on the top of the ground and dug a hole down until he penetrated a water vein or "zone of saturation." Most of these dug wells were shallow but some wells do go down to nearly three hundred feet, much of this even in solid rock.

The homesteader setting out to dig where there are no other wells should consider these main points: He should be above the sanitary facilities. That is, his well should be located on a higher slope than the outdoor privy or septic system so he won't have sewer or other seepage from his "bathroom" in the well. He should also locate the well close to the cabin so the water won't have to be carried too far. The third consideration is that he had just as well locate it in some natural depression because even a depth of three feet below the nominal surface of the ground will save that much digging, and three feet, when you are digging a well, can be as much as two days' work!

When starting to dig your well and curb it up you will quickly see that a square hole or a rectangular one is much easier to work in than a round one. One can work in a rectangle three feet by four feet most efficiently.

The chief tool for digging a well is a short-handled shovel. Most shovel handles will probably be too long and therefore should be cut off. Also a pick will probably be useful plus a bar to pry out boulders, etc. The pick handle too will have to be cut off some. Once the hole gets five or six feet deep you will have to have some special means of getting the dirt up out of the hole. This can be a bucket with a rope attached, to be raised and lowered by someone on the top of the ground or it might be a device that can be operated by one man.

One such device for use in getting in and out of a deep hole and also for carrying the dirt up is a crane pivoting on an upright pole. This is known as a "bridge crane" and its base consists of a six-inch hardwood post sunk in the earth to at least a six-foot depth. This post is drilled four feet above the ground and a ½-inch bolt inserted through it so that its ends project. A guy wire is used to hold the post upright. A section of eight-inch pipe is put over the post so it rests against the bolt. This forms a pivot point or collar. Now one end of a four-foot length of two-inch pipe is welded to this collar and the outer end is drilled for installation of an eyebolt from which a pulley and rope are suspended. The main advantage of a bridge crane arrangement is that it can be pivoted out of the way so the bucket can be dumped without lifting it. This permits use of a much heavier bucket, it

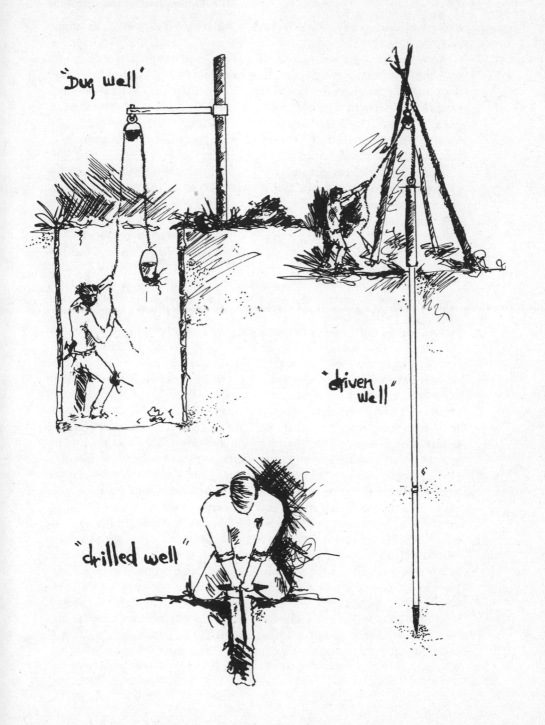

"Dug well"

"driven well"

"drilled well"

also permits one man to dig and dump by attaching a system of pivots and lines to the bucket.

Another arrangement which is widely used and is simple and economical is a tripod built over the hole. Its apex should be at least four feet above the surface of the ground. The tripod consists of strong poles and one-inch rope. Extra strength is needed since it will be used to raise and lower a person when the hole gets too deep for a ladder. As the well deepens it must be curbed to prevent a cave-in. Again, it is easier to curb a square or rectangular hole than a round one. The curbing can be lumber or stone and clay or cement tile can also be used if available. Some wells have been curbed with poured concrete. Whatever material is used it should seal out surface water and seepage. The top of a dug well should be covered and a pipe and a pump should be used to lift the water. Before a well is used it can be sterilized by mixing a tablespoonful of calcium hypochlorite to a quart of water and adding it to the well. This should be left in overnight and then pumped out completely.

Perhaps the easiest and most economical well to bring in is the driven well. Well points for driven wells are sold in hardware stores almost everyplace in the country. They consist of a perforated steel pipe, tapered on one end so that it can be driven into the ground. The opposite end is threaded with 1¼-inch pipe thread. It is used by attaching a length of 1¼-inch well pipe to a driving point. Then at the other end of the well pipe there is attached a heavy-duty coupling or drive cap. (All of these supplies are commonly sold where well points are sold.) Place the sharpened end of the point into the ground and start driving it. It helps considerably if you use a posthole digger first to go down about three feet before starting the point. Be very sure to keep it straight up and down when you start. If the ground is fairly soft you can pound the point in with a heavy sledge. If a sledge doesn't produce the desired results, build a tripod or bridge crane arrangement over the pipe and install a pulley. Next find a length of pipe about three feet long that will fit over the drive-pipe cap. This would commonly be a piece of two-inch pipe. Take this pipe to a blacksmith and have him weld a piece of round stock in one end of it for weight. The pipe should weigh about thirty pounds after this is done. Also weld a loop of heavy rod over the top for attaching a rope. Then thread a rope through the tripod pulley, tie it to the loop in the end of the drive weight, slip the weight down over the pipe and start lifting and dropping it. It also helps if a set of handles is welded to the drive weight so a helper can slide the pipe up and down thereby keeping it straight and assisting in the driving as well.

In using the point, keep it full of water. This is for lubrication and it will also indicate when water is reached. Water in the point will quickly run out to the depth of water encountered. Additionally, the amount of water which can be poured into the point at a given time will indicate how much water can be taken out. It is a startling fact that water-bearing sand or gravel will absorb about the same amount of water as it will give up.

Most points drive fairly rapidly even in hard soil. If downward progress stops it indicates a boulder has been encountered and the point can't penetrate anymore or it has hit either a layer of extremely hard soil or a ledge of rock. Usually the point will indicate whether the obstruction is rock or just dense soil. A boulder or ledge stopping the point will be signaled by the ringing sound of the driver against the pipe. Also the driver and possibly even the pipe will rebound. If it rebounds you will have to pull it and start over. Don't give up too easily though as sometimes the boulder will move out of the way. If a posthole auger is available try turning that down to the obstruction. In fact many times it is necessary to use a posthole auger in conjunction with a drive point to penetrate rocky soil. And shallow wells have been drilled with the posthole auger alone.

Remember as you add additional lengths of pipe to the point that they will stay permanently in the soil. Therefore the joints (as pipe is added) must be coated with sealer and they must be very well tightened when pounded down. One of the best ways to do this is to turn the pipe while pounding it. Even if you don't turn the whole column you will still be able to turn and tighten the last pipe. The importance of keeping the pipe going straight down cannot be everemphasized. This makes it drive easier, insures that the pipe joints will be at maximum strength and of course will make it easier to pull if you have to bring it back up.

The task of bringing the pipe back to the surface with the point still attached depends on how deep the point is and how hard the soil is. Usually it can be pulled from coarse sand or clay but seldom from hardpan or very fine sand. At best it will require a considerable pull such as had by using a jack or a chain wrapped around it and connected to a long pole or lever. Two jacks under an I-beam which is chained to the pipe will work also. Of course if time is not at a premium you can always dig it out. Points have been pulled by keeping them full of water for a few days or by pumping water down into them where pumps and water are available. If an auger is available, drill down beside the pipe to loosen it. If a lot of pipe is down in the ground and you wish to retrieve as much of it as possible the pipe can be speedily cut off by dropping dynamite down the open end of the pipe. *Use all the precautions relating to dynamite and get well back from the site before the explosion.* Typically, a half stick of 40% dynamite should shear the pipe at its most rigid point, usually where it enters the drive point. The shock also loosens the pipe in the ground so it can be retrieved. Similarly, one homesteader I know was able to pull 16 feet of pipe and the attached point up from tough clay merely by dropping large firecrackers down the open end of the pipe; the shock waves loosened the pipe enough so it would come up.

As mentioned before, the pipe should be kept full of water. If the water seeps away slowly but completely, you are drilling in dry soil, but if it runs out to a certain level and then stops, and subsequent fillings of the pipe confirm the same results you could possibly be in water-bearing soil. If so, attach a pump, prime it and try to pump. When the drill encounters water-bearing soil it is usually signaled by the point suddenly becoming very easy to drive. Once in a while, however, the point will get so clogged up from drilling that it won't let water in even though the point is submerged in it. Then it has to be flushed out. A pitcher pump works very well for this. Just pump very hard for a few minutes, then drop the handle and let the water run back down again. This reverse flow of water will usually clean the screen. If it doesn't, the drill and pipe will have to "soak" or be pumped again in reverse. Even a good well will yield a lot of sand and dirt at first. Sometimes it takes two or three days of alternate pumping and resting to clear up a well so that the water is good and clean.

Having described three methods of drilling a well by hand, let's examine the feasibility of using all three methods together for bringing in a well in a particularly stubborn place. First, go to the library and/or write to the water regulatory board of your state or talk to local residents and find out how deep the water table is in the area. For instance, let's say it is fifty feet deep with a layer of rock at 15 feet. Before planning our strategy we know that we can't turn an auger or drive a point through a layer of rock. Therefore it is mandatory that we somehow dig down to that level. Using the method for the dug well, we dig a rectangle three by four feet straight down to the rock, curbing as we go. When we get to the rock ledge we find it's so hard that we have to star drill and chip it out a little at a time. Finally we make a hole through the rock about one foot square. Directly under the rock is the hardest most dense sand we have ever seen. To penetrate this we use an auger such as usually used for drilling postholes. Soon though we get into some easier digging, clay soil interlaced with gravel. We are not surprised at these layers because we have done our "homework"—we have a pretty good idea of the geology of the area. Our auger penetrates for another six feet and then we get into some moist sand. We are looking for this also and know that this moist soil overlays the water-bearing sand and is called fringe water. Now we know we are going to have to go yet another six to ten feet to reach the water so we couple up a sand type driving point and drive it down. It goes very well and pretty soon it's moving as much as three inches at each blow of the sledge. We keep on driving until we are sure the point has penetrated to its full depth in water. All that remains is to fill the hole up again, adding lengths of pipe to reach the surface of the ground. Since we won't be able to use a pitcher pump with this well, we purchase a long-handled regulation farm pump and build a concrete foundation for it around the base.

Some homesteaders are going to settle in areas where it is practically impossible to bring in their own well. This means they will have to have a well-driller do it. Before buying the land, find out how much this will cost and figure it in for the purchase price of the land. Typical prices for drilling a six-inch well are $10.00 to $12.00 a foot. The advantage here is that the well will almost always be a good producer and, like the banker says, it will add that much to the equity you have in the land if you should decide to sell. In fact, it might be impossible to sell a piece of property without a drilled well in some areas.

CLEANING AN OLD WELL

There are old wells usually on old abandoned farms. All a homesteader has to do with these is clean them out. Usually they are full of rocks; children love to drop rocks down a pipe just to hear them hit the bottom; plus maybe small animals, dead birds, pieces of metal and other objects that have fallen down through the casing. Well-drillers encounter this frequently enough to have special fishing tools for their removal. Having a well cleaned out is much, much cheaper than having a new one drilled. If you decide to clean your own, borrow a spiral or hook-shaped tool called a ram's horn for lifting the rocks. One homesteader we know removed the rocks from his well casing by dropping sections of pitchforks at the end of a rope down the casing. His formula was to use two tines from a three-tined fork for large rocks and to use three tines from a four-tined fork for the smaller ones. The rocks jam between the springy tines of the fork and are lifted by pulling on the rope. Probably other easily procured tools would work as well. Beneath the rocks the well is frequently filled with sand. The latter can be removed by pouring water down the well and pumping the sand out. If the sand is hard it can be loosened by lowering ¾-inch pipe into it. Fill the pipe with water and raise and lower it quickly by hand. Hold your thumb over the pipe when you raise it and remove your thumb when you lower it and the sand will be loosened by the jetting action thus produced. When the water and sediment is in suspension it can be pumped out easily enough.

WASTE DISPOSAL

Once the well is in and working the homesteader will find himself faced with the next consideration, the disposal of water and waste.

Most homesteaders will know exactly what to do with their meat scraps, vegetable peels and pieces of organic kitchen wastes. They will add it to the soil either through a compost heap or by burying it directly in the garden. Cans and bottles, though maybe few in number since most homesteaders won't be buying too much retail food stuffs, do pose their problems.

Tin cans can be disposed of by cutting out the tops and bottoms and then flattening them and burying them or saving them for a recycling center. Bottles can be recycled by taking them to a reprocessing center or by converting them into useful objects with one of the glass or bottle cutters made for that purpose. Many times walks between the domicile and out buildings can be paved with glass and glass ground fine enough can be used for road paving, as a mix for concrete and in dozens of other uses. In areas where lumber and other building materials are scarce glass bottles have been used for building material by adding them to concrete or adobe. A little thinking will put the conscientious homesteader on a par with the Indian who had no word for scrap or waste simply because he left none.

Human waste and its disposal is best handled via using a rural septic system or an outdoor privy.

The septic system can only be used with a pressure water system. It consists of sewage lines connected from inside the house to a septic tank outside, one usually buried in the ground. This system carries the waste into the tank where it is decomposed by bacteria and then the resulting "clean" water drains from the septic tank into a "dry well" where it seeps away into the surrounding soil. For drainage, some systems use a leach bed or a series of pipes leading away from the discharge spout of the septic tank instead of the dry well.

The actual installation of a rural sewage system can be quite a hassle. The first consideration, of course, will be where to put it so that it doesn't drain into some nearby watercourse. Almost all areas have regulations which govern the installation of these systems so it would be well to check first with the "Powers That Be." Lacking specific regulations, a few rules of thumb should be kept in mind. The first rule is: end the system at least one hundred feet away from a watercourse. The second is to bury it deep enough so it doesn't freeze. The third is to make it large enough to handle the load. In areas where septic tanks are available for purchase it is probably easier to buy one than to make one, but almost always the tile will have to be purchased. Manufactured plastic or organic tile can be procured by mail. Burying the septic system, that is, digging the holes for the septic tank and dry well and digging the trench for the pipe or tile, can be done by hand or much faster with a backhoe digger. Machinery of this type is expensive to hire or even rent, but since such a large amount of

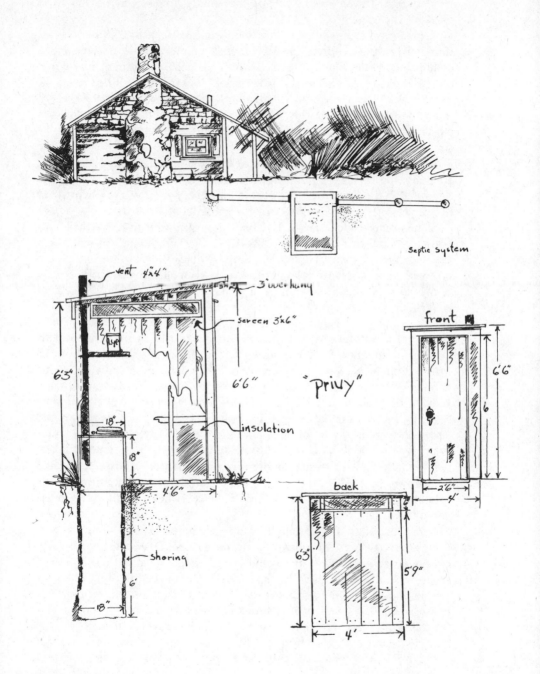

septic system

vent 4"x4"   3" overhang

screen 3"x6"

"privy"

insulation

6'3"

6'6"

18"

8"

4'6"

shoring

6'

18"

front

6'6"

6'

2'6"

4'

back

6'3"

5'9"

4'

hand digging is involved perhaps machinery use would be the most prudent way to go.

A much more sensible way for handling human waste, to my way of thinking, is the outdoor privy compost method. This doesn't mean complicated systems and concrete structures such as used in many foreign countries either. All the homesteader has to do is to build a little shed. Half of the bottom has a bench or seat area built into it. The other half is floored as any building would be. The bench part of the floor has one or two holes cut into it. It will rest upright over a hole in the ground. Add lime every time you use it and when the piles get to within three feet of the top of the ground dig another hole to one side of the first and slide the shed over it, covering the first one with earth. Now for the best part, the waste deposited in the first hole will be turned into very good, very rich fertilizer in two years. It will then in no way resemble its original state.

Some homesteaders, however, aren't going to want to move their outhouse now and then. That's fine also. Just dig the hole under your favorite shade tree or back behind the clump of lilac. Shore up the side of the hole with whatever material is at hand such as an old culvert, rocks, bottles cemented in place, treated lumber or do a real good job and build a cement wall about six inches thick. The bottom of the hole should be left as it is to permit drainage. This hole should be about six feet deep. Around the outside build a wall by setting stones or cement blocks in the ground. This wall is a foundation for the building so that it doesn't sit directly on the soil. See plans. Now for the secret of an odor-free, practically antiseptic permanent bathroom. In addition to screening the windows and vent and keeping the holes covered and the door shut, take one can of common household lye and shake it down the holes once a month. One can should decompose all the waste for one family. It will also keep the rats and mice away, kill the odors and "eat" up the piles so that there is no buildup. Additionally, at least once a month mix up a solution of disinfectant and wash down the inside of the building very thoroughly, making sure that the solution gets into all the cracks and crevices where roaches and other vermin live.

Some fastidious folks plant flowers and herbs around their outdoor privy also so that it is like visiting a flower garden. Of course the door will have to be equipped with inside and outside latches and there should be a spring to shut it automatically, especially if you have children.

One objection to the outdoor privy is that it is cold in winter. Our outhouse is insulated and in real bitter cold we set up a kerosene heater which keeps it very warm. The last one to use it at night shuts it off and the first one to use it in the morning lights it. In frosty but not bitter weather we keep the seats inside the cabin and carry them with us when we go. I have used outdoor privies in Canada that had fur lined seats which felt warm in any weather.

Don't forget the mainstay of winter-bound folks everywhere, the chamber pot. It can be used inside and taken out to be dumped.

Keep the interior of the outhouse painted and clean, provide enough window space for illumination and keep a few copies of your favorite magazine in a little rack inside. Who needs an indoor bathroom? Remember what the Indian said? "White Man, he crazy, eat outside and 'eliminate' inside."

WATER USAGE CHART

Person	8 gallons per day minimum
	30 gallons per day average
Cow	15 gallons
Sheep	1 gallon
Hog	3 gallons
Horse	12 gallons
Hen	⅓ to 1 gallon
Goat	2 gallons
Rabbit	⅛ to 1 gallon

(Based on actual observations by homesteaders.)

Booklets

Well Drilling Operations
Army and Air Force Technical Manual
AFM 85-23
U. S. Government Printing Office
Washington, D. C. 20402

Manual of Individual Water Supply Systems
U. S. Department Of Health, Education And Welfare
Superintendent Of Documents
U. S. Government Printing Office
Washington, D. C. 20402

Sanitation Manual for Isolated Regions
Department Of Health And Welfare
Ottawa, Ontario, Canada

Excreta Disposal for Rural Areas and Small Communities
The American Public Health Association
1740 Broadway
New York, New York 10019

Water Supply for Rural Areas and Small Communities
The American Public Health Association
1740 Broadway
New York, New York 10019

Suppliers

Pumps and Windmills
Denster Industries
P. O. Box 848
Beatrice, Nebraska 68310

The Heller-Aller Company
Corner Perry and Oakwood
Napoleon, Ohio 43545

Baker Manufacturing (pumps only)
Evansville, Wisconsin 53536

6

ORGANIC GARDENING AND FARMING

ORGANIC GARDENING IS the science and art of raising plants without using chemical fertilizers or chemical sprays. Simple as this statement is it embraces a whole way of life and a whole group of intelligent foresighted people whose concern for the environment and the earth with all its people overshadows the thought of immediate gain or profit.

It is widely held that plants raised organically or with natural fertilizers taste better than plants of chemically forced growth. It also follows that since a plant is made up of what it grows in, the vitamin and mineral content of organically produced plants should be greater than that of the chemically forced plants, thus affecting the health of the consumer. Also, since farm animals eat plants produced on the farm, their meat and milk will also better benefit the health of the consumer. It is my private theory that the body has evolved over eons to handle what has been put here by the Maker. Try to produce food artificially and the body will react negatively since it isn't "programmed" to handle artificial substances.

Anyway, the first step in developing the organic garden is deciding on a plot and this will be influenced by the condition of the soil.

LOCATING A GARDEN

To judge soils with any accuracy it is first necessary to understand what soil is. Soil is finely ground rock mixed with decayed organic matter. It may be local in origin or it may have been carried for hundreds of miles from its birthplace by wind, water and great glaciers. Thus over a thousand soil types have been formed and often six or seven kinds will be found on a single farm.

83

The fertility of the soil or its ability to feed plants is a result of the mineral content of the parent rock it was formed from and the organic material that decomposed upon its surface and which has been incorporated into it. A soil's ability to feed plants and its willingness to feed plants are not always parallel since the size of the soil grains, the looseness of its texture and the amount of moisture it receives, will affect its ability to give up plant nutrients.

Soil is not a dead substance but a seething storehouse of living organisms ranging from the microscopic insect to the larger visible earthworm. These organisms are at work at all times changing and altering the structure and composition of the soil.

Since soil is such a delicately balanced substance the addition of chemical fertilizers is thought by many to be harmful since this could destroy much of the life of the soil even though it does stimulate many growth forms.

The topsoil, which contains the organic matter, is the layer that all plants grow in and it thus supports all life. Directly under the topsoil is the subsoil and beneath the subsoil the hardpan. Topsoils range in depth from several feet to only one or two inches, subsoils can be several feet deep, and the hardpan can go to the rock core of the earth.

In judging soil a homesteader can dig a vertical hole at least one foot in diameter to permit viewing the side walls and then by smoothing the sides of the hole he can tell where the topsoil ends and the subsoil begins. If he is selecting a garden spot, the darker topsoil layer should be at least six inches deep. Also the subsoil should be soft enough to be penetrated by a shovel without undue effort. If the subsoil is too hard moisture probably will not enter it and drainage will be poor. If it is too porous or composed mostly of gravel or very coarse sand the water will probably drain through it too rapidly and the topsoil above it will always be leached out. Thus a good garden spot will have at least a half-foot of topsoil which is loose and mellow and probably dark colored since this is an indication of the organic material found in it, and the subsoil will be loose or soft enough to allow the water to drain away without permitting it to run away too rapidly as would be the case with a large-grained or gravel subsoil.

Soil experts like to point out that dark looking topsoil does not necessarily mean that it is rich. They cite the case where swamp soil is very dark and rich looking but is grossly deficient in plant foods. This is true, of course, but as a general rule if the topsoil is dark and found on well-drained land, it will be rich and able to support luxuriant plant growth.

Many homesteaders judge soils by the squeeze test. They pick up a handful of topsoil and squeeze it. If it falls completely apart when it is released it probably does not contain enough organic material in its present form to be good garden soil. If the soil sticks together and stays together after it is released it could contain too much clay and not enough organic matter to be "good" soil. The ideal soil, which contains enough organic material to be porous while still maintaining a bond between the soil grains, will partially break apart into smaller pieces when it is released.

Testing soil takes a qualified expert. Almost all those who have tried the do-it-yourself soil testing kits say they tend to test everything as deficient even when it isn't. Some of the richest garden soils have been tested this way and found wanting. A mighty good way to test the soil of a prospective piece of land is to gather a few quarts from different sections of the land, label each one and send them off to the nearest state agriculture department for testing. County agriculture agents also have facilities to test soil and some fertilizer and feed mills do it as a convenience. The nearest feed mill would be a good place to find out where you can have the soil tested. It might cost a few bucks but it is worth it.

Forested or virgin lands, contrary to popular belief, are usually soil deficient in something. On the other hand, we don't know of soil anywhere that is perfect in all respects. Conversely, there is scarcely any soil in its natural state that won't raise some type of garden if it has optimum moisture.

Almost all gardens that are super plant beds have been cultivated for years. They have had either already made compost added or organic matter added that decomposed into compost.

Some desert soil is good for growing crops if it is watered. Remote areas can sometimes be gardened by building sand dams to catch the runoff from the very infrequent rains. Of course "Big Brother" has irrigation projects going on all the time and possibly a prospective homesteader will be able to lease or purchase water from the government.

On the other side of the coin, even though the most fertile soil might be found on the low wet ground it too has its drawbacks. Very low ground has a short growing season, "sour soil" and presents a drainage problem in some areas.

How to find the ideal place to establish a garden spot then? First, judge the soil by its growing vegetation. If some of the acid-loving plants like sheep sorrel or sour dock are present it's a sure bet the soil is high in phosphorus. On the other hand if alfalfa and sweet clover are present the soil has to be alkaline. Tall weeds such as burdock give some indication that the soil is rich and will grow crops. Of course since weeds characteristically need a more alkaline soil than many vegetable crops, some slight sulphur or organic matter might have to be added to get top yields.

If it is habitually wet or dry this will show up in the type of plants growing. Large rank cattails or smartweed indicate too wet, sandburrs and low tough grass indicate too dry.

Homesteaders wanting to garden in the Prairie states should realize that these areas don't get enough rain to raise trees; this affects gardening there somewhat. In this case they will want to locate close to a source of water such as a creek or a well, and they should plan on having to water and mulch their garden. Then there will be those gardening in rainy regions such as the Pacific Coast. There, if the weather is warm, is a great place to grow anything but the garden location should be on a grade or some drain tile dug down or other contrivance provided to assure good drainage. Also there is the novel situation produced by the north slope of a high mountain. Spring comes later, the days are shorter, the sun shines less and winter is more severe on the north slope of a mountain. Thus the best garden spots should be on the south side. This will not be true in tropical regions, however, where the north slope can be an ideal place.

When planning the garden space remember that plants require full sunlight most of the day. Do not locate your garden where it will be shaded by trees. This can be qualified if necessary to permit shading during the early morning or late evening when the sun is very low in the horizon anyway.

One other point to remember is to locate the garden patch as close to the cabin as feasible. There are figures to prove, and every gardener knows, that the more you are forced to look at your garden the more time you will spend in it! The more attention you give a garden the better the plants will grow! Maybe even from the plants sensing good "vibes", as experiments seem to indicate. Of course being close to the house is an asset when carrying compost and other matter to the garden and when bringing in the day's harvest of fresh vegetables.

TILLING A GARDEN

Once the garden spot is located, tilling it will be the next consideration. Tilling a garden can be done by hand or it can be done with a variety of mechanical contraptions. Not much needs to be said about a roto tiller since it is simple to operate, but remember a garden can be tilled by hand, especially in conjunction with the use of some light inhibiting mulch such as a thick covering of wood chips or large leaves to cover and hold down unwanted weeds and grass. Also animals, especially pigs, will till a garden very nicely and add organic manure at the same time. Just place adult pigs in a portable enclosure and let them root up the place. When they have all the weeds and vegetation dug up in one area move them to another. Pigs do a very thorough job of cultivation and prospective garden areas offer them good fresh pasturage.

When clearing new land or farming an unused piece of field we usually mow off the area and spade up strips as wide as the shovel or fork, making sure to get all the grass and roots out of the spaded strip. Pick the sod up on a fork and shake it off back into the hole. Where the roots or weeds aren't too thick just turn them under by digging out a spadeful and turning it over. These strips are dug as long as the garden patch and about a foot apart, then we plant in the dug-up strips and cover the space between the plantings with strips of black plastic or a layer of ten-inch thick hay or other mulching. The undisturbed grass won't grow or use moisture as long as light cannot get to it and the roots and the top vegetation gradually die and add their humus to the soil. The next year the grass between the strips is well-rotted so it then can be dug up for planting. By following this method we have opened up strips of new ground without the shriek of machinery or noisy exhaust fumes spoiling the tranquility of our homestead. Gardens that have already been tilled merely need to be spaded up. Larger patches can be tilled with horses as an alternate to machinery use.

PLANTING

After the garden is tilled the next step is planting the seeds. These are readily obtainable from the seed catalogs, neighbors, feed mills and other sources. The most important thing about seed selection is that the seeds should come from plants that have flourished in the same locality or conditions where you intend to garden or farm. This means that a tomato strain developed in the tropics probably would not do well in northern Wisconsin, for instance. A drought-resistant variety might not do well under extremely moist conditions. It is possible and feasible to develop your own strain or variety of vegetable which will be acclimated to local conditions and its seed will be especially desirable.

Obtaining your own seeds is as simple a process as letting the plants mature and reach the seed stage, then picking and drying the seeds. Hybrid plants tend to regress into an original state; try not to use hybrids.

The seeds from the tomato plant can be harvested by letting the tomatoes from the largest, heartiest and best plants get dead ripe. Then take them up and cut out the seed pulp. Put the pulp containing the seeds in water and wash the seeds loose by swirling the pulp around. Then place the seeds on a cloth or absorbent paper and dry them well. They can then be placed in fruit jars with tight-fitting lids or in absorbent bags and stored in a cool dry place, such as in an attic, dry basement or on the rafters of the cabin.

Radish and lettuce seeds are gathered from plants which have been allowed to go to seed. They must be dried well and kept in a dry container.

Cabbage seeds are gathered or produced by a unique method. The plant is started and allowed to grow until just before it heads out. Then it is taken up and allowed to dry out until it is almost dead, then it is replanted and kept well watered. When it starts growing again it will produce seeds instead of heading out. In some areas of little rainfall like Arizona, for instance, the irrigation is withheld from the plant and it is allowed to dry out and wither on the ground. Just before it dies the water is supplied again and it produces seed instead of heading out. Cabbage seeds are started in a pot before they are set out in the garden.

The fruits such as raspberries and blackberries are propagated from roots or young plants as are strawberries and other perennials. Pears, apples, peaches and cherries can be grown from well-dried seeds.

All pulpy seeds are washed out well and dried. All hard seeds are shelled out and dried. Beans, peas, pumpkins, watermelon, corn, sunflower, peppers, cucumbers, onions, citrons, etc. can all be grown from seeds.

After the garden site is selected and the seeds and seed beds are prepared and planted the question of plant food or fertilizer becomes paramount. As it stands in its natural state most land lacks at least one of the plant foods necessary to proper plant growth. Even if the soil is very good for the first year, if good gardening procedures aren't followed returns will diminish with each successive crop grown. Thus a knowledge of what the soil lacks is important. As mentioned before it is therefore important to have the soil tested. If a homesteader doesn't like to or can't test his soil there are plant indicators that will offer some clues to soil deficiencies.

Deficiency	Indicator
Nitrogen	Yellowish green leaves and drying older leaves
Phosphorus	Very dark green leaves with a tendency to develop reddish and purple colors
Potassium	Yellow streaks in the leaves. Mottling of older leaves.
Magnesium	Yellowing, drying, bronzing and reddening of older leaves
Sulphur	Younger leaves turn yellow and finally all leaves turn yellow

| Copper | Top leaves of plant wilt and do not recover |
| Zinc | Same as copper. In addition the plants may have a bitter taste. |

The chief kinds of fertilizers are calcium, potassium, nitrogen and phosphorus. Organic sources of calcium are wood ashes, ground limestone and burned lime. Natural sources of potassium are potash and wood ashes. Organic sources of nitrogen are manure, bone meal, castor beans, fish meal, cottonseed meal, soybean meal and dried blood. Legumes such as clover and alfalfa which have the ability to remove nitrogen from the air and supply it to the soil are also good. This is called green manuring. Natural potash is produced from mined phosphate rock. Fortunately the homesteader has a readily available substance that will supply most all the needed ingredients (compost).

MAKING COMPOST

Compost is simply a name for organic substances such as plant and animal products that are piled up and kept watered until they decompose into a dark substance that can be added to the garden or to individual plants to supply the fertilizer that might be needed. Compost can be made in a heap or it can be made by spreading organic material on the soil itself and letting it decay by action of the soil bacteria. The mulching method has the advantage of retaining all the minerals while the heap method of composting has the disadvantage of losing some minerals and nutrients through leaching.

For various reasons though it will still be desirable to make compost in a heap. For heap composting a very definite procedure can be followed which will give good results.

The first step in composting is selecting a site which will be protected from the wind and from the direct overhead sun. Thus a desirable location is under a tree having a nearby wall or natural rise of ground to prevent the prevailing winds from blowing directly on the pile. Wind stops the composting by cooling the fermentation. The next consideration is the distance of the pile from the garden and the availability of a water supply. No need to have to carry either water or the finished compost too far. Some people make a crib or box to contain the material but it isn't really necessary as long as the heap is well made and kept watered.

The raw materials for compost are piled in layers. The first layer should be green material such as grass, hay, weeds, cornstalks, flower stalks or other green plant material. This layer should be six inches thick and about six feet in diameter. Next put on a two-inch layer of manure, kitchen scraps, egg shells, meat, fish heads, fish products, etc. In the case of pure meat products the layer need be only about one inch thick. Next "salt" the pile with ground limestone or preferably wood ashes and on top of the lime or ashes sprinkle a thin layer of the richest earth available. Then start the layering all over again, green material, manure, limestone, etc. and keep adding layers until the heap is about five feet high. Don't pack it as air must penetrate the mass to generate the composting process. The compost heap must be constructed like a pyramid with each succeeding layer, starting from the bottom, getting smaller in diameter. This is to keep the pile from falling over or sliding apart. The top layer of earth will be much heavier and it should enclose part of the sides. When applying this last layer of earth it will become apparent that the more the pile tapers, the easier it is to apply this last layer. As a final step the whole pile can be covered with a layer of straw. This permits its frequent watering without making it fall apart.

After the pile is constructed use a pointed 2 x 4 board or other piece to poke air holes from top to bottom. These holes should be five or six inches in diameter and about three feet apart.

When the pile is completed it should be well watered and kept moist while it is "working." After about three weeks the heap must be turned. Turning is done to get the outside of the heap to the inside and vice versa. This distributes the composting bacteria throughout the pile and greatly hastens the process. The next turn should be made about five weeks after the first one. In both the first and the second turning be sure the materials are well mixed. The compost is ready to use when it is dark and has cooled off. It should be applied immediately to the garden or else turned frequently to prevent its complete decomposition. A sure sign of well-made compost is if it can be compacted into a ball.

Compost can be made faster using finely ground material. This might involve using a shredder or it could be ground up perhaps with a hand lawnmower. Large quantities of leaves can be shredded between the fingers in a short time and added to the compost heap, but use gloves in this if you have just come from the city.

There is evidence that the soil can be made too rich through the overuse of compost over a period of years, but this certainly would not concern the beginning homesteader.

MULCHING AND WEED CONTROL

While we are close to the subject let's not forget the advantages of mulching. Mulching is piling organic plant material such as hay around growing plants. This conserves the moisture in the soil and keeps weeds down. When the crop is harvested the mulching can be dug into the soil to provide humus. Many people believe that mulching with plant material will overcome almost any soil deficiency and many garden, orchards and berry plantations have been made highly productive just by adding mulch.

Weeds—usually the enemy of every gardener—make almost the best mulching material. This is because weeds can penetrate far into the soil and bring up trace minerals and plant food from the subsoil. Tree leaves rate highly for mulch as do many hay plants. People who live where it can be trucked in even use seaweed with excellent results. I have also used algae from ponds with good effect and broad-leaved marsh plants such as cattail and pond lilies are second to none.

EARTHWORMS

Along with mulching the extensive propagation of earthworms will bring a gardener almost unbelievable results. Earthworms burrow in the soil creating tiny tunnels which carry water down to the plant roots and decrease water runoff. Perhaps the most valuable addition of the earthworms are their "castings" from soil passing through their digestive system. Some feel that topsoil is largely created by earthworm castings. In addition, earthworms furnish as much as a thousand pounds per acre of highly nitrogenous fertilizer as they decay. Earthworms penetrate the soil to a depth of six feet and move minerals and plant food up from the subsoil. They also eat fungi and harmful insect eggs that they find in the soil.

Because of their general asset value, many people raise earthworms and add them both to their soil and compost piles. In fact, instead of maintaining a compost heap some homesteaders put all their organic trash into a pit and let the earthworms turn it into good and valuable compost. Earthworms are raised commercially and can be purchased, but good soil practices will cause earthworms to increase to the optimum point naturally. Should you want to raise them you will probably want to procure your breeding stock from the brantling or red worm. This worm adapts very well to extensive breeding in a small space. Some people raise them under their rabbit pens where they turn the manure into an odorless humus which can be applied to the garden or greenhouse.

INSECT CONTROL

Once garden plants are started you may be troubled with insect pests and feel like reaching for the poison spray. Fortunately there are better ways. In the first place healthy soil and plants attract few insects. Certain insects seem to be nature's way of destroying that which is unnatural. Thus the over-fertilized or artificially-fertilized plant may be attacked by insects first as being the deficient or abnormal. Occasionally all that you or nature can do to discourage the insect hordes is not enough and some other corrective measures must be taken. Fight back by encouraging other insects to destroy the unwanted ones—encourage the predator and parasitic insects.

Turning to the use of predator insects is becoming more and more important as we gradually discover that poison sprays kill and damage more than do the insects they are used against. The turning of one insect against another isn't new, it has been going on in the United States since 1888 when the lady beetle was imported to control the cushion scale in California citrus fruit. The lady beetle was credited with saving the citrus industry at that time. Lady beetles are extensively raised in California and though their production is expensive they represent one of the best measures for control of citrus fruit parasites. Gardeners who are troubled with such pests as fruit tree and scaly parasites would do well to encourage the reproduction of lady beetles on their lands. The next insect in order of importance might be the caterpillar-eating ground beetles. First imported in 1905, this species—of which there are almost two thousand varieties—is largely credited with controlling the gypsy moth. These hungry bugs range the earth at night hungrily eating and killing. Some of these insects live to the astounding old age of four years and will devour hundreds of harmful caterpillars during their lifetime.

The familiar firefly which brightens many a summer evening feeds largely on snails and slugs and a good population of fireflies could be very helpful as a control measure during moist years.

The bane of the ant hill is the assassin bug, which exudes a poisonous substance which clings to its hairs. The assassin bug stations himself near the ant hill, the ants come to him and eat the poisonous nectar and then are paralyzed, after which the assassin bug eats them.

Dragon flies are ferocious predators on other insects, preying especially on mosquitoes while the blister beetles especially crave fat grasshoppers. One of the most ferocious of all is the praying mantis, which devours every bug it comes across, from aphids to caterpillars. And so it goes throughout the insect world as whenever there is an unusual abundance or good supply of plant-eating insects there is also a family of predators which feeds upon them. Man, when he sprays with poison, kills harmful and beneficial alike and when the harmful raises a new generation they grow exceedingly thick because of the lack of natural enemies as predator insects reproduce much more slowly. Harmful insects also promote plant diseases. Predatory insects can be encouraged by planting so that some nectar and pollen-bearing plants are in bloom in the organic garden at all times. Where native populations are low some desirable insects can be purchased through garden and organic publications.

The next most important factor in the control of insects are birds, consequently every homesteader should encourage them whenever possible. Provide water and nesting facilities for them.

Another important insect control is crop rotation. Keep planting potatoes year after year in the same place and you will soon have a leaf-stripping crop of potato beetles. Skip potatoes for a few years and your next crop probably won't be troubled.

Grasshopper and other insect eggs can be destroyed by late fall and early spring plowing which turns up the eggs. Many beetles can be picked off by hand and destroyed, for instance the cabbage worms, tent caterpillars on fruit trees, and the potato bugs.

WHAT TO PLANT

At this point some readers may say, "Fine, now I know where to plant and something about how to get the soil ready to plant, but I still don't know what, when or where to plant!"

Sorry, there are so many variables involved that I can't tell you this. Don't throw the book away though because the source of seeds for your first planting will solve all of these problems for you.

Chances are you won't be bringing your seeds with you when you come to the country and chances are equally good that you will be getting them locally or from some seed company that knows your conditions locally. Okay; sit down with pencil and paper and figure out what foods you like and need for "radiant health." They include corn, potatoes, peas, radishes, carrots, cabbage, melons, tomatoes and cucumbers—to name a few. Browse through the seed catalogs and read the free information. Notice that the average yields are given for each planting. To be on the safe side halve these for your first attempts. Notice also that the planting dates are given for each plant in each locality. Seems like everything is covered then except what sort of vegetables you will eat the most of, and nobody knows this any better than you.

Of course if you buy your seeds from the local feed mill or general store, the proprietor or friendly gardening neighbor can give you the same information in much more accurate detail than the seed companies can. Remember to prepare your seed bed thoroughly, spading or tilling it up so all the lumps are gone and then raking the ground smooth before you plant. A hoe handle can be used to make the furrow for small seeds and its blade will dig the hole for large ones. Naturally the hoe must also be used to keep the weeds down throughout the summer unless you mulch heavily. But don't be discouraged if your first attempts at gardening are frustrating. Gardening is a skill, like learning to drive, keypunch or do plumbing, but of course much more satisfying.

Further suggested reading for organic gardeners:

Magazines

Organic Gardening and Farming
Emmaus, Pa. 18409

Books

Rodale, Robert, *The Basic Book of Organic Gardening.* New York: Ballantine, 1971.
Cocannouer, Joseph A. *Organic Gardening and Farming.* New York: Arco, 1954.
Darlington, Jeanie, *Grow Your Own.* New York: Random, 1971.
Stout, Ruth, *How to Have a Green Thumb Without an Aching Back.* New York: Cornerstone, 1955.
Philbrick, Helen, *Companion Plants, and How to Use Them.* Old Greenwich, Connecticut: Devin, 1966.

Pamphlets

Suburban and Farm Vegetable Gardens (Robert Wester) 40¢
Superintendent Of Documents
U. S. Government Printing Office
Washington, D. C. 20402

Seed Catalogs

Gurney Seed and Nursery Co.
Yankton, South Dakota 57078

Earl May Seed and Nursery Co.
Shenandoah, Iowa 51601

Stark Brothers
Box D29712, Louisiana, Missouri 63353

Jung Seed Company
Randolph, Wisconsin 53956

7

GROWING AN INDOOR GARDEN

NOTHING IS MORE beautiful or tasty than fresh green vegetables plucked from your own organic indoor garden in January. Along with sprouts, meat and stored crops the garden fresh lettuce, radishes, cabbage and watercress he can grow in an indoor garden will keep the homesteader as well fed as a bureaucrat and he need rarely go to the grocery store.

The location for the indoor garden is important. It has to be where the temperature can be kept from 60 to 70 degrees; slightly lower temperatures are permissible since they can be corrected.

The "garden" can be as simple as a succession of plant pots or it can be a completely enclosed box where the temperature and environment can be rigidly controlled. Since by far the best results can be obtained with an enclosed "green box" and since building one requires very little outlay of capital and minimal skill, it would seem better to build your own.

BUILDING A GREEN BOX

The size of the green box is governed by the amount of plants to be grown. For raising radishes and lettuce only a small two foot by two foot box would be sufficient. For raising an elaborate garden a large box eight by ten feet would be needed. If the homesteader's family numbers four and if he eats the normal amount of greens to promote good health he will need a green box measuring about four by six feet. One person could get along by raising his garden set in flower pots around the house under various lights.

95

In appearance a family mini-garden will resemble a rabbit hutch. The list of material is four two by two's, each 45 inches long for the corner posts. Four one by six boards, six feet long for the top and bottom corners of the frame. Four pieces of one by six's, four feet long for the ends.

Nail the six-foot lengths of one by six boards to the corner posts with 6d nails to form a rectangle measuring six feet by 45 inches. This will frame the sides of the mini-garden. Nail the four-foot lengths of one by six's across the ends to complete framing the box. Now obtain a piece of heavy clear plastic, the super-clear kind sold for storm window use and completely cover the sides and ends with it. This plastic can be stapled, taped or tacked to the frame. Now turn the box upside down and cover the bottom with one by six boards. Turn it right side up again and put a piece of plastic, old linoleum or other waterproof covering across inside the bottom so the wood doesn't rot from coming in contact with the drainage from the pots. The drainage will be taken care of by slotting one end of the box between the plastic on the sides and the boards on the bottom. Thus the box is set at a slight slant so the water will drain to one end and drop into a container. Naturally the mini-garden will have to be placed on saw horses or boxes to allow space between the box and the floor. Also it had just as well be raised high enough to permit care of the plants without a lot of stooping over.

The slot at the end of the box for drainage will allow air circulation to

the plants also. This is almost as important as watering. Should your basement be stuffy and airless and the plants don't do too well some amazing
results can be obtained by opening a window a little ways.

LIGHTING THE MINI-GARDEN

The life of this mini-garden will be from the light made to shine upon it.
Thus the top will have to be made to hold the light, which can be a fluorescent light fixture. The double-type fixture with four-foot clear tubes
should give adequate lighting. The frame for the fixture can be two seven-
foot lengths of two by two's nailed across the length of the top of the
mini-garden. The lamp is supported from the frame by means of adjustable chains, thus the light can be moved and kept to within four to six
inches of the plants for maximum lighting. The type of lights sold in
garden stores for growing plants indoors can be used at a slightly greater
distance from the plant. The only time they should be used though is when
you have to buy a new light anyway; then only buy the tube or bulb. The
fixtures can be obtained from wrecked buildings, second-hand stores, etc.
The light should be left on for 16 hour a day intervals. This cycle will make
a stronger healthier plant. However, if you occasionally forget to turn off
the lights it will do little harm. The frame for the light should be installed
so it offers a smooth surface to the mirrors which are placed across the top
to reflect light. Old mirrors can be picked up around second-hand stores,
junk yards and at flea markets for very little. Mirrors are sometimes used
at the ends also as this helps increase light intensity. But don't restrict
the air movement with the mirror arrangement, however. It is much better
to leave one end of the top up or leave a peephole open so that air can
circulate through the plants. The top also has to be removable for watering. The openings not covered with mirrors are covered with white
cloth.

To boost the heat to the 60 to 70 degrees that the plants need, an incan-
descent bulb can be placed in the box also. But keep the bulb far enough
away from the plants so they don't burn or shrivel.

NECESSARY — THE RIGHT SOIL

The next consideration is the containers for the soil and the soil, itself.
Soil for growing plants is always important but in the mini-garden it
becomes so important and critical that it must be controlled and regulated
to the finest degree.

The soil should be clay or silt loam. Where can you find clay or silt
loam? Every creek bank is a source as are low-lying areas in open fields.

Conversely the black soil found in the woods under trees is not always the best since it can contain growth-inhibiting qualities such as from pine needles. How do you know if you have found good soil? Well, one way is to give it the mud pie test. Moisten it and mold it into a mud pie about one inch thick. Then break the pie. If it sticks together and bends it contains too much clay. If it crumbles apart it contains too much sand. The right mixture will bend slightly and then break into pieces which stick together. As a point of interest most of the soil sold as potting soil is picked up along creek banks or in fields. Of course if you have a good supply of compost this is better yet.

There is one thing that must be done to the soil when you bring it in from the outdoors if you desire it to be perfectly safe for your growing plants. It must be sterilized, a very simple process. The soil should be watered very heavily first. Then place it in the oven and heat it to 275°, leaving it in for one hour. The whole mass of soil should be steaming and starting to dry out when you bring it out from the oven. After this sterilizing, the soil will have to be screened to restore its former fluffiness. It can be screened through a ½-inch wire mesh.

AUTOMATIC WATERING

Indoor-grown plants must be watered at least twice a day. It is possible to make an automatic waterer by putting a pan of water in the mini-garden with sections of lampwick or other very porous cloth conducting the water to the soil of each pot. Water will automatically transfer to the dry soil. But even with this method it will need frequent watering for optimum growth.

STARTING AND TRANSPLANTING PLANTS

There are two ways that you can start plants in the indoor garden—from seeds or by procuring them already started. The homesteader will probably use seed and then transfer the started plants to the mini-garden.

One of the usual problems when beginning from seeds in pots under lights is that the plants are apt to come up too thick or too thin. If planted too thickly they later must be thinned and this, of course, disturbs the roots. This still avoids transplanting, however. Despite this most plants are started in seed flats and transplanted to the mini-garden later. Some claim this enables selective breeding since they can eliminate the slow-germinating weaker plants.

Transplanting can be done after the second leaf shows or 24 hours after the plant first shows on the surface or even anytime in between.

For that matter, if the seed flats are large enough they may even be transplanted later on at the grower's option. Germinating seeds need little light.

Young seedlings are easily transplanted with an ordinary kitchen knife. Just slide the knife under a row or bunch of seedlings and flip them out to the top of the ground. Make a hole in the soil of the mini-garden with a pencil tip and very gently set the tiny transplants into the holes, then press the soil around the roots. The holes should be bigger than the roots so that no roots will be broken.

The seed flat is generally a large pan containing 1 to 1½ inches of water. The seeds are set ½-inch deep for large seeds and just barely covered for small seeds in pots of vermiculite. The pots are then set in the water in the pan. This keeps the vermiculite constantly damp and promotes germination and growth. Peat moss or sphagnum moss are also good mediums for starting seeds. We have achieved very good results by germinating seeds in a sprouting battery and then moving the sprouts to soil. Our seed-sprouting battery consists of pieces of wire screen framed with wooden strips to form eight-inch squares (see Chapter 11).

Plants growing from seedlings must be well watered or they will stop growing and may die. The lampwick method for watering plants will do the job. Seedlings also require frequent fertilizing which underscores the importance of feeding the indoor garden.

The frequency of fertilizing mini-garden plants varies from once a week in the case of seedlings to once a month for mature plants. However, don't overfeed plants either. If so they will quickly burn up and die. If you must err, do it on the side of starving the plants rather than overfeeding them.

There are only two good ways to determine if your plants need fertilizing; test the soil or closely watch the plants for cessation of growth. Soil testing can be done with the kits that are available or it can be done professionally. Many people complain of the lack of viable results from the soil testing kits so unless you are an expert it will probably be well to have it done by a garden store or county agent or someone with expertise. Feed mills usually do this or have contacts with fertilizer companies who do.

The fertilizer mix to use will vary according to the type of plants grown. Vegetables generally do well on one of the commercially prepared mixes or you can make your own liquid fertilizer by incorporating rotten fish and liquid manure into a mixture. Liquid manure is made by mixing horse or cow manure with water (urine is the best) and letting it turn to liquid. Almost always if the pot is large enough for the plant or plants in the first place the soil itself will carry a crop for one year very well. Next crop mix up a new batch. Test again and proceed from there. Naturally you will want to keep the plants thinned out so their roots don't crowd each other.

Vegetables which do very well in indoor gardens are asparagus, broccoli, brussels sprouts, cabbage, carrots, cauliflower, celery, cucumbers, eggplant, lettuce, muskmelon, onions, parsley, radishes and tomatoes. All of these can be grown by just keeping them watered and warm. The light needed for these plants is approximately one hundred candlepower, the amount of light transmitted from a fluorescent tube four inches away from them.

Flowering plants will have to have their flowers fertilized by transferring pollen from one blossom to another with a small soft paintbrush or similar aid.

Indoor greens will often do better if they are crowded since this seems to keep the soil from drying out, especially if they are top-watered. Leaves that turn yellow can indicate a lcak of nitrogen, a very common deficiency in mini-gardens.

Lack of electricity doesn't mean that you can't have a garden. If you live in a small cabin without a basement you can still raise plants in winter, especially the greens which are the most needed and sought for their Vitamin C content. All you have to do is keep them warm, moist and near as much light as you can. It is surprising what can be raised in this manner. Smoke and lack of air in tight stuffy cabins are more of a menace to such gardens than lack of light. Mirrors, too, can be used for reflecting light to an indoor garden. Many wild plants are accustomed to low light levels as are alfalfa and clover, and they do well indoors.

In the fall just before the ground freezes dig up dandelion and chicory roots and plant them in a box of sand. Keep their roots moist and in a warm place in the cellar or corner of the cabin and the roots will send up crop after crop of useful leaves that make delicious salads and soups. This procedure can be kept up all winter if the roots are not all used at once. Just leave the spares outside and bring them in as needed.

Watercress will grow on the windowsill as will lettuce, radishes, etc., in fact, don't be afraid to try whatever plants you like. If you can raise flowers in your cabin you can almost certainly raise vegetables with just a little more care.

8

MAKING YOUR OWN SUGAR

AS TO MEETING the needs of his own household, the production of such sugar-containing items as honey, maple syrup, sorghum molasses and sugar or syrups made from fruit is usually within the homesteader's capabilities. Depending on individual interest and the degree of part or full-time effort, these productions could lead to a rewarding business enterprise. Since beekeeping and raising honey is not uncommonly a full-time occupation in many parts of the country, let's consider that first.

HONEY AND BEEKEEPING

The first step is procuring the bees. If one lives in an area where a lot of bees are located he might get a swarm from one of the wild colonies that periodically decide to find new homes. These are occasionally seen in the summer, swarming off to take up new residence, perhaps in a hollow tree. Possibly they move because of internal strife in the hive or a lack of food or water.

En route they may stop and cluster on a tree branch or church steeple or even on a fence post while the worker bees search for the new home. The bee hunter can often capture one of these clusters for his own hive if he proceeds with alacrity.

Before trying to capture a "wild" swarm put on a pair of hip boots and a jacket and tie the jacket sleeves tight around the wrist or use one with tight-fitting wrists. Now button the jacket collar up tight around the neck.

101

Then put on a pair of thick gloves and a wide-brimmed hat—over the hat put a mesh sack with mesh large enough to see through yet small enough to keep the bees out. This bag must be pulled down over the collar and tied tightly enough to keep bees from getting beneath.

When certain of being protected in all areas and being sure not to have any rips in your clothing, take the hive in one hand and a brush such as a large paint brush in the other, and slowly and quietly walk up to the swarm. When within arm's reach hold the hive under the swarm and brush the bees into it. Keep brushing until they're all captured. It is very important to get the queen bee in the hive since without her the rest will want to leave the box and swarm after the queen again. The queen is usually found deep at the center of the cluster. Be very careful and gentle while brushing or shaking the bees into the box since if the queen is injured the workers might die from starvation or search for other hives. Similarly you don't want to unnecessarily kill or injure work bees.

Once all the bees are in the hive carefully place the cover on it and put the hive in place. Chances are, the little laborers will go right to work within an hour, cleaning out the hive and starting to gather honey.

Sometimes a hive can be just placed down near a swarm and they will go into it, especially if they have not yet decided on a specific location. With luck a swarm may be induced to enter a hive simply by placing it near a good flower field or source of water, especially if some sugar water, honey or other bait is put in it. Another way of getting a swarm is to find a bee tree. Bee-tree hunting is a fascinating sport requiring patience, keen eyesight, good mobility and a little simple equipment.

The homesteader desiring to find a bee tree can place some honey or syrup in small cans and place the cans in likely places in his locality. Sooner or later if there are bees in his area he will have some coming to them. The next step is to bait one station heavily so a regular string of bees come and go. When there are regular flights to the bait the bee hunter can watch the little workers when they leave and, since they fly more or less in a straight line, he can learn the direction of the tree from the bait station.

The next step is to get a rough idea how far away the bee tree really is. This is done by marking one bee, using a straw dabbed in white paint. Then note how long it takes this bee to leave and come back. This is where patience comes in. Move the bait a little closer towards the tree each day. Move it only a few yards a day and keep it baited. Sooner or later you will get close enough to the tree so that a marked bee will leave and come back within five minutes. When this happens you are very close. Then start examining the trees around for hollows which could likely contain a bee colony. The openings to bee trees are distinctive because they have been polished smooth by millions of bees going in and out and also, when the bees are working, there will be several flying around the entrance all the time. If the trees are tall a good pair of binoculars or a telescopic rifle sight is a definite asset.

Once the tree is located several possibilities arise. If it is late in the season and the flowers are about done blooming for the year the homesteader may elect to cut the tree down, take the honey and sacrifice the colony. An alternative is to wait until cold weather, then saw the tree down and take the section home containing the bees and honey. Next spring the homesteader will have a colony of bees which can be smoked into another hive or it can be retained in the same hive by making some closures for the ends of the tree trunk, a subject that we will get to in more detail later.

Still another alternative is, if it is early in the spring, to borrow a bee excluder from a commercial apiary and tack it over the hole so the bees can come out but not get back in. Before doing this though fasten another hive containing a queen bee cell and some honeycomb directly outside the entrance to the bee tree. The workers will eventually go into the new hive and eat away the sugar cell enclosing the queen bee and quite happily start building a new colony.

Still another way—if the tree has a hollow going from the ground to the entrance hole (which may be many feet aboveground)—is to place another hive directly in front of the entrance and smoke every last bee including the queen out of the tree hollow and into the new hive. This is easier than it sounds and it is accomplished by building a smoky fire at the bottom of the tree so the hollow will act as a chimney to carry the smoke up into the bees. With luck the bees, including the queen, will walk right out of their old home and into the new one, especially if it is baited with honey. Then close up the entrance to the new hive and take it to its permanent location. Of course then you can cut down the tree and get the honey. The bee larvae that is sure to be found in the hive at that time of year is the best fish bait known to man, when impaled on a hook and lowered into a favorite fishing hole.

Still another method of harvesting honey is possible if the bee tree is large and looks like it will contain all the honey that the bees need. Just take a chain saw of the direct-drive type and saw a doorway into the hive. Use this doorway to take out the honey you need and then wire the cut section back in place. The bees will seal it again with propolis and when the next season honey flow is complete you can go back and open the same door, using a pry bar this time, and collect another supply. Two or three such trees should easily supply all the honey that a homesteader would need. But of course some homesteaders are going to want to have their bees close by, which will probably involve building a hive.

Honey bee, delightful friend of man that he is, does not need an

hive →
wood
cover

10q

wood
covers

"wild hive"

'bee gathering"

elaborate home. All the colony requires is shelter from the weather and about three cubic feet of space for the bees and the honey. This shelter can be a cylinder, a pyramid or a box.

Cylindrical hives can be made from hollow logs, tree bark or clay. Sometimes a log may be found that just fits the purpose. It should be at least three feet long and have a 14-inch diameter opening in its center. If the inside is very rough it should be smoothed up and all the rotten wood removed. If you don't do this the bees will, and it diverts their time from making honey. Both ends of the hives should be closed off with one-inch boards or the equivalent. One end board should have a ¾-inch diameter hole drilled in it as a flight hole for the bees and the other end should be removable for taking out the honey. The flight hole should have a one-inch cleat under it for the bees to land on.

Clay hives can be made of good quality clay impregnated with straw. They are built by laying ropes of clay on top of each other, building a cylinder until the inside dimensions are at least three cubic feet. If the homesteader knows how to fire this clay so that it will be hardened a very good weathertight hive results.

Straw hives are widely used in some countries, even today. They are usually made of ropes of straw coiled on top of one another to form a completely tapered cylinder or pyramid. The holes are usually in the top, and the bottom rests on a board.

In remote areas hives are suspended from tree limbs to keep them away from bears and skunks. Hives that aren't suspended should be placed inside a building or on a platform to discourage these invaders.

The homesteader in rural but populated areas can probably obtain plastic or clay tile already made or secure wooden boxes from municipal dumps to make bee hives. Also he may be able to secure scrap lumber to build his own which may as well be of the Longstroth type since it is standard-sized and if he obtains some commercially made supers or covers they will fit.

A Longstroth hive is a rectangle 20 inches long, 16¼ inches wide and 9¾ inches high. It is made with a separate cover and bottom. The bottom has a ¾-inch-thick cleat nailed around it on three sides of the floor for the hive. The fourth cleat is omitted to form the flight hole for the bees. The floor piece is made large enough so that about an inch and a half extends forward so the bees will have, in effect, a landing field in front of the entrance. It is also wide enough to extend slightly beyond the sides. The under surface of the floor should have at least three cross-cleats to prevent it from warping or splitting. These cross-cleats will also form legs to support the hive.

The top of this hive is formed by a false cover of the same dimensions as

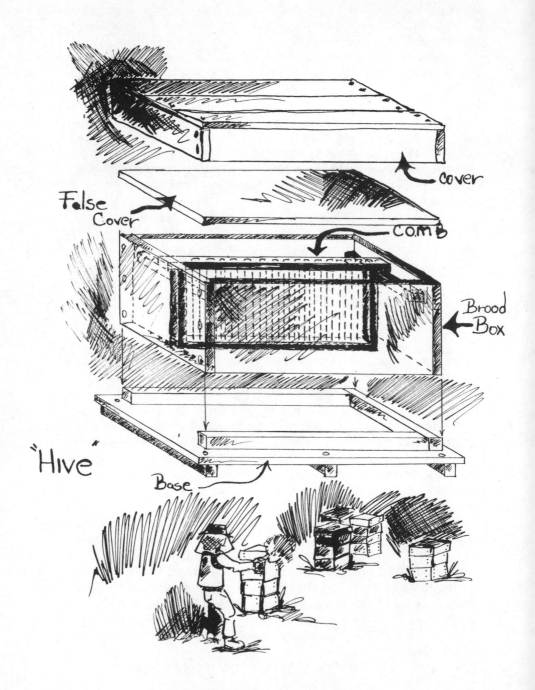

cover

False Cover

C.o.m.B

Brood Box

"Hive"

Base

the top. Over that is placed a cover which has sides two inches wide to enclose the false cover and extend down the sides of the hive two inches. Naturally this top has to be covered with building paper or other waterproofing. It doesn't hurt to paint the entire hive also, the wood lasts longer that way.

Inside the hive frames are placed on which the bees can build their brood and honeycomb. These frames are made 17⅝ x 11¼ inches wide with the top bar 19 inches long. This top bar holds the frames in the hive by resting on a cleat nailed just inside the brood box. The frames are covered with screen or artificial honeycomb on which the bees can build.

After the bees have the first story or brood box full of brood and honey the removable cover is lifted off and a second story known as a "super" is added. This super is usually screened from the first story or brood box with a screen which keeps the egg-laying queen from getting up into it and laying eggs. This insures that all the comb in the super will be filled with honey only, and not alternate honey and brood, as is the case with the honey in the first floor. Additional supers can be added when the bees have the first one full. The honey in the supers is harvested by the beekeeper for his use. The bees have the honey in the first floor for food during the winter. Frames almost identical to the brood frames are placed in the supers for the bees to build their honeycomb on.

All sorts of bee equipment is available commercially and reams of literature are easily obtainable on beekeeping. The homesteaders who wish to have a modern efficient business will find a variety of labor and time-saving devices to be had. Many different varieties of bees can be purchased and all sorts of population and variety manipulations are possible.

MAPLE SYRUP AND SUGAR

Another good sweetener is maple syrup. Homesteaders who live in the northern tiers of states and in the mid and eastern provinces of Canada or wherever the maple grows can make their own sugar and syrup by tapping the trees and boiling down the sap. The maple with the highest sugar content is the sugar maple but all maples can be tapped and all will yield syrup and sugar if the sap is evaporated enough.

The equipment for making a few gallons of maply syrup can be chiefly homemade, a drill for making holes in the trees being the only exception. Its bit should be large enough to drill at least a ¾-inch diameter hole. Besides the drill a collection of spiles or tubes are needed and a hammer for driving them. These spiles will be inserted into the holes drilled into the trees to carry the sap into the waiting buckets.

The buckets can be any plastic, metal or wooden pail that will hold the sap. They should be at least of two gallons capacity. The buckets can be suspended from the spiles or from a nail driven in the tree above the spile so the bucket will hang in the right place to catch the sap.

Wooden spiles can be made of sections of sumac limbs or trunks of the right or approximately right diameter. They make good spiles because their centers are filled with a soft, white pithy material that can be easily pushed or burned out. Make them by sawing off as many six to eight-inch lengths of sumac as you need spiles and trim the limbs off very close. Then heat a wire red hot and push it through the center of the spile, burning out all the soft material encountered. All that remains is to whittle one end so that it will fit in the tree.

Sometimes tubing is procurable which will do the job as an alternate to wooden spiles. Also remember that it is not necessary to have a complete tube. A half-tube will work, as will a section of birch bark rolled into a tube or a tin can lid bent to form a trough and inserted in the hole. Commercially-made spiles can be obtained also.

Besides the drill, buckets and spiles, the maple syrup maker will need a large pan or evaporator for boiling off the sap. Ideally this pan will be two feet square with sides about four inches high, but if such a pan is not obtainable just use the largest pan on hand.

The heat for boiling the sap can be a stove or an open fire, but the stove is preferable since it will cut down on the flying ashes which tend to fall into the sap when it is boiling.

Sap flow, which starts in March, varies considerably, with some good trees yielding thirty gallons or more and some barely yielding five. Since it takes about thirty gallons of sap to make a gallon of syrup you can regulate the number of taps accordingly.

The days of heaviest flow will be warm days following cold nights.

The sap should be collected and boiled down every day since it may otherwise "sour". It takes a long time and a lot of reduction in bulk to convert sap into syrup. About the easiest way to check the sap for being cured is to check its temperature with a candy thermometer. When the temperature is 219° sea level the sap is done. It should have a specific gravity of 31.5.

Now here is where custom syrup making comes in. There is nothing in the world wrong with cooling a bit of sap and tasting it from time to time. If it is sweet enough to fit your palate, stop boiling and bottle it up. Personally, I find the sugar content of commercially-prepared maple syrup far too high so I stop boiling quite a while before it gets this sweet.

After the homesteader has as much syrup as he wants he can, if he wishes, make some sugar. This is done merely by continuing to boil the syrup for a while after it reaches 219° at sea level. Care must be exer-

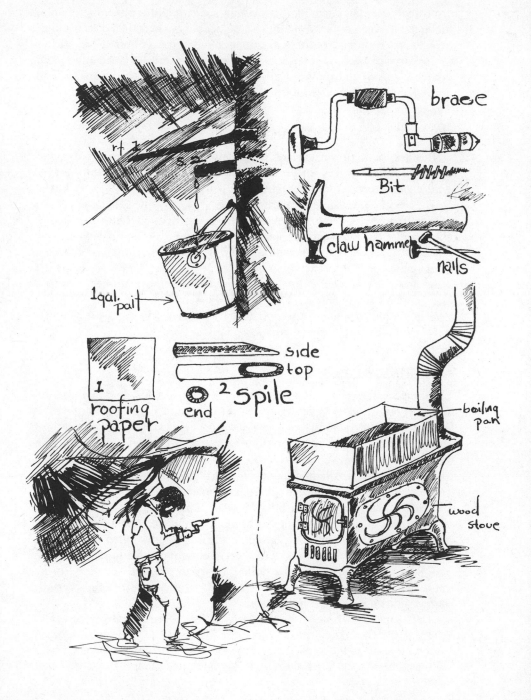

brace

rt

Bit

claw hammer

nails

1 gal. pail

side
top
end ²spile

roofing paper
1

boiling pan

wood stove

cised that it doesn't scorch. We do our sugar making inside with small amounts of syrup on a stove that can be heat-regulated since it is a rather delicate procedure. Note that the longer the syrup is boiled the harder the sugar will become after it is allowed to harden. Soft sugar is what you really want and the most all-around useful unless you want to mold animal or other shapes from it.

SWEETS FROM FRUITS AND BERRIES

Besides making syrup and acquiring honey the homesteader has access to other sources for producing a refined sweet—fruit and berries. The exact procedure for making syrup or a concentrated sweet from fruit is very simple. Just put it on the stove and boil it slowly until enough water has been driven off to leave it sweet enough for use as a syrup or jelly. Jelly making without commercial pectin and with little sugar is almost a lost art nowadays. Old Timey women used to combine sweet and sour fruit containing natural pectin and let it plop away on the stove until the desired color was reached. Then they strained it into a jelly jar and let it harden. One of the best fruits for pectin are green apples. Green applejuice also combines very well with other juices and a very good jelly can be made of ripe and green apples.

SORGHUM MOLASSES

Homesteaders with a half acre or so of land which will raise sorghum have access to another very good sweet, sorghum molasses. Sorghum is generally raised in southern states such as Tennessee and Kentucky, at present. However, in times past there were sorghum fields located on nearly every farm, even in the Midwest.

Sorghum cane is planted like corn in hills about 18 inches apart. The rows are usually kept far enough apart to permit cultivation. The cane is cut when it is fully mature, but before it starts to dry. Then the leaves are stripped off and the stalks crushed between cane rollers or by a press to squeeze the juice out. The extracted juice is finally boiled down to the required stage for sweetness. Most sorghum cane juice is distilled into molasses but it can be further boiled down to produce sugar. Also the molasses can be poured through flannel to strain out the sugar crystals, thus requiring no further boiling.

The homesteader who lives in areas where there are no machines to crush the stalks could probably cook his chopped cane stalks down enough to extract their juice. Cane rollers could also be constructed by a clever homesteader. Some say a washing machine wringer will work. Even

wringer (press)

pan

"NORGE"

"Washer wringer"

boiling pan

open fire

"Sorghum molasses"

if it wouldn't, it would still probably be a good start toward making a crusher.

Books

Nearing, Helen and Scott, *Maple Sugar Book: Together with remarks on pioneering as a way of living in the Twentieth Century*. New York: Schocken, 1971.

Booklets

ABC & XYZ Of Bee Culture (A. I. Root)
A. I. Root Company
Medina, Ohio 44256

Starting Right With Bees (A. I. Root)
A. I. Root Company
Medina, Ohio 44256

Sorghum Making
Tennessee Department Of Agriculture
Tennessee Agriculture Center
Nashville, Tennessee 37204

Bee Culture Branch
National Agricultural Library
U. S. Department Of Agriculture
Beltsville, Maryland 20705

Suppliers

A. I. Root Company
Medina, Ohio 44256

Walter T. Kelly Bee Supply Sugar Market
Walter T. Kelly Company
Clarkson, Kentucky 52726

9

MEAT, MILK AND EGG PRODUCERS

MANY HOMESTEADS WILL have animals as part of their self-sufficiency scheme. Animals which have proven successful on small farms are goats, rabbits, cattle and swine. Traditionally the goat and rabbit have been the mainstay of the farmer in the poorer or underdeveloped regions of the world. This is probably because these animals can thrive under even marginal conditions of food and shelter.

There are three well-known classes of goats: the Swiss with erect ears, the Nubian with heavy drooping ears, and the group that grows wool—the Angora and the Cashmere. Development and crossbreeding has produced at least five well-known milking breeds: the La Mancha or American goat with very tiny ears, the French Alpines with no set color pattern but with erect ears, the Saanens with erect ears and almost white hair, the Toggenburg with erect ears and a brown coat with light stripes down each side of the face, and the Nubian with heavy drooping ears and a dark brown coat.

GOATS

Some goats are very good milk producers with one French Alpine doe producing an official 4,551.8 pounds of milk in ten months. Generally speaking the Saanens are the heaviest producers of milk and they are sometimes called the "Holsteins" of the dairy goat world, inasmuch as the Holstein milk cow is the heaviest producer among dairy cattle. Conversely, the Nubian produces the richest milk and in that respect may be compared to the Jersey dairy cow. There is much variation in milk production between individual animals though and no one breed should be excluded from consideration by the prospective goat raiser.

Like the cow the goat is a grass eater, but unlike the cow goats will browse on woody plants. They have a special stomach so they can hastily swallow their food and yet bring it up again later to chew. Most domestic goats weigh from 100 to 120 pounds when mature. They have cloven hoofs, short horns and short tails. Like the female or doe goat, the male or buck goat has a beard, but unlike her, he has a strong odor. Goats can thrive on poor or dry land but they will do better on richer food. Most of them will not do well in a damp climate.

The goats or kids are born about 22 weeks after the doe has conceived. They can be single, twins or triplets. Goats are born fully haired with their eyes open and they can run and jump within four hours. They may take milk from the doe for six months before they are weaned and they have a life expectancy of about fourteen years.

Buying a goat is about like buying anything else; you buy the best one you can afford. The best milk goat will be the cheapest one in the long run because offsetting the cost of the feed she eats will be the good return in milk. A scrub goat may sell cheaper and even eat a little less, but she may produce almost nothing. It is usually advantageous to buy a doe goat that is about to freshen. Freshening means about to give birth to a kid. The advantage in this is that you will soon have two goats and one of them, the doe, will be giving the most milk that she ever will. Picking out a good milker, especially when she is dry, does take both knowledge and a little luck. Once a doe is milking, her udder will give a clue to her ability to produce milk, and incidentally, to produce kids that will be good milk producers, too. Specifically, if the udder is carried high and the "attachment" or the skin that supports the udder is tight and holds the udder up to the abdomen, she has good potential. The top of the udder at the attachment should be large enough so that a normal-sized pair of hands can't reach around it. Some does with pendulous or low-hanging udders give a lot of milk but they are forever kicking their udder when they step which can cause infections and other problems, and they can be hard to milk since the udder hangs so low to the ground. Some goat raisers say they have to be milked in a pie plate!

Prices of goats vary from about $5.00 for a scrub goat to as much as $200.00 for a prime purebred. The highest price stock will make one a successful goat raiser faster, all other things being equal. However, many scrub does milk very well. Happens you don't have any "bread" at all but you want a goat very bad, there are ways of getting one. First try to get well acquainted with a goat raiser. Maybe he will be a neighboring homesteader. Then when he has a surplus of bred does, offer to take some of the does and care for them in exchange for kids. Almost all breeders are susceptible to this suggestion at the right time because (a) they have more mature does than they need, (b) feed is unusually high, (c) they just lost one of their markets for milk and they are overproducing, and (d) they would like to get other goat raisers established because they raise high-grade animals and new breeders buy them. Goat raisers are generally a friendly bunch anyway and it's not hard to bargain with them.

Other ways of acquiring goats pop up from time to time also, such as buying them at commercial farm auctions where they are sometimes sold very cheap, but probably the best way to get a goat is to visit as many raisers as you can and talk to them about the possibilities.

It is possible to get by with just one milk goat, breeding her artificially or borrowing a buck from the neighbors. A very good goat will keep a family in milk. Many homesteaders have two or more does, however, so they will have a more or less continuous supply of milk since while one is dry the other can be producing.

Feed is a very important part of the cost of keeping a goat. Goats should be fed a good-quality hay such as alfalfa and this should be supplemented with grain. Many people figure the cost of keeping a doe goat is at least $5.00 a month. If this outlay is a problem use your ingenuity to shave the cost, by harvesting hay from out of the way places such as back roadsides and hand-picking wasted grain and field crops. Hay can be stored in your barn or under canvas or plastic and the grains can be kept in sheds or stored in a root cellar.

Goats of course will do very well on weeds or wild edible plants also. This takes some knowledge of what they like, however. In summer many raisers put a collar around the necks of their goats and stake them out with a length of chain and a tub of water so they can forage their own food. The location can be changed once or twice a day to keep the goat in fresh pasture. When they dry up and feed isn't so critical they can be staked out near whatever patches of brush that need clearing. Also they make good lawnmowers, chewing the grass off and fertilizing the soil at the same time with their manure, but don't expect them to graze like sheep. Tethered goats have to be guarded to prevent dogs from worrying or killing them.

Kidding or birthing is usually very easy and the new addition is born without any help. Occasionally, however, a crisis develops. Multiple births tend to get mixed up and while a head is being born on one goat the front legs may appear on another. Nothing for the herdsman to do then but be a midwife and push one of the babies back in the birth canal and let the other be born first. Sometimes there will be a birth where the new arrival is trying to arrive sideways or with the front legs first and the head doubled back along the body. Here too the herdsman must reach in and turn the baby so that it is born head first.

Okay, helping the goat give birth is usually very simple but how do you know if she needs help? A mother needs help in delivery if the kid is partially born, if one foot or the head appears and nothing else happens for 15 or 20 minutes even though the doe is obviously in labor and straining very hard. She also probably needs help if she labors for an hour or more without anything happening. Help means scrubbing the hands and arms very well and then gently reaching in the uterus and feeling around until you can tell which part of the kid is foremost. Happens that the first part you touch is the backbone, you know the kid is sideways. As gently as you can, turn it until the head is forward.

The afterbirth should be passed very soon after the birth. If it is not, tug on it gently or go exploring again to try to find out what is happening. Sometimes there will be a still birth or a partially developed fetus that must be removed before the afterbirth will pass. If the afterbirth is still not passed after about twelve hours it might be well to call a veterinarian.

Shelter for the goats can be as simple as a small draft-free shed or as elaborate as a barn with separate stalls for exercise, milking and feeding. The homesteader with two goats can build from whatever scrap material that is available to make a tight, dry, draft-proof shed. The building can be as small as 8 x 10 for a temporary arrangement. A milking stand can be built in one corner and small closet for storing the forks, brooms and other utensils for cleaning the barn and milking. The rest of the shed can be partitioned into two box stalls with a manger at one end to hold hay and grain. Since goats have a great desire and ability to climb, partitions must be made so that they span the distance between floor and ceiling. They should be made from wooden bars or wire so that the goats can see each other as this way they will be more contented.

As you acquire more goats and wish to sell milk, more elaborate housing is necessary. Many commercial dairies have a row of tie stalls where the goats are kept except for milking and exercising time. These tie stalls have concrete floors and gutters to make cleaning the stalls easier. When the stalls are being cleaned the goats are turned into an exercise pen or outside. Frequently milking machines are used to milk the goats and everything is kept spotlessly clean. The hay ration and grain ration is kept fresh.

Many goat raisers butcher their surplus stock and the meat is delicious. They are usually butchered when they weigh about one hundred pounds. With the intestines and the skin and head and legs removed they lose about half their weight.

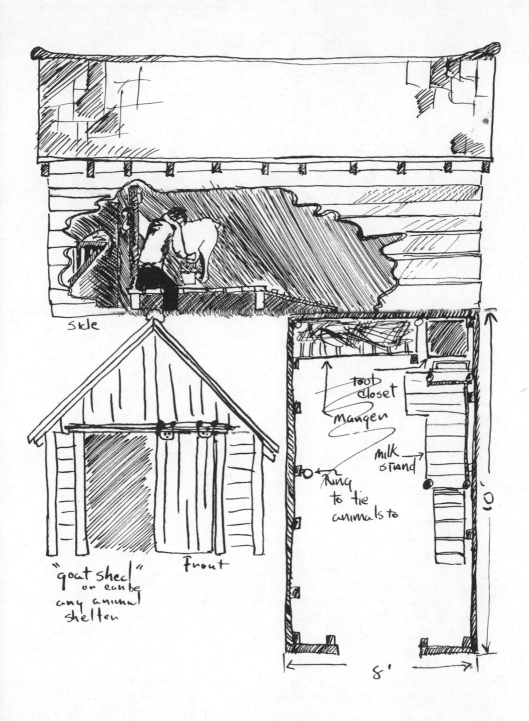

side

"goat shed" or canbe any animal shelter

Front

tool closet

manger

milk stand

Ring to tie animals to

8'

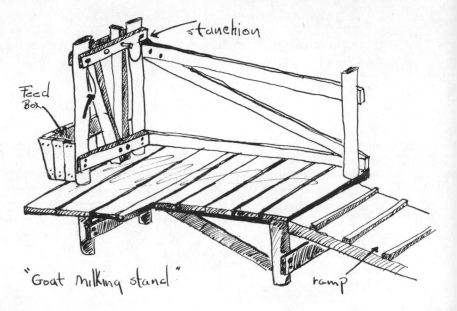

"Goat milking stand"

RABBITS

Another good meat animal is the domestic rabbit. There is not much that can be said against the domestic rabbit as a meat producer. It compares very favorably with the cow and pig in feed conversion. The meat is richer in calories than most other domestic animals, it can be raised anywhere, even in the backyard of city residents, it costs very little in capital or time to get started and a return is quickly realized. In addition rabbits are such quiet, affectionate animals that many people derive a deep satisfaction from keeping and caring for them. It will surely follow that as people get thicker and compete with the larger animals for the world's supply of grain, rabbit production will be increased. Many European countries, with their dense populations, already depend heavily on the domestic rabbit for meat. Britain, for example, once had a total of seven and a half million breeding rabbits.

The homesteader has a choice of several different breeds of rabbits. If he wishes to raise meat simply for his own use any one of the meat breeds will do quite nicely. They include the Flemish, the Belgian Hare, the Californian, the Dutch, New Zealand, English Spot, Lops or almost any one of the sixty odd varieties of rabbits. It is probably well to stay away from the extremes of rabbit size unless a specific reason makes it advisable. Thus the Himalayans and Tans, which only weigh when mature about four pounds, and the huge American Chinchilla and Flemish Giant, which can weigh near twenty pounds, probably will not give as good results as the Californian or New Zealand Whites, which weigh about ten pounds when mature.

Commercial raisers strive to produce a breed or herd of rabbits that will produce nicely finished friers running at 3¾ to 4½ pounds at two months of age or weaning.

In addition to the meat rabbits there are rabbits bred for the Angora wool they yield. There are the English Angora and the French Angora, for instance. The meat from the Angora rabbits is as good as the meat from the short-furred rabbits but they are slightly harder to raise.

After the homesteader has decided on a particular breed or type of rabbit he can obtain lists of breeders who have rabbits for sale by consulting classified ads in newspapers and magazines. A word of caution here though. Don't be misled by the claims made in some ads which state, "Make thousands of dollars raising rabbits for us." These folks usually charge so much for their breeding stock and pay such low prices for the rabbits that they do buy back, if indeed they even buy them back at all, that it is almost impossible to realize a return on their "deals".

A better way would be to deal with a local breeder with a good reputation. You can of course find out what you will have to pay for breeding stock by writing to several breeders. In this way you can be a good judge of whether or not you are being overcharged for a certain animal. It is usually advisable to start with mature animals because the return is much faster. This means start with a bred doe if possible. Don't accept a doe that looks as if she is about ready to kindle, however. There is a good chance that placing the prospective mother in unfamiliar surroundings immediately before she gives birth will cause her to eat or abandon her young.

One other advantage of dealing with a local breeder, if you are short of "bread", is that you can often lease a doe or does and pay for them by returning part of the litter to the original owner. This may include two does or all of the litter or all of the does or some other arrangement that can be worked out.

Other ways that rabbits can be obtained without actually purchasing them is to raise the young on shares, work for the rabbitry in peak loads and take your pay in rabbits or perform some special service for the breeder like watching the herd so he and his lady can take a weekend off once in awhile. There is hardly anything as valuable to the fledgling rabbit breeder as having a friend who is in the business, especially one who has been in the business for a long time.

Even before you obtain your breeding stock you are going to have to give some thought to housing the furry little creatures. Housing for rabbits can be as simple as wooden boxes with one end protected with wire mesh, or it can be a battery complete with sprinklers, lights, feed boxes and a host of other gadgets.

Rabbit pens or hutches have been made in every conceivable way but they have evolved mainly into a standard rectangular or square box that contains about a square foot for every pound of breeding rabbit to be enclosed. Thus a ten-pound rabbit would have a pen that would measure 2 feet by 5 feet long. This pen should have a wire bottom of 16 ga. welded wire with ½-inch mesh. The sides can be one by one inch galvanized wire. The top can be lumber or it can also be wire. However, rabbits have to be protected from rain, snow, cold and hot weather so all wire cages will have to contain a box made of waterproofed wood filled with straw, hay, shredded newspaper or something dry and warm for the rabbit to burrow into. In hot weather the hutch will have to be shaded. Doors for feeding and watering and removing the animals should be at least one foot square. If a wire mesh floor is used the pen should be placed on legs to allow the droppings to fall through. Also since it has to be placed on legs it might as well be made high enough so that not much stooping is necessary when caring for them.

The young animals being raised for meat can usually be kept in the same pen with the doe until they are marketable age, especially if the bucks have been castrated.

Feeding your rabbits is equally important to housing them. A homesteader can buy a complete ration from the commercial feed houses or he can produce his own ration. Buying the ration all but insures the rabbits getting a reasonably well-balanced diet but it is expensive. More in keeping with the strived for independence of homesteading is feeding all the home-produced greens, grain and hay that you can. Rabbit feeding though is a complex undertaking and any changes to the diet should be

"Rabbit" Hutch

side   front

done slowly and carefully. For example if you are feeding commercial pellets and hay don't suddenly start giving them all the greens that they can eat. You could kill the whole bunch. Instead start with small amounts such as one small cabbage leaf per animal. If no harm comes of this in one week double the amount, meanwhile keeping hay and pellets in front of them. Almost all the green plant trimmings from the garden and most leafy weeds are good rabbit food. In addition dry bread, very often obtainable from bakeries, cull apples, oranges, grapefruit, cooked potatoes and their peelings and cow or goat's milk are good food.

Study of the nutritive requirements of rabbits plus careful observation of the reaction of your stock to various feeds will enable one to bypass the feed mill eventually in favor of locally or self-produced foods, some often free for the taking. Proof of this are the millions of healthy rabbits produced by European raisers, some of whom have never heard of buying feed nor using a scientific ration. Good rabbit meat, rich in body-building elements, can be produced by feeding sprouted alfalfa seeds, oats, barley, corn, soybeans or other cereal grains.

One thing that you may have to buy for your rabbits is salt. Rabbits should have this available at all times. Water is also a necessity, especially when feeding dry hay and pellets. Some small raisers who feed sprouted grains and considerable greens report that their rabbits don't drink any water except in the hottest part of the summer, but always keep fresh clean water in front of the animals, summer and winter.

Doe rabbits are usually bred at about four months of age for the smaller breeds such as the Tans, at about six months for the medium breeds such as the New Zealand, and at about nine to ten months for the large ones such as the Flemish.

Once mated, the doe may be bred often enough to produce four litters a year. Allowing for a gestation period of 31 to 32 days and a suckling period of eight weeks the doe can be rebred when the litter reaches the age of two months and has been weaned.

For mating, take the doe to the buck's hutch as most does will not accept a buck in their hutch and may injure him. Once mated, take the doe back to her own hutch.

Does are "in heat" or ready to receive the male when they become very restless in their pens and show signs of wanting to join other rabbits or rub their chins on their water dishes or pen. Unlike some other animals, appearance of the vulva does not provide an indication of a "heat" period. Only the best does and buck should be kept for breeding purposes.

One of the most accurate indicators of good or complete rations is the condition of the litter upon kindling. If the baby rabbits are large, healthy and vigorous the ration is apt to be good. Many dead babies or thin weak ones suggest improper rations being fed to the doe. Too fat or too thin does will result in poor kindling also. Cannibalism is also a result of poor rations.

Very little help need be given to the doe when she is kindling, in fact, the caretaker's presence could cause the doe confusion and anxiety. This is usually not a problem though since the kindling usually takes place at night. All does should be provided with a nest box 27 days after mating. This box should be large enough to hold the doe and litter and contain enough soft absorbent material so the doe can make a bed. Material for the nest can be straw, marsh hay, leaves, or wood shavings. Avoid rough hay, paper, excelsior and peat moss since these can be harmful to the babies.

Sometimes a doe will kindle a litter too large for her to suckle. In this case some of the young will have to be removed and given to a foster mother. This means picking up the young and giving them to a milking doe, either one that has lost her litter or one that has more than enough milk. A foster mother will readily accept the new young and rabbit breeders divide up young to equalize the litter sizes as a general practice. Be sure to remember which doe the young came from though so you can make a decision as to which ones to keep for breeding stock. Usually a tattoo mark is put on the rabbit's ear.

After the doe has kindled she will pull hair from her belly to make a covering for the young. This is very necessary, especially in cold weather and the caretaker should inspect the nest box to make sure that this is done. If the young are not well covered the caretaker should pull hair out of the doe until there is enough to keep the young warm. Once in a while a doe will get overzealous about the amount of fur she needs to add to the nest and will pull two or three times more than needed. If there is another doe kindling at the same time with insufficient fur for her nest some of the surplus can be given her. Too, it may be placed in a paper bag and stored for future use.

All strangers and animals should be kept away from the rabbit pens when the does are kindling. Just the sight of a strange dog or cat can make a doe so anxious that she will dive into the nest box and harm her babies.

A little arithmetic can illustrate how much meat a well-fed doe can produce for her keeper in a year's time. First, if she produces four litters in a year, which is a reasonable production figure, and the young are weaned and butchered at two months when they weigh four pounds, the total production can be 120 pounds of meat. All this from a 10 or 11-pound doe, and some does beat this figure. Thus the homesteader who kept one doe for each member of his family plus a couple of extra would be virtually assured of a continuing and adequate supply of meat.

The food necessary to supply this much meat including feeding the doe will be about four to five pounds of balanced ration per pound of meat produced. If a homesteader feeds his own grown ration he may have to supply a bit more food.

Rabbit meat can be covered and frozen like any meat, it can be canned, salted, smoked or dried. Whichever way you cook it, it offers good flavor and nutrition.

Rabbits will have few diseases if the housing is kept spotlessly clean. Some of those to watch out for are colds, sore hocks, bloat (mucoid enteritis) and ceccidesis. When an animal appears to be "droopy" or otherwise unhealthy he should be quarantined until the illness is identified and treated. If a large number of rabbits come down with a specific ailment there is usually an underlying cause such as improper feed, dirty pens, too many people handling the rabbits, dogs or cats sleeping on the bedding material or the contact of other animals with the rabbits.

If a disease cannot be identified and the rabbit doesn't improve in a few days he should be destroyed and the carcass buried or burned to prevent an epidemic. Identifying diseases requires the help of a veterinarian or experienced rabbit raiser.

THE FAMILY COW

Those who would like to keep a family cow will find that one of the smaller breeds such as the Guernsey, Jersey or Ayrshire are best. Since they are smaller they do not take up so much room, don't eat as much and are easier to handle than larger breeds such as the Holstein. They don't give quite as much milk either but one good cow will still keep even a large family in milk and butter.

In buying a family cow it is well to get one that has had at least one calf. Sometimes a dairy farmer will want to cull out a cow that isn't a real top producer but still milking well enough to be a good family cow. These are the kind to watch for. Commercial dairy farmers are continually upgrading their herds for better production. Here again, if you want to get a cow but don't have any "bread", offer to work for the farmer whenever he needs help and take the cow as your pay. It may take a while to earn one this way but remember you will be gaining experience as you go.

One advantage of cows over goats for milking is that they produce a bigger offspring. Thus whether a cow is used for meat or sold, it is of more economic value than a goat.

The feed costs for a cow vary greatly depending on the availability of hay but usually they will be about $100.00 to $200.00 a year. Besides three to four tons of good hay a year, a milking cow needs about two tons of a grain concentrate. If good pasture is available the cost will lower considerably and if an acre or so of land can be used to grow corn for the milk cow, this too will help. Many family cows are staked out on halter and chain to graze along the country roads and lanes and on other patches of good green grass during the summer.

When the cow is staked out, provide a large container such as a discarded bathtub or a wash tub and keep it filled with water, especially in hot weather. A milking cow can consume an unbelievable amount of water. Without a nearby water supply, the cow should be led to the water at least three times a day and allowed to drink all she wants.

In winter she should be fed all the hay she will eat and a good grain ration, especially when she is milking. Commercially prepared rations can be used or you can mix your own. A good grain supplement for a milk cow is ground corn and wheat bran with a little soybean oil meal added. The amount of grain she will need will depend on the hay quality. The better the hay the less supplement needed, but a rough rule of thumb is to feed a pound of grain for each two quarts of milk produced. The gauge for this will be the milk flow. If it drops off considerably she probably is not getting enough grain.

In winter the cow will have to have a warm dry building to stay in. The space allowed for the cow will have to be about 6 x 10 feet if she is confined to a stall. A pen can be used which will allow the cow to move around but it will have to be kept very well bedded or she will lie in her manure and be a problem to keep clean.

The cow can be tied in a stall with a rope or chain to her halter and thus her manure will all be in the same place and make it easier to keep the barn clean. She should be curried or brushed each day and her bag and teats washed before each milking. A cow confined like this will be happier if she can be let out to a lot or pasture for exercise on warm days.

In summer, if the flies are not a terrific problem the cow can be milked outside where she is tethered or pastured. This saves all the hassle of taking her into the barn. Before she is milked she ought to be brushed to remove dirt and loose hair. If tethered on a chain, the chain should be snubbed short for milking. Sometimes the flies will be so bad that some kind of repellent will have to be wiped or sprayed on her, but never do this around milking time.

SHEEP

Aside from possibly a little trouble at lambing time, sheep are about the easiest of all to raise. They will graze on almost any rough ground, feeding and doing well on pasture that would never support cattle.

They do need housing in winter, medium good hay and some grain. In return they yield very good meat and of course wool for the homesteaders who spin or can sell it.

As an animated lawnmower the sheep has no equal, being far superior to goats in this. They can be tethered with a collar around their necks wherever it is desired to keep the grass short, but like tethered goats they have to be protected from dogs and they have to be kept well watered. Homesteaders should not overlook the possibilities in keeping sheep, but we will leave the topic since helpful information on this is widely available.

PIGS

Pig or swine breeds are the Yorkshire, a white streamlined pig; the Berkshire, a black chunky pig; Poland China, black with spotted white legs; Spotted Poland China, a black and white hog; and the Hampshire, a black pig with a large white belt around the shoulder and rib cage. Two other breeds are the Chester White, a pure white pig; and the Tamworth, a red, lean-bacon-type hog.

The homesteader who only wants to raise a pig or two for his own use can often buy the young ones at about weaning age from livestock barns or local farmers. Sellers sometimes want to sell a whole litter to you or none at all. We solved the problem by finding three other homesteaders who wanted to raise pigs also and split the litter. Young pigs sell from $5.00 a piece to $15.00, depending on the market at the particular time.

Reading in various magazines about how much it costs to feed a pig always amazes me. We habitually buy them for about $12.00 at weaning time. We buy one bag of starter food from the feed mill, worm them good and that is about all of our commercial costs. After they are started good we feed them garden produce, gleaned grain, dried bread, tons of weeds, cull apples, unsalable produce from the supermarket, wheelbarrow loads of acorns and oak leaves (yes, they like leaves) raked up in our wood lot and water weeds from our fish pond, cooked cull potatoes and anything else we can lay hands on to provide them carbohydrate. For protein we feed them bones from the butcher shop, whatever pest animals have to be eliminated from the garden, the frozen and cooked carcasses of carp fish that are to be had by the dozens in the marshes in early spring and surplus bluegills from our fish ponds. The pigs grow well, they are very happy and their meat is delicious. They cost us about 15¢ a pound, live weight, when they are ready to butcher, not counting the time we spend on them, the gasoline for the pickup, or depreciation on the housing. However, these costs are small.

Regardless of the picture many people have of pigs lying around happily in filthy mudholes they will be even happier and do better if they have a clean, dry pen. The pen need not be large but it should be well fenced with woven or board fence at least four feet high and its bottom buried in the ground to keep them from rooting out. A shed should be provided for housing that will be large enough for the mature hogs to sleep in out of the rain and sun. They must have water available at all times and ready access to food.

Hogs can be butchered at home by anyone who has even only a rough knowledge of animal anatomy. Some people scald the pig and some skin them but regardless of the way you get the hair off they must be suspended by the hind legs and eviscerated and then the meat is cut into pieces. Almost all of the hog is edible, this includes the feet and the head. Hogs are usually butchered when they are six months old and weigh about 200 to 250 pounds. (See next chapter.)

Hogs are very compatible with poultry, such as chickens, ducks and geese.

CHICKENS

Chickens can furnish eggs and meat for even the smallest homestead. They come in various sizes and colors, some of them bred exclusively for the production of eggs and some of them bred for both meat and eggs. Chickens bred exclusively for egg production are the Leghorns and those bred for both meat and eggs are the Rhode Island Reds and New Hampshires, among others.

Unless the homesteader wants the chickens as a source of income immediately he will not want to start with White Leghorns but he will get one of the dual purpose breeds such as Rhode Island Reds instead.

Chickens can be purchased from local hatcheries or be bought by mail from hatcheries that advertise in magazines and papers. Almost all of the large mail-order retail houses sell day-old chicks by mail as do most of the seed catalog firms. In addition large chicken raisers rotate their flocks on a continuing basis to get rid of poor layers. The hens they cull out are usually sold for about 50¢ apiece and of course they are mature chickens, some of them still laying quite good.

If you have a building and enough room to let them run you can take a flock like this home, put them in your building and give them access to pasture. The chickens allowed to forage for themselves will produce good sweet meat from the natural food. Also you will notice that the good layers will be found setting in the nest boxes quite regularly. These individuals can be marked with a dab of paint and, presto, you have culled out the layers from the non-layers! Butcher the non-layers, keep the layers.

If you have poultry houses in your vicinity or large commercial raisers you can offer to work for them for a time during some peak season and take your pay in the form of cull chickens. A week's work might pay for a whole flock.

Food for the flock in summer should include as much pasture as possible. Chickens are the world's best foragers and if they are allowed to run free and select their own food they do very well indeed, especially if a little grain such as oats or cracked corn is fed to them. In winter, however, they will have to be fed a good balanced ration to keep them laying well. Also they have to be kept warm and dry and have plenty of water available. Commercial rations can be obtained from feed mills and the county agent can supply a list of ingredients for making up a complete ration should you want to mix your own.

If you have the time to sprout seeds, a ration of sprouted seeds including corn, wheat, barley and soybeans should cover most chicken needs. Add a little protein such as the chopped up carcasses of small animals or fish.

DUCKS AND GEESE

The easiest birds to raise for the table are ducks and geese. About all that you have to do with them is hatch the eggs under a banty hen or in an electric hatcher and feed them chick-starting mash for a few weeks. As soon as they have their second feathers they can be allowed to run and forage. After that they will need neither food nor housing until it is time to butcher them. Some people like to fatten up the geese on corn for a few weeks before butchering but it is not really necessary. Ducks, if they have access to a pond, will fatten themselves fairly well. They also can be thrown a little corn as butchering time nears.

Some people keep ducks for egg production also. In fact the world's record for a year's production of eggs belongs to a duck, not to a chicken.

For Additional Information Contact:

Magazines

Dairy Goat Journal
P. O. Box 1908
Scottsdale, Arizona 85252

Countryside Magazine
Route 1, Box 239
Waterloo, Wisconsin 53594

The Mother Earth News
Box 38
Madison, Ohio 44057

Books

Mackenzie, David, *Goat Husbandry*. Levittown, Long Island: Transat-
lantic, 1961
Templeton, George S., *Domestic Rabbit Production*. Danville, Illinois:
Interstate Printers & Publishers, 1968
Diggins, Bundy and Ronald V., *Livestock and Poultry Production*.
Englewood Cliffs, New Jersey, 1969
Stamm, G. W., *Veterinary Guide For Farmers*. New York: Hawthorn,
1963

Associations

The American Dairy Goat Association
P. O. Box 186
Spindale, North Carolina 28160

American Rabbit Breeders Association
1007 Morrissey Drive RW
Bloomington, Illinois 61701

Superintendent of Documents
U. S. Government Printing Office
Washington, D.C. 20402

Write to the above address for the following pamphlets:

Animal Diseases Yearbook of Agriculture 1956
Catalog No. A 1.10: :956 S/N 0100-0103 $2.00

Raising Ducks
Catalog No. A19 :221512
S/N 0100-0070 10¢

Raising Geese
Catalog No. A 1.9:2251
S/N 0100-1584 10¢

Breeds of Swine
Catalog No. A 1.9 :1263/13
S/N 0100-0012 10¢

Hog Castration
Catalog No. A 1.35 47313
S/N 0100-0208 10¢

Raising Livestock on Small Farm
Catalog No. A 1.9 :2224/2
S/N 0100-1617 15¢

Brooding Chicks with Infrared Lamps
Catalog No. A 1.35 : 3975
S/N 0100-0186 10¢

Housing and Equipment for Laying Hens for Loose Housing
Catalog No. A 1.38 : 72813
S/N 0100-0428 25¢

Lighting Poultry Houses
Catalog No. A 1.9 : 222912
S/N 0100-0082 10¢

Newcastle Disease in Poultry—How to Control It
Catalog No. A 1.35 : 45113
S/N 0100-0201 10¢

Commercial Rabbit Raising
Catalog No. A 1.76 : 30912
S/N 0100-1376 35¢

Selecting and Raising Rabbits
Catalog No. A 1.75 : 358
S/N 0100-2640 15¢

10

HOW TO DO YOUR OWN BUTCHERING

IT IS VERY convenient to be able to do your own butchering, especially if you live some distance from a commercial meat processor. Many folks say that the job of loading an animal up, taking it to the slaughterhouse, then unloading it and making yet another later trip to get the meat—not to mention the expense involved—is as much work as doing the whole job yourself.

HOGS

Butchering takes some equipment and knowledge of farm animal anatomy and how to handle meat. The equipment involved is a .22 rifle usually, or a heavy maul for stunning the animal and a hoist of at least a half-ton capacity for lifting the carcass. Three good sharp knives, one having an eight-inch blade, scrapers such as dull knives or paint scrapers—useful for scraping a pig after it is scalded—and a gambrel device for placing and holding the hind legs of the carcass when it is hoisted.

A cool or cold day is preferred for butchering since it takes a while for meat to cool. Animals to be butchered should be kept without feed for 12 hours, but allowed plenty of water. Not feeding empties the intestines somewhat and makes them easier to eviscerate. Very dirty animals should be washed before butchering, if possible, especially if they are coated with manure or caked mud. If they can't be washed they can at least be bedded in a clean place for a few days prior to butchering.

Before butchering a pig, many homesteaders will isolate the animal in a small pen at least 24 hours beforehand and withhold his feed. The pig should be bedded with clean straw and have all the water he wants so he doesn't become nervous and excited since this can affect the taste of the meat. It is desirable that the pen be located close to where the butchering is to be done. If the carcass will have to be moved before dressing it, provisions should be made for this beforehand. Two strong men can drag a pig or a tractor or horse can be used if available. If the homesteader and his 98-pound wife are doing the butchering the pig can probably be moved by wheelbarrow or small wagon to the scalding or skinning site.

For the easiest handling, the pig should be killed and bled right in the pen. Shoot the animal in the head with a .22 rifle and when he is dead or badly stunned, which should be instantaneously, stick a knife in his jugular vein. Both bullet and blade must be placed correctly. The bullet should be placed directly above the cross formed by the ears and eyes. As soon as he drops immobilized, he should be turned over on his back and the throat cut to drain the blood. Thrust a sharp sticking knife in midway between the head and the front legs, at the hollow of the throat. The idea is to cut the large veins located almost between the front legs which lead from the heart to the brain. With the knife at least six inches deep, turn it back and forth to make a sizable cut. With the veins properly cut, they will release blood in quantity. With the sticking done, the carcass is rolled over to bleed out, but it should be hung up head down as soon as possible to promote blood drainage.

Meatpackers, Morton Salt and some Old Timey farmers recommend sticking the animal without shooting him, feeling that the hog bleeds better that way. I don't agree with this because it unnecessarily invites trouble. Besides, it is almost impossible for one man alone, or attended only by his wife, to throw and hold an animal so he can be stuck without first killing or stunning him.

As soon as possible the carcass should be hung up to drain. As to the merits of whether it should next be skinned or the hide left on and the hair scalded off, some feel the meat is easier to handle and store with the hide left on. With modern cold freezer storage the frozen meat is as easy to handle one way as the other, however, and sooner or later the hide is going to have to come off, consequently quite a few farmers today will as soon skin the hog at this stage and get it over with. There was a time, of course, when pork pieces used to be put in dry storage, suspended from the walls or ceilings of garrets, etc. For this kind of storage or in case the pork is to be smoke-cured, the hide will usually be left on. Anyway, if the pig is to be scalded, this is the time to do it. Have a fifty-gallon barrel or the equivalent handy, full of water heated to about 150°. In very cold weather this water should be 160° since it will cool more rapidly. Some old timers pour the water in boiling hot and allow it to cool to just where it doesn't bubble and then try an experimental dip. The first dip should be very quick. If the hair doesn't slip, the next one can be longer and so on until the right immersion time is found. Then if possible the whole carcass should be dipped including the ends of the legs and even the tip of the nose. This brings up the point that a carcass can be scalded in a barrel by dropping it hind feet first with a hog hook in the jaws easier than by dropping it head first. Some carcasses will be too large to scald all at once. Then half the carcass has to be scalded and scraped at a time. Bell scrapers, which can be obtained at farm auctions, borrowed, made or purchased from farm supply stores, are about the best thing for scraping. However, if the scalding goes well, almost anything will work including the back of the butcher knife, blade of a knife, a large spoon or even a tin can with the ends cut out. Pour more water over patches of hair that initially resist scraping.

Another way of scalding a hog is to just cover a small patch of the skin at a time with four layers of burlap and apply hot water to it, soaking it well. This holds the heat long enough to loosen the hair. When one patch is scraped clean move to another and keep at it until one side is done, then roll the carcass over and do the other side. This method is best when working with a large hog.

Hogs are sometimes skinned out instead of scalded. Skinning a hog carcass is almost exactly like skinning a beef, except much easier. The carcass is hung head down and skinning is begun at the inside of the hind legs where a slit downward is made, then a cricle is cut around the hock and the skin cut away. Almost all the skin on a hog carcass has to be cut since it has so much fat attached to it. When the orifices are encountered they should be tied off to keep the meat clean. Once the body is reached the skin can be slit down the belly. If the skin is not to be kept and used it can be slit down the back also. The head is usually skinned out down to the end of the nose. Preserve the hide after skinning by sprinkling five pounds of salt inside it and then rolling it up.

The hair or hide now removed, the next step is to gut it. If a wooden or steel whippletree device called a gambrel has not already been inserted, now is the time to do it. Make a lengthwise slit back of the hind heels; this will expose three tendons. Carefully work them out with your fingers and slip the ends of the gambrel between the tendons and the bone of the hind legs. The gambrel keeps the hind legs spread and provides a way to lift the hog. Attach a lifting device at the center of the gambrel stick and hoist the carcass well off the ground for working convenience.

The first step in gutting the carcass is to remove the head. Make a deep cut all around behind the ears at the first joint of the backbone. Keep cutting deeper until you have cut through the gullet and windpipe. Now you can either continue this cut horizontally and cut the jowls off with the head or you can cut vertically from the ears to the eyes and out at the point of the jawbone. This will leave the jowls on the carcass.

Now make a shallow slit from a point between the hind legs and forward of the bung to the point where the animal was stuck. Place your sharpest knife in the center of the neck at the sticking cut and cut upwards to split the breastbone and the first pair of ribs. When this cut is complete go to the top of the original slit between the hind legs and cut deep enough to expose the intestines but be very careful not to cut into them. When it is possible to insert the fingers into the cavity to do so, grasp the knife in your other hand with the blade cutting edge out, then cut downward using the fingers inside the cut to push the intestines away from the knife. Carefully continue this cut down to the severed breastbone. When this cut is completed the intestines will be hanging forward.

The next step is to cut the aitch or rump bone (also—crotch bone). Cut deep enough between the hind legs to hit the bone. This cut has to be directly in the center since the aitch or crotch bone has a seam in its center by which it can be split. Place the point of the knife against the seam and pound on it with your palm. Sometimes the aitch bone is so tough you have to hit it with a meat cleaver to break it. If the direct center of the aitch bone isn't reached a heavy knife or cleaver can be used to cut it. Once the crotch bone is cut the hind legs will spread and the bung can be worked out.

Working inside, cut the bung loose from the carcass until the external orifice is reached. Then with the point of the knife cut all around it. If it hasn't been tied off before tie it now. Some butchers cut deep enough around the anus to tie off the bung before they start gutting. Once the bung is free it can be pulled down to the intestines by cutting loose the fat and membrane otherwise holding it to the backbone.

Now place a large tub under the carcass and cut and pull the intestines until they are loose and will fall out. The tub should be clean since the liver and leaf lard are usually retrieved later.

Next wash out the carcass with cold water and remove heart and lungs. Then split the carcass in two by sawing directly down the center of the backbone. Leave enough meat at the neck to hold the halves together so they don't slide off the gambrel stick.

The meat has to be cooled before it can be handily cut any smaller. It should be allowed to hang and chill at least twelve hours. This is why a cool or cold day is preferred for butchering. In Wisconsin butchering is usually done in November. I can remember my grandfather sniffing the air and saying "Tomorrow is a butchering day" and he'd hit it right on the head every time—the coldest day in November, which in this state can mean below zero. It isn't too good to let the meat freeze before it is cut up but pork can stand quite a while in bitter cold weather without freezing.

While the meat is cooling the liver can be processed. Cut it loose from the intestines. There is a little green bag called the gall bladder attached to the liver. Cut this loose without spilling any of the gall on the liver and discard it. Now remove all of the leaf lard from the intestines and the inside of the carcass. This leaf lard is fat hanging in "leaves" or bunches and it is usually loose enough to pull out.

If the weather turns out milder than expected the meat may have to be artificially chilled. If you have ice, use that; if not, use the coldest water obtainable. Some spring water runs about 39 degrees. Don't salt any meat until it is well chilled.

One way to cool meat with water is to quarter the carcass and then cut each quarter in half. Follow the standard cutting lines used by professional butchers if possible and then place the meat in a tub or barrel filled with cold water. Let it stay there and chill. A homesteader in Alabama once wrote me that he and his wife took turns getting up at night to pump cold well water on a tubful of fresh pork. It worked too, the meat was the best he ever had. Sprinkling a little salt on the ice is recommended by some, if you have ice. This hastens its melting and helps lower the water temperature. Meat should be cooled at least 12 hours and 24 hours is even better.

If chilling is just not possible, there is no alternative but to cut the meat into as small pieces as you can use and salt it. Meat can also be placed in brine to cure. But pork spoils easier than beef.

BEEF CATTLE

Butchering a beef is different from butchering a hog since the hair does not have to be scraped off and you have a much larger animal to work with. Beef can be butchered when they weigh around a thousand pounds, but practices vary. Young cattle under fourteen weeks are called veal calves and their meat is called veal.

The method and steps in slaughtering a beef parallel those recited for butchering hogs. To facilitate draining the blood, the carcass is hung up as early as practicable, the head being removed at the last neck joint to expedite drainage.

With the carcass bled out but before it starts to cool, the hide should be removed. Circle the hind hoofs with a knife cut and then slit down the inside of each hind leg so the cuts run together at the crotch. Then continue the skinning cut down to the neck area. Return to the hind legs and start working the skin off around the hock and peel it down over the legs, working on one leg at a time. When the crotch is reached circle the anus and reproductive organs and slit the skin down the center of the tail, continue cutting the skin loose and pulling it down over the body. When the front legs are reached circle the hoofs with the knife, cut the skin and continue pulling and cutting the hide loose until it drops free. Raise the carcass higher as you skin so that when the front legs are free the skin is easily removed. Then immediately spread the hide out and sprinkle about five to ten pounds of salt on the inside and roll it up for later disposition.

The carcass should be lowered near the ground before removing the guts. The job is very similar to that of removing them from a pig.

Sometimes no facilities will be available for hoisting a carcass as large as that of a beef. Then all the skinning and gutting will have to be done on the ground. This is a little less conveinent but does not pose too many special problems.

When it is bled, roll the beef over on its back. Slit the skin from tail to head and then slit up inside each leg, circling the hock to remove the leg skin. Either skin or cut off the head and proceed to skin out the carcass as much as possible without moving it. Then spread the loosened portion of the hide out around the carcass (it will still be attached at the back) and do the gutting. This is done much the same as if the carcass was hanging up except offal and other material will have to be dragged out by hand. At the point when the heart, lungs and intestines have been removed but before skinning anymore, the beef can be cut in half. Locate the last two ribs. With a sharp knife cut between them to the backbone. Do this on both sides. Then with a hatchet or meat cleaver sever the backbone but be very careful not to cut the hide. Skin out as much as you can reach of the hide at the end of the severed backbone. This will free the carcass halves so they can be easily rolled around until the skinning is finished. The hide will flex enough to permit this. As soon as the hide is removed from one half, that piece can be propped up and sawed down the center. The carcass will then be divided into quarters and hung up to cool. This will put even the largest beef into manageable proportions.

Beef, like pork, should be thoroughly cooled before it is cut up or frozen. Beef also can be chilled by placing it in cold water or on ice if the weather is too warm.

A very simple hoist can be made by which two men can lift a beef. Simply place a piece of 1¼ well pipe between the carcass' hind legs. It should be long enough so its ends stick out a ways at each end. Hang two stout ropes from a tree limb and to the free end of each tie a two-foot length of pipe. Pass these pipes beneath the pipe going between the beef's hind legs, then raise the carcass by winding it up. Each man holds his piece of pipe perpendicular to the horizontal pipe supporting the carcass—you could say each holds his pipe piece vertically, winding the pipe he holds around the pipe going between the carcass legs. In other words, the pipe between the carcass legs serves as a fulcrum for each winding pipe. As the hoisting proceeds, the lines from the tree limb are gradually wound around the piece of horizontal pipe supporting the carcass. When the winding handles are to be secured another long piece of pipe can be placed across the ropes to prevent them from unwinding.

The beef head can be opened and the tongue and brains removed. The tongue is removed by slitting the lower jaw from the bottom and pulling the end of the tongue down. When it is pulled as far as possible severe it at the base. The brains can be removed by splitting the skull. The tongue should be cleaned and scraped and it and the brains immersed in clean cold water.

SHEEP

Lamb and sheep are about the easiest animals to dress for meat. A lamb, which normally weighs about 80 pounds, is hung by his hind legs, head down and stunned by a sharp blow to the top of its head with a hammer. The head then is very quickly removed completely at the last joint of the neck and the carcass is left to drain. Following this it is removed from the hoist and put on its back for skinning. The sheepskin or pelt is opened by cutting a narrow strip of skin from the front of the front legs and the back of the hind legs. Then, using the fingers, the skin is pulled off the brisket, belly and flanks. The process is usually called "fisting"; with one hand pick up the fleece and pull the membranes tight; with the other hand strike the junction of the inside of the hide and the carcass. The knife may have to be used to loosen small areas of skin.

After the legs have been skinned and the pelt fisted off the belly, insert a gambrel stick between the tendons and hocks of the hind legs and raise the carcass. Then slit the pelt down the center of the belly and skin out around the hind legs, pulling the skin away from the meat, and work it off over the head.

With the pelt still attached at the tail, the colon can be tied off to prevent meat contamination. Cut clear around the anus and pull enough of the colon out so it can be tied off. Then the pelt is fisted loose from the tail and cured.

The intestines are removed by slitting the carcass from the anus to the neck. Follow the colon and large intestines down, cutting wherever necessary, and roll the paunch out. When the gullet goes through the diaphragm cut it off and drop the paunch and liver in a clean pail. Then cut out the diaphragm and roll the heart and lungs out of the carcass. Clean all organs by soaking them in clean cold water. Wash out the inside of the carcass with cold water. Naturally the brisket must be split to allow the heart and lungs to come out. Cut the gall bladder away from the liver.

The fat from sheep and lamb is usually kept for soap stock. It can be pulled away from the intestines by hand. The carcass of a lamb or sheep is usually not split down the center before it is cut up.

GOATS

Goats are usually slaughtered by stunning and sticking them. They must be skinned with a knife. They are eviscerated like sheep. The meat from all but old buck goats is very good. Many people say it tastes like venison. Goats and sheep are the two cheapest meat producers since they will thrive on grass and brush without expensive grain or other feed especially if not being milked.

Cutting up the carcass can commence after it has cooled for 12 to 24 hours.

Many homesteaders get a good carcass chart such as the one put out by The Morton Salt Company. Study it well, flop half the carcass on a clean surface such as a table or bench and start cutting. A good sharp knife is used for the meat cutting and the meat saw or even a wood saw is used to cut through bone. When the cuts are reduced to desirable size they can be wrapped and frozen or cured under one of the methods described in the next chapter.

In many rural areas there are locker plants where meat can be taken for freezing when the weather is otherwise too warm for proper curing. All meat will keep in cold water long enough so that it can be canned or dried or salted, however, if no cold storage facilities are used.

GAME ANIMALS

Game animals such as deer and moose can be handled the same as sheep and beef. A good way to clean squirrel and wild rabbits is to remove the head, feet and tail. Then make a slit crossways of the skin in the center of the back. Insert the forefingers in this slit and pull the two halves of the

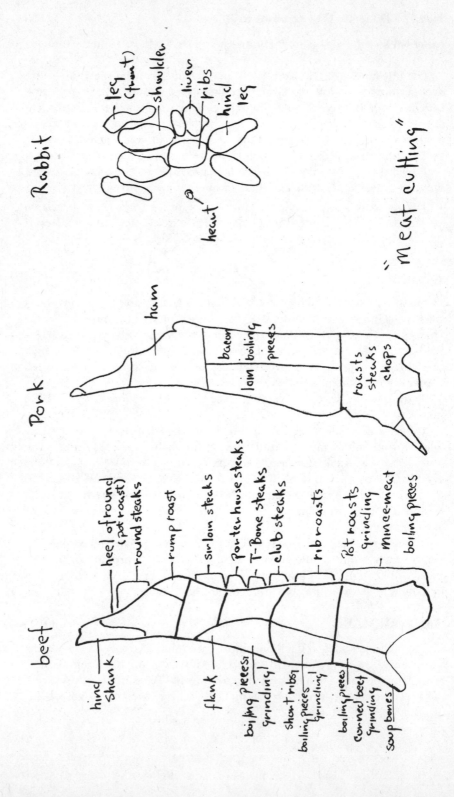

Rabbit

leg (front)
shoulder
liver
ribs
hind leg
heart

Pork

ham
bacon
loin
boiling pieces
roasts
steaks
chops

"meat cutting"

beef

hind shank
heel of round (pot roast)
round steaks
rump roast
sirloin steaks
porter-house steaks
T-Bone steaks
club steaks
rib roasts
pot roasts
grinding
mince-meat
boiling pieces

flank
boiling pieces
grinding
short ribs
boiling pieces
grinding
boiling pieces
corned beef
grinding
soup bones

hide away from each other. Continue pulling until the skin comes off over the animal's legs. Then hold the carcass in the left hand in the center of the back so that the belly faces you. With a sharp knife carefully cut into the crotch enough to expose the colon and urinary tract. Then reverse the knife and make a slit down through the belly lining through the ribs and bring it out at the neck. Go back to the crotch, cut the colon loose by cutting on each side of the anus and pull the colon towards you while slipping the forefinger behind the intestines. When the colon is free down to the large intestines flip the viscera out with the forefinger. Use the forefinger and thumb to pinch out any unwanted pieces still remaining in the carcass.

RABBITS

Raised rabbits are usually butchered when they weigh about four pounds. Hold up the rabbit by his hind legs with one hand and with the other hand rap him sharply behind the head at the base of the neck with a short piece of iron rod. Quickly then hang the rabbit on a nail or hook by one hind leg and remove his head. Allow him to drain, then skin him. Remove the other hind leg at the hock, then skin down the inside of the remainder completely across the crotch and up the inside of the other hind leg. Circle the suspended leg at the hock with your knife and start the hide peeling down the leg. Return to the other hind leg hock, start the skin loose there and pull it down along both legs to the crotch. Cut around the vent and reproduction organs so that half the hide will pull around the back of the legs and the other half around the front. With one hand on each half, pull the skin down over the carcass to the front legs. Peel the legs out of the skin and continue pulling until the hide comes off the neck.

Since rabbit skins are salable in some areas the skin can be put over a fur stretcher, allowed to dry and then be sold.

Eviscerate the rabbit by slitting the abdominal wall from crotch to the breastbone, but do this carefully so no intestines are punctured. Remove the vent and reproductive organs by cutting on each side of the base of the tail to free it and reproductive organs (female). Gently pull on the tail and cut until the rectum is removed. Continue pulling and cutting forward and remove all the intestines up to the diaphragm. Next cut out the diaphragm and remove the heart, lungs and liver. The carcass is usually cut into seven pieces. The hind legs are severed across the back just ahead of the hips and separated. The next cut is across the back just behind the ribs. Then the front legs are cut from the rib cage and the latter is split down the center of the back. Rabbit meat should be chilled at least 12 hours before being prepared for the dinner table. This chilling can be done before or after cutting up the carcass.

POULTRY

Poultry are dressed on the farm by chopping the head off and then removing the feathers. After the head is removed and the fowl is drained, it is immersed in hot water to loosen the feathers. The temperature of the water should be just below boiling. Dip the chicken quickly the first time and repeatedly dip until the feathers are easily pulled off. The hairlike pin feathers are then singed off with a piece of burning newspaper.

Ducks are handled the same way. Sometimes it is necessary to dip the fowl in hot paraffin and then flake the paraffin off with a knife to remove all the small feathers.

Poultry are eviscerated by removing the intestines through the hollow between the legs. A deep horizontal slit is made through this skin and the intestines pulled out. The crop and the gullet must be pulled out through the opening under the neck. Poultry such as ducks and chickens are usually cut into six pieces.

Larger fowls such as geese and turkeys are butchered in the same way as ducks and chickens. The gizzards of all poultry must be opened and cleaned immediately after gutting. Poultry should be immediately chilled and processed upon butchering.

Books

Ashbrook, Frank, *Butchering, Processing and Preservation of Meat*.
    New York: Van Nostrand Reinhold, 1955
Levie, Albert, *Meat Handbook*. Westport, Connecticut: AVI, 1970

Booklets

A Complete Guide to Home Meat Curing
Morton Salt Company
110 North Wacker Drive
Chicago, Illinois 60606

11

FOOD WITHOUT FARMING

THOSE WHO HAVE the instincts and inclinations of a nomad or hunter or who don't or can't raise a garden for some reason still can pick up all the food they can possibly use from the earth. A thorough study of edible wild plants will allow anyone to gather food almost anytime in every green region of the world.

Besides the wild foods there's the waste from cultivated crops. One good example of this is the thousands of bushels of corn left lying on the ground by mechanical corn pickers. Another is the potato which the machine-driven digger drops back to the earth. Still another is the tomato, the cucumber and the pepper left over after the canning companies have made their selective pickings. I have never met a farmer who wouldn't let people go out to the fields and pick all this potentially wasted food when told I was going to eat it. Any homesteader living in the farming regions could live very well for virtually nothing on the tons of field crops wasted every year. I have picked enough waste potatoes from one eighty-acre field near us here in Wisconsin in two leisurely days to more than see us through the winter. I have also picked enough waste corn to feed two pigs and supply us with cornmeal and cornbread for the year in one day of more strenuous picking.

In fact, there is so much easy to get food to be found that we can think of the months as being divided into free-for-the-taking food sections.

JANUARY AND FEBRUARY

The snow which is piled deep outside the cabin window would seem to put an end to all wild food harvesting. Not so. There is still an abundance of food for the wild food forager.

Almost everywhere in the deep snow will be the tracks of the cottontail rabbit, jackrabbit or snowshoe hare, depending upon location. The food forager will follow these tracks, especially upon a fresh snow, because at the end of these will be a tasty meal in form of delicious rabbit.

The cottontail rabbit, most familiar of the well-known rabbits, is also the most easily hunted. He can be trapped in a box trap made of scrap lumber, baited with a piece of carrot, cabbage or apple, or he can be snared or harvested with a slingshot, bow and arrow or more easily with a .22 or shotgun.

Snowshoe hares can be trapped, snared or shot but jackrabbits, because of their habits of living in the open and not traveling so much in trails, must almost always be harvested with a high-speed projectile.

Once the rabbit is procured he should be skinned and dressed as quickly as possible. He can be dressed the same as domestic rabbits. Rabbit meat can be salted, peppered and rolled in cornmeal and broiled or fried or it can be made into stew. Any good chicken stew recipe will do for this.

There has been occasional talk about people starving to death on rabbit meat. This could only happen if that was all you ate.

To my way of thinking fishing through the ice is more enjoyable and probably as fully productive as fishing in summer. Panfish, pike and trout are the species most apt to bite.

The procedure for all ice fishing is to select a pond, lake or a river known to have a good fish population. Possibly one of the same places where you catch fish in the open water seasons. Good locations for the winter fishing will be about the same as in summer fishing. Fish seek the coolest water in summer, which is the deepest water. Conversely, the warmest water in winter is also the deepest water. Almost always a narrow neck between islands or an opening in an obstruction such as a bridge across a long manmade fill will also be a good spot. The fish sometimes are scattered out all over the place, though, feeding or seeking food, and then there is little else to do but hunt around for them.

The ice fishing hole can be most speedily cut with one of the ice augers sold expressly for this purpose, but it can also be done with an ice chisel or axe. An ice chisel can be improvised by sharpening one end of an old car axle so it is pointed like a spear. Another way to make the chisel is to weld an eight-inch length of old car spring to one end of the axle and sharpen that on one side only so that it has a chisel edge. Or ice chisels can be purchased. The size of the hole depends on size of the fish you expect to catch. A four-inch diameter will be large enough for any but large pike and trout. A six or eight-inch hole will take care of almost everything. If you manage to hang a huge whopper of a fish and can't get him up through the hole you can enlarge it by chiseling with one hand while keeping a tight line on the fish with the other, but don't chisel your line though! Bait for ice fishing can be artificial spoons or natural bait such as goldenrod grubs, horsefly larvae or garden worms. Tackle is either a set device called a "tip-up" or a short pole having a spool to store line. Either can be easily made at home. The sporting magazines and public libraries are well supplied with plans for making your own.

Down in the marshes where the cattails grow there are open areas of very thin ice, even in late winter. The thin ice can be found by going out into the cattail marsh with your ice chisel and chopping away in different areas, especially places where water stains the ice. Mark these in your mind because you may want to come back many times to them during the winter.

The purpose of finding the thinnest ice possible is to make it easier to chisel through since now you have to open a good-sized hole through the ice in order to make the cattail root accessible. Once you have found them, sections can be hooked out with a rod that has a right-angle bend at the bottom. The procedure is to work the rod down into the mud under a root or collection of roots and pull them up. A garden rake works for this too. Better yet though, if the water is shallow, use a posthole digger of the clamp type. This cuts the roots off and makes them easier to lift out. Swish the mud and muck off the roots before you take them home. Cattail root processing is covered a little later.

Greens such as winter cress, black mustard and strawberry leaves can be found by examining the southern slopes of hills and earthen banks during periods of thaw, or by kicking the snow aside over areas that you know contain these hardy plants. Chances are you won't find a bushel of them but you may find enough to whet the palate and supply your system with Vitamin C and A.

MARCH AND APRIL

Praise God, spring is beginning to show and the maple syrup is running in the trees! Greens are also showing on the south sides of hills. Dandelions, mustard, and mayflower greens are showing signs of life.

Making maple syrup is a very popular activity at this time among homesteaders who live where the sugar maple tree grows. Why not, since it is one of the few ways to get unrefined sweets which are so healthful and good-tasting.

In very early April the new heads of the dandelions start to appear. They will look like a miniature ball of purple string that someone dropped on the ground. These are the first very tiny leaves and stalks the plant sends up. Directly under these little leaves is the white crown of the dandelion. This is very good food indeed. In taste it resembles broccoli and in appearance the lower stalks of celery. It can be dug up and eaten raw or combined with other vegetables to make a salad or it can be sautéed or boiled the barest minimum of time to make a delicious boiled food.

Very soon the first leaves of the dandelion will appear. These first leaves are very tender and usually of such little bitterness they are palatable raw. As they progress beyond that point they may have to be boiled in a little water and the water discarded before they please.

The dandelion is a three-layered food plant. Under the crown are the roots, wide, long and usually forked. They are dug up in early spring, washed very clean, peeled and boiled. Roots that are as thick as a pencil or larger can be sliced lengthwise. All roots can be cut into bite-sized pieces before being cooked. Sometimes the water has to be changed once to eliminate all bitter taste. They are served with condiments and butter.

As the dandelion season progresses farther the leaves will get taller, greener, and unfortunately, more bitter. Of course when you cook them you can always boil the leaves, change the water and bring it to a boil again, and keep this up until they are neutral enough to satisfy your palate. The only minus factor to this method is that every time you change the water you are throwing away some of the dandelion's considerable vitamin and mineral content. Another way to keep the dandelion from getting bitter is to partially blanch it. To do this, cover the plants about a week before you eat them with a layer of straw or other light material to keep the sun away. You won't have to shade them completely to achieve the taste you want. It takes a little experimenting the first time and results are affected by the amount of sun and rainfall during the blanching time. But if you care to blanch them completely you can mix in a few unblanched green leaves (for Vitamin A) when you make salad without affecting the taste much. In short, the right combination of blanched and unblanched leaves will deliver all the vitamins that your system needs without such bitterness that the leaves must be repeatedly boiled to make them palatable.

Dandelion roots make a good coffee substitute, too. The procedure is to dig, wash and peel the roots. Then place them in a slow oven and roast them until they are dark brown and brittle enough to break like a stick. They are then made into coffee by grinding the dried roots very fine and using one teaspoonful to each cup of boiled coffee desired.

The leaves of chicory look much like the dandelion's. They are larger and darker green, however. The chief distinguishing factor is the long tall stalk that springs up in the center of the plant. Sometimes this stalk gets as tall as a man. The chicory stalk also grows small blue flowers. Chicory leaves, stalks and roots can be used just as dandelion leaves, roots and stalks.

Much welcomed additions to the menu are the onions found growing wild all over the nation in early spring. They are a little hard to spot at first since they have flat leaves like grass in some species. (Some species have round leaves like onions, however.) A good way to find them is to look for bunches of green "grass." Taste the grass until you find a wild bunch of onions, then you'll notice that the leaves are a little thicker than grass leaves and that they are of a little different color. After your first find you won't have any trouble discovering the next. Use them for delicious salads, creamed onions, hot dishes, soups and other wild meals.

Thistles are a menace to livestock and life and limb when they are fully grown. Before they are grown, when they are less than six inches tall, they make tremendous food. Just put on a pair of gloves, take a pair of scissors or a knife and cut them off just below the leaves. Wash them well, boil until the thorns are soft and serve them with your favorite dressing. Plain yogurt goes well.

There are about thirty different varieties of willow. All of them have new shoots in the spring. Many of the new shoots are good food, either raw or cooked. Pick them when they first start growing.

Along about the last of April the cattail will start sending up its new plants. These miniature cattail plants are some of the most tender, best-tasting food to be found anywhere and they can be eaten raw right out in the field. Just grasp the leaves of the emerging plants where they come up from the lake bottom and pull gently until the tender white stalk comes loose from the base. This white stalk is the edible part. The leaves are not good even when very young. The white base can be cooked and used in soups or as a side dish for meat or baked fish also.

Since spring is a spawning season when many fish congregate in large numbers to migrate up small streams this is one of the best times to procure them in large quantities.

Suckers are classified as rough fish in most places; hence unlimited numbers of them may be taken either with spear or net. The homesteader can procure a few hundred pounds of this very excellent fish in spring and preserve it as a source of protein for his family.

At almost the same time as the sucker run in the spring the smelt come to the shores of the Great Lakes to spawn. They are taken mostly with special smelt dipnets or with small seines. Smelt are very high in food value and they, too, can be frozen, salted, smoked or canned for future use.

Homesteaders who are lucky enough to live where there is a special season on black bear in the spring can very often procure one for summer meat. They will usually come to bait better in the spring than any other time. The trick is to get one with some fat left on him. Lean thin bears in the spring are apt to be strong-tasting. However, even a thin bear at this time of the year will make good bacon.

Chances are that the homesteader will know watercress when he sees it in the supermarket. March and April is the time of the year when water-cress is usually abundant in the streams. Just keep watching for a small green opposite-leaved plant growing up from the bottom of the stream. It is almost always found in flowing streams but the streams can be as small as the width of a handkerchief. If there is none growing in your area but there is at least one clean, clear stream there it will certainly pay to plant some so that you have a crop. Some people cook watercress like boiling greens. Personally I wouldn't anymore think of cooking them than I would think of cooking a radish. I eat all I can get raw or mixed with other greens for a salad.

MAY AND JUNE

During the two months after April some of the wild greens will get tough and bitter. They can be restored to almost their original goodness by cutting off the mature plants and harvesting the new ones when they come up.

May and June also has its own considerable collection of greens, one of these being the well-known violet plant. Both the leaves and blossoms of the violet are very delicious, very vitamin-packed. Violet blossoms and leaves can be eaten raw or cooked. They also combine very well with sheep sorrel or watercress to make a violet salad.

Another very important May-June plant is milkweed. Milkweed produces greens, buds and pods and all are very delicious and vitamin-packed. The greens are eaten when the plant is small and immature. They are harvested by cutting the plant off below the bottom leaves. Then the plant is placed in a pot on the stove and boiling water poured over it. The water will stop boiling temporarily and when it starts again dump it and drain the greens. Serve with butter and condiments. Sometimes the greens will still be bitter after the first boiling. Simply repeat the procedure until they are neutral.

As the milkweed matures a cluster of flower buds will appear on each stalk, usually just below the forks of the leaves. When these bud clusters are full and "ripe" snap them loose and treat them to a boiling water bath. Serve with butter and condiments as you would any green side-dish vegetable.

Still later after the flower is gone bunches of small green pods will appear. These pods are about the best vegetable found in the wild. Their preparation is about the same as for the greens or flower buds. One thing to remember about boiling out the bitter white sap from milkweed pods is not to use salt in the water. Salt seems to cause the bitterness to "set" in the plant. Also it doesn't work too well to pour cold water over the plants and bring them to a boil. This also seems to perpetuate a faint hint of bitterness. I find as I eat more and more milkweed that I am parboiling them less and less though, and I seldom boil them more than once anymore.

Of course the parboiling doesn't cook the plant parts. That must be done by further boiling them until they are tender. This takes about five minutes for pods and about three minutes for the flower buds and small plants.

After the pods are cooked they can be used as a side dish for roast meat (wild or tame) or soup. Cover them well cooked with goat milk gravy and you have almost a complete meal in itself.

The pods will keep very well if you have a freezer. They can be frozen before or after the boiling out process, with slightly better results obtained from boiling them out before they are frozen. When you boil out the plant parts you will notice they turn from a fuzzy off-white to a deep, delicious, emerald green.

As asparagus is a very familiar plant, almost everyone has eaten it at one time or another. What some people don't notice is that this prolific plant grows along almost every roadside in the rural parts of the U.S. Growing as it does among the roadside grasses, it is hard to spot. Later as it matures and the familiar plant projects high above the grass it is easy to see. When prospecting a new territory for asparagus the homesteader is first apt to spot these mature plants. Cut them off and wait about two weeks until they grow back again. Naturally, after he has found three or four such bunches he will only need to keep them picked at the right time to have all the asparagus he will need. Most areas have tons of this very succulent plant going to waste every year.

Purslane, that well-known garden weed, is found growing in cultivated fields. An immigrant from India where it is cultivated for a vegetable crop, purslane has spread to almost the entire United States. It can be eaten raw, boiled or wilted. Unlike some other plants it needs no special handling. Just pick it, wash it off and work your culinary magic on it. I like it best washed and wilted in a slow pan of peanut oil. It seems to fill one up like meat and many times I have eaten a complete meal composed of one huge purslane plant. Purslane never gets tough like some other plants.

A plant that no one should overlook is the wild strawberry. Much sweeter than most domestic strawberries, the wild variety grows in shade

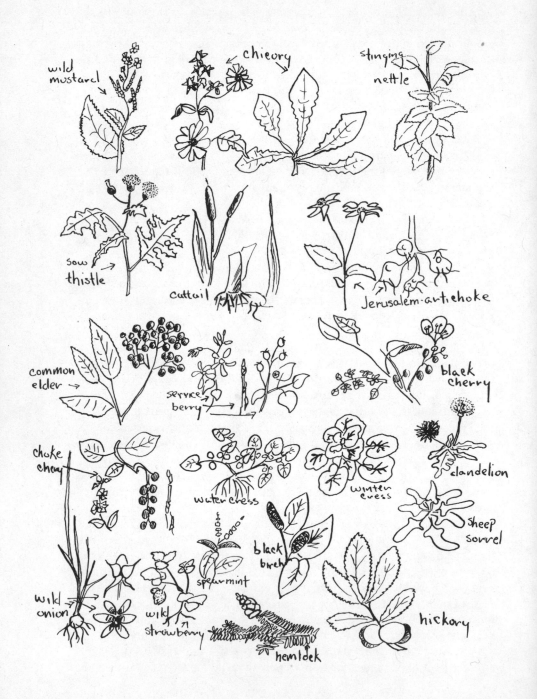

wild mustard

chicory

stinging nettle

sow thistle

cattail

Jerusalem artichoke

common elder

service berry

black cherry

choke cherry

water cress

winter cress

dandelion

sheep sorrel

wild onion

wild strawberry

spearmint

black brch

hemlock

hickory

and secluded nooks throughout most of the northern forests of this hemi-sphere. The procedure for finding them is to locate a patch of wild straw-berry plants and then stoop down and part the leaves and look beneath them. You may get a big surprise. Down under the thick green leaves com-pletely hidden may be a considerable quantity of sweet strawberries to be had for the picking. Preparing and eating wild strawberries is just like preparing and eating the tame variety. Pick off the hulls and eat their sweet little bodies.

May and June of course are almost the best months for fishing; about all anyone has to do to secure some fish is to show up at the fishing hole with tackle and natural bait such as worms and he can load up with some species of fish. This is also a very good time to catch frogs and turtles. Frogs can be caught by hand with a frog spear or they can be caught like fish by dangling a small artificial fishing fly in the front of them on six feet of line tied to the end of a long pole or rod. Ol' frog thinks that the fish fly is good to eat and he jumps and bites it just like a fish. All the homesteader needs to do then is reel him in.

Turtles can be caught by looking for their tracks in the sand and then tracking them down and by feeling along the banks under the water where they frequently hide. The all-around best way to get them though is to place a set line equipped with a treblehook, baited with very tough meat in places where turtles are sure to be found.

Sometimes in late May or early June snapping turtles come ashore to lay their eggs. They can be found then by going out at night, especially in warm rainy nights and walking or cycling along sandy roads that border marshes. Old Snapper is liable to be out there trying to find a nest for her eggs. Pick her up by the tail and drop her in a gunnysack and take her home. Put her in any cool place and she will keep well and comfortably until you are ready to use her. When you are ready, cut off her head, let her bleed out and then cut all around the shell under the bottom rim and turn her inside out. Cut off the claws, skin the legs out and serve her according to the cookbook recipes for stewed snapper.

Crayfish too are abundant in June. They usually are located in shallow water, especially where rocks and vegetation are found. They can be caught on hook and line or they can be grabbed by hand or caught in special crayfish traps. Anyway they are procured they make a good meal. Drop them into boiling water until they turn a bright red. Then remove, cool and twist the tail to one side so it comes out of the shell. Peel it and eat it with melted butter or your favorite fish sauce.

Two good beverage plants are alive and accessible in June also. They are mint and black birch. Mint is a tall green plant often found along road-sides and in fence rows or at the edge of marshes in deep woods. There are several varieties of mint. Possibly the easiest way to identify them and find them is by smell. Walk through likely places in early mornings or on damp days and chances are you will smell the mint if it is about. If the odor is present but you can't tell which plant it's coming from try checking the stalk. The mint family has a square stalk. Of course the crushed leaves will have such an overpowering odor and taste of mint that it will remove any doubt. Both spearmint and peppermint are good beverage plants. The chopped leaves can be steeped green or they can be dried and used. Steep like tea.

Black birch is a large dark-colored tree with leaves like the white birch. The chopped small twigs and the inner bark can be steeped for a wintergreen-flavored drink. This oil is volatile though; so it shouldn't be boiled away.

JULY AND AUGUST

July is the month for cattail pollen, cattail corn-on-the-cob and cattail new shoots and the old standby, cattail roots. Cattail pollen is the yellow "dust" that clings to the flowering spike of the cattail after the corn-on-the-cob or flowering buds are gone. It is harvested by bending the stalks into a pail or even a paper bag and shaking them slightly to dislodge the golden dust. Don't shake too hard though since it is easy to dislodge undesirable objects such as leaf bits and insects into the bag also. When you have the cattail pollen home, mix it with soup or pancake flour or biscuits to add a golden color and "corn" taste. When you are harvesting pollen there is sure to be a supply of flowering spikes that haven't matured yet. They will be just an enlarged tube near the top of the bloom spike. Narrow-leafed cattail has a double tube, the wide leaf only one. If the thickening is double pick the top one. Peel the husks away and reveal a tiny ear of corn. Pick all these you can find; they can be used for corn-on-the-cob, a soup vegetable or in any one of a hundred ways. They also freeze or can very well for future use. Pull up the cattail roots and use every part of them—the tender new shoots and the root between them. Use the pointed shoots for salad or a cooked vegetable. Squeeze or pound the starch out of the cattail roots and make biscuits or bread. Peel the roots and bake them and then grind and sift the fibers out and use this flour for biscuits also.

July and August is the time when berries ripen in many places. Nobody has to be told what to do with berries after they get them but picking them efficiently does take some experience. Berries that you stand up and pick such as blackberries, mulberries, pin cherries, plums and wild cherries, can be picked much faster with a picking can hung around the neck. Just take an old coffee can, tie a string from a hole in each side of the can and put it over your head. This leaves both hands free for picking and eliminates stooping and moving to find the pail.

Don't forget the mayapples, ground cherries, black cherries and early apples either. This is the time to start preparing for winter. Put away at least 25 pints of berries and early fruit this month for each adult member of the family. This can be dried, canned or frozen.

SEPTEMBER AND OCTOBER

If you can, turn your eyes from the colored leaves and harvest Jerusalem artichokes, sunflowers, hickory nuts, walnuts, butternuts and acorns.

Acorns are a special gift of Providence for hungry homesteaders. Pick them up under oak trees, using the biggest ones you can find. Better pick up at least a bushel. When you get time shell them out with a hammer or nut pick and grind them in your grain mill or a food grinder. When they are all ground up build a lazy fire outside and set your biggest pot filled with water on the fire. Put a good layer of acorn flour in the pot and let it boil for a while. Carefully dump this water off and add some more. Boil this again and change it when the water won't get any darker, which will probably take about twenty minutes. Dump this water off and taste the flour. It should be sweet by now. If it isn't boil it again. When it's done spread it out in the sun to dry and then store in quart fruit jars or the equivalent. Use acorn flour for bread, cake and cookies.

This is also the season to harvest bee trees, assuming you may have found one earlier, and don't forget wild grapes for sauce, juice or even wine. The cranberries will be ripening also, their bright red faces showing among the lacy plants in the marsh. While you're on low land look for the arrowhead since this is too good a vegetable to waste. Arrowhead will push potatoes off my plate anytime. Better harvest some elderberries too, for fruit, juice and for mixing with other plants.

Naturally this is the month to lay in a supply of protein; squirrels will be fat and juicy, pheasants will be at their prime and wild ducks and geese will offer many satisfying meals.

This is the month for filling the drying bins, freezers and canning shelves. If you are new to the homestead, store three times as much as you think you will need and then lay in a good supply of dried acorn flour, salted meat and dried fruit to see you over the low periods.

NOVEMBER AND DECEMBER

Harvest and store in these months also. Deer and moose will be about as good as they will ever be this season and the weather should be cool enough to give you some time to prepare the meat. If the fish are biting, might as well catch as many as you need and fire up the smoke box. Smoked fish will get you through many a hungry week.

Plenty of plants are still green, also on the bottom of fast-flowing streams and on the south side of hills. Check the storehouse again and if it looks a little bare go see the friendly farmer next door who just finished picking his thousand acres of corn with a mechanical picker. He will probably let you wander around on his fields with a bag picking up the dropped ears. Don't gather huge amounts at one time, though, as this might worry him. Take the corn home and dry it in a rodent-proof, well-ventilated building or hang it in the barn in burlap bags. When you get hungry for cornbread or corn mush, corn fritters or any one of the other three or four dozen good corn dishes, grind it in your hand gristmill. If you live in wheat country go help the farmer for a day or so put his machinery away for the winter and then take your pay in wheat. Grind this also with your hand gristmill, for maybe the best-tasting flour you ever ate. Don't forget that oats can be ground if they are as easy to find. They are hard to cook up though.

Well before Christmas your sprout battery should be operating. Use mung beans, corn, oats or wheat sprouts for health and succulence. Use anything that can be kept moist for sprouting but you may as well make a sprouting battery since it is so easy. Follow the directions to be given shortly. While you're building one though you can tie a rag over the mouth of a wide jar with the grain inside. Soak for ten hours, dump the water off through the cloth and keep the jar inclined to let all the water drain off the grain. Flush two or three times a day. The sprouts should be ready to eat in about five days or less. Most sprouts are about a thousand times as healthful as the kernel of grain. The easiest to use are mung beans.

Make your sprouting battery to supply green and tender plants in the dead of winter. Nail strips of wood together to form one 8-inch square for each adult member of the family. Tack screen, copper, plastic or galvanized, on the frames. Stack the frames up with the screened surface separated by the width of the frames, in a sink or in a large pan where they will drain. We like a pan so we can set it in the window to receive the light, but some people keep them covered all the time so they don't turn green.

To use the sprouting battery place on each screen four teaspoons of grain that has been soaked overnight. Then flush the grain every four hours by pouring water over the grain in the top frame. This of course will dribble down and moisten all the kernels on all the frames. Make sure each kernel gets wet. Harvest when the sprouts are just starting to leaf out. The fastest is mung beans, the slowest, corn. Don't forget that many of the wild seeds will sprout also. We have sprouted acorns, smartweed seed, burdock seed and even some juneberry seeds, and eaten them all.

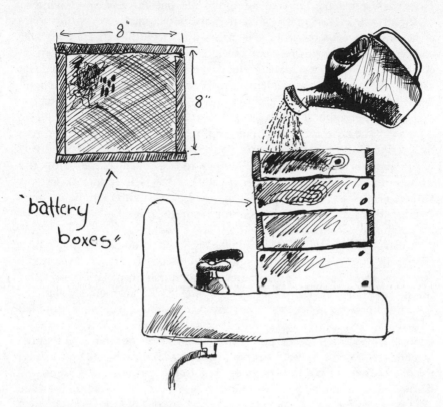

`battery boxes`

YOUR OWN FISH POND

Any sizable fish pond will raise all the fish a family will eat if good management methods are followed. It attracts wildlife, it is a place to swim and toughen the canoeing muscles in summer and it can be a skating rink in the winter. An additional consideration is that fire insurance companies will frequently give a rural place a lower premium rate if one has a good dependable supply of surface water that the fire department could use in an emergency.

Upon thinking about possible pond sites, but before giving the project too much more thought, arrange to visit your nearest U. S. Soil Conservation Office and talk it over with an SCS representative. These officials will provide all kinds of help and expert advice, send you home with perhaps a barrelful of fish pond literature, and possibly show up at your homestead within a few days to look the situation over—perhaps even run some soil tests for you. It pays throughout to have them on your side and to follow their advice.

An early consideration is selecting the site, and this is where having an expert advisor at hand really pays off. Naturally if you have a spring or artesian well on your property you might want to utilize that for a water source. If it happens to be on a hillside, a site below the well might be good. Water from artesian wells can be piped long distances across level ground and even slightly uphill by using inexpensive plastic pipe so a pond could probably be located to either side or slightly uphill from such a spring. Springs almost always form watercourses leading downhill so there might be a site along one of these. If it happens that there is no spring or artesian well on your property you could possibly dam up or divert water from whatever creek might happen to flow through your property. This, however, brings up questions under the jurisdiction of various authorities so be sure to secure permission or clear with them before proceeding. Possibly a canal could be dug from the creek to the pond but of course this might be too expensive.

A private fish pond is not simply any random basin or low area which holds water—there are technical features to its construction which must be observed, some benefiting the chances of good fish propagation, some for safety and sanitation and others for compliance with laws and regulations. Prolonged periods of heavy rainfall could easily enough cause a fish pond to overflow and for this and other reasons ponds have to have water level control provisions. In some places there are in fact requirements that the owner must be able to drain his pond within a specified time period, and the disposition of the drainage water must follow a stipulated or approved method. The design and construction of your pond is therefore best done after consultation with local authorities and your SCS representative.

Once the pond is ready to accept fish the chances are good that some government agency may help stock it. If a cold water pond, trout fingerlings may be procurable through the Bureau of Sports Fisheries and Wildlife, assuming the pond has been built to qualify for such help. The same agency may also provide an initial stocking for a warm water pond. Some state conservation agencies require the pond owner to first obtain a fish stocking permit, but assuming the pond was properly designed and constructed, this should prove no big problem.

Generally speaking, the pond will be ready for fishing about two years after the fish have been planted. If it is a warm water pond containing panfish such as bluegills and sunfish as well as larger species, it will be nearly impossible to anywhere near fish it out, particularly in the case of the smaller species.

Naturally high concentrations of fish in ponds are going to lead to a shortage of natural fish food. Commercial feed is available and it costs surprisingly little to feed fish compared to the gain they make. Insects can be attracted to fish ponds by hanging a light bulb over the water or even by keeping a torch burning over the water. The brighter the light the more bugs it attracts. The bugs fall in the water and the fish gulp them down.

In winter ice can cause a fish pond to "freeze out". A freeze-out is fish kill caused by oxygen deficiency, since the ice seals the water from the atmosphere, but oxygen can be introduced to the water by pumping air into it with a compressor through a hole in the ice, by churning the water with an outboard motor through a hole in the ice, or merely by cutting large holes in the ice and keeping them open as much as possible.

Plowing the snow away from the pond surface also helps since it allows sunlight to penetrate the water and stimulate the growth of water plants such as algae. As they grow they exude oxygen, taking up carbon dioxide from the water. Fish ponds require control of rooted vegetation and weeds since too many are undesirable and some may rot, poisoning the fish.

There is certainly no shortage of information on building and maintaining fish ponds and anyone who has a source of water can develop his own fish supply.

Magazines

The Mother Earth News (Issue No. 8) *Fish In Your Own Pond*
Box 38
Madison, Ohio 44057

Fish Farming Industries
Sandstone Building
Mount Morris, Illinois 61054

Books

Farmer, Charles J., *Creative Fishing*. Harrisburg, Pa.: Stackpole, 1973

Raising Bait Fishes
Circular 35
Fish and Wildlife Service
U. S. Department of the Interior
Interior Building
Washington, D. C. 20240

12

PRESERVING FOODS

STARTING WITH THE Indians, people living in rural and remote areas of the country have had to preserve some of their food to bridge the gap between times of plenty and scarcity. As might be expected, several different methods of keeping food edible for months or even years have been developed.

OUTSIDE WINTER VEGETABLE STORAGE

Plant foods such as vegetables are canned, dried, salted or simply kept cool until they are ready to be eaten. Specifically, potatoes, rutabagas, turnips, parsnips, Jerusalem artichokes, apples, cabbage, sweet potatoes, squash, pumpkins and some other root crops can be kept all winter in a cool dry place. The storage conditions found in root cellars (35 to 50 degrees) are almost ideal for this type of crop. Small root cellars can be built in a few hours with a hand shovel by any homesteader. We have even used a trash can sunk vertically with its top two feet below the surface of the ground. An amazing amount of potatoes or vegetables can be placed in one of these. And you can use more than one trash can. The important thing to remember when sinking the trash can is to place it on top of a knoll or small hummock where the water from rain and melting snow will drain away from it as rapidly as possible. Of course the cover has to be placed on the trash can very tightly to keep moisture from entering. A six-inch layer of dirt can be placed on the cover and then the hole filled with packed straw or leaves up to ground level. On top of this a mound of leaves should be piled about two or three feet high. Over this mound put a waterproof layer of plastic or canvas held down with rocks. When the contents of the can are desired, dig down through the snow or leaves and find the canvas. Then push it aside and dig out the loose fill and open the can. Alas, when you dig up one of these cans it cannot be reburied with the same results guaranteed unless the day is far above freezing! So the safest way is to take the contents, once dug up, into the cabin. For this reason an amount to be consumed by the homesteader and his family over a certain period should be the maximum amount stored in one can. Thus instead of the logical practice of placing all apples in one can and all potatoes in another, a can will probably be stored with ⅔ potatoes and ⅓ apples. Or even a mix of apples, potatoes, carrots and cabbage in one can. It takes a little experience and depends on what you expect to want to eat during the period.

CABIN STORAGE BIN

It takes a little watching, but even homesteaders without a cellar can have an indoor storage area where root crops will keep very well, too. For this build a bin along one inside wall of the cabin or house. A louvred window or a series of holes through the wall are used for cooling. These holes are fitted with plugs and screened on the outside against mice. The bin must be fitted with at least three inches of fiberglass insulation or the equivalent. A good place to put this box is along one wall where it can serve as a bench. The bin size should afford storage space of at least six square feet for each member of the household. It should be placed on the north wall, if possible, unless the climate is very cold. This box is so versatile it can be used for vegetable storage, a freezer or as an indoor garden when the produce is used up.

The bin is fitted with a thermometer and the temperature kept between 35 and 50 degrees by controlling the amount of cold air allowed to enter. At night the storage bin is cooled to 40 degrees and then sealed to keep it from getting too cold while left unattended.

If you don't need the bin as a vegetable cooler you can still use it for a freezer just by letting the winter air freeze your meat solid. Cap it tightly on warm days. During warmer days the top shouldn't be opened or removed any oftener than necessary. The top for the freezer should cover the center three feet of a six-foot bin. To make things handier, especially when it is to be used as a freezer, a small door about one foot square can be provided in the larger center door. This smaller door, of course, is to allow removal of food without affecting the stability of the inside temperature.

If it happens that space is at a premium this box can be placed on the porch or entryway or even outside if the top is roofed. An old freezer or

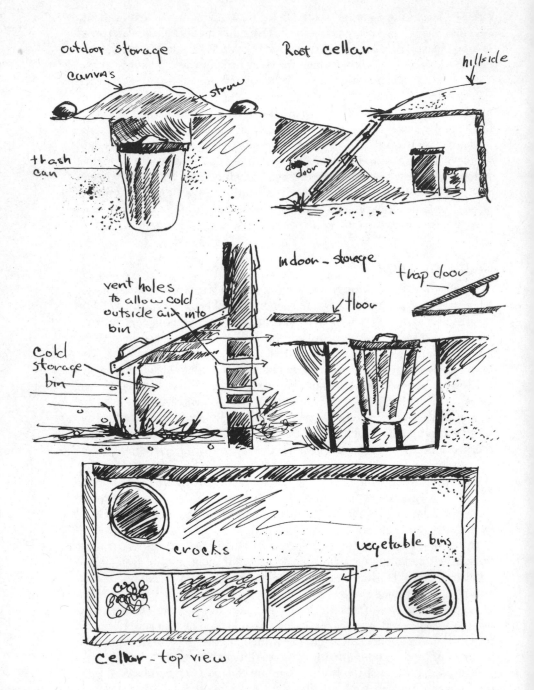

outdoor storage

canvas

straw

trash can

Root cellar

hillside

door

vent holes to allow cold outside air into bin

cold storage bin

Indoor - storage

floor

trap door

crocks

vegetable bins

cellar - top view

icebox works very well for this. It might help to place some salt inside the box to keep the moisture content low, although most cabins are so dry inside that humidity is not a problem.

CELLAR STORAGE

The cellar or hole in the ground under the homestead dwelling has been used for untold years for keeping vegetables and fruit in an edible condition. A good practice is to have one bin at least three by three feet filled with the driest sand available. This bin will be used for burying carrots. Jerusalem artichokes, rutabagas and turnips that will keep in splendid condition when so stored for the winter. If they are not buried they dry out and wither. This doesn't necessarily make them inedible, but very unattractive.

Besides this bin in the darkest coolest corner of the basement a wooden bin is built for potatoes. This can be a simple rectangle of slats separated from the floor by at least two inches for air circulation. This bin should contain at least thirty square feet. Potatoes to be stored must be clean and dry. They also must be handled carefully to avoid bruising them. A bruised potato or a potato with a cut or gouge spoils very quickly.

Cabbage should be wrapped in at least two layers of newspaper or the equivalent. When cabbages are stored for the winter they should not be trimmed except for the two large outer leaves since these protect the inner cabbage. Cabbage should not be stored until the weather has cooled and there has been frost a few times. Celery and cauliflower can be stored this way also but the cauliflower has to be used within a few weeks to be at its best.

Both cabbage and potatoes can be stored outside in trenches dug below the frost line and covered with straw if the climate isn't too cold.

Peas and beans are usually dried for cellar or loft storage. To dry them pick the beans and peas when they are at their peak and lay them out in the sun. When they are thoroughly dried they are taken to a corner where a gentle breeze is blowing and rubbed between the fingers. This breaks the husks off and leaves just the bean or peas. When husked they can be placed in glass cans or cloth bags and stored in the loft or basement.

Tomatoes, one of the most useful vegetables known to man, can be dried also for home storage. They are picked, washed clean and cut into thin slices, then dried in the sun. At night or during rain they must be covered or brought inside. Some sprinkle a little salt on the slices before they are dried. Tomatoes attract insects so a screened-in or windowed area which will allow the sun to fall on the fruit is ideal.

Green beans are a favorite dried vegetable. They can be made into

Rhubarb
Wash stalks and cut into ½-inch pieces. Cover with boiling syrup. Process for 20 minutes in boiling waterbath.

Berries
Pick over, wash, pack closely in jars. Fill with boiling syrup. Process 20 minutes in boiling waterbath.

Tomatoes
Scald fresh tomatoes one minute. Then dip in cold water to remove skins. Cut out cores; quarter. Pack loosely in jars. Fill with boiling water. Add one teaspoon salt per quart jar. Process 30 minutes in boiling waterbath.

Beans, Green
Wash, remove tips. Break into small pieces. Precook 5 minutes. Keep juice, pack, heat juice to boiling, pour in jars, add one teaspoon salt. Process 40 minutes at 10 lbs. setting in pressure cooker or 2¼ hours in boiling waterbath.

Greens
Use fresh tender greens. Wash and pick over. Steam 8 minutes; pack. Fill jars with boiling water. Pressure cook for 1¾ hours at 10 lbs. pressure or cook 3½ hours in boiling waterbath.

Grapes
Use sound grapes. Wash and stem. Cover with boiling syrup. Process 20 minutes in a boiling waterbath.

Corn
Cut from cob. Add one pint of boiling water and one teaspoon salt. Heat to boiling; pack. Process for 45 minutes at 10-pound setting in a pressure canner or 2½ hours in a boiling waterbath.

Muscle meat, steaks, roast, etc.
Remove bones, gristle and most fat. Precook in oven by cutting into one-pound pieces. Roast for 20 minutes at 350° or until pink color is gone. Pack hot and cover with boiling liquid in which cooked. Process pints for 1¼ hours, quarts for 1½ hours in pressure cooker at 10 pounds pressure or process pints for 3½ hours in a boiling waterbath.

Hearts
Wash, trim, precook in water for 20 minutes. Pack, add salt and boiling broth from the precooking. Process pints for 75 minutes, quarts for 90 minutes at 10 pounds pressure or process pints 3½ hours in boiling waterbath.

Meat trimmings for stew
Cut into one-inch cubes. Add boiling water to cover. Simmer until red color is gone. Pack hot, cover with boiling broth. Process pints for 75

minutes, quarts for 90 minutes at 10 pounds pressure or process pints for 3½ hours in boiling water.

Poultry

Use mature chickens. Dress and separate backs, necks, wings into one pile; legs, thighs, breast in another; giblets, heart, liver in another. Simmer backs, etc. to make broth. Add broth to legs, etc. and simmer until done. Pack legs etc. into pints. Pressure cook 65 minutes at 10 pounds pressure, quarts 75 minutes. Eat or freeze backs and giblets, etc; don't waste jar space on them.

SMOKING MEATS

Experts say the practice of smoking meat followed the ancient methods of drying foods and probably was an accidental method discovered when fires were built under racks of drying meat to keep the flies away and aid the sun in meat drying. The practice of smoking meat gradually developed, finally becoming a more acceptable method of preserving it rather than just drying it. We know now that smoking meat is actually subjecting it to chemical treatment since smoke contains various preservative chemicals that retard or destroy the organisms of decay and spoilage. Also since salt is usually used in the treatment before smoking, it combines with certain substances contained in smoke to drive the water out of flesh. Naturally the less water in a substance the less medium for destructive germs to breed in.

Aside from its preservative qualities, smoke imparts a delicious flavor to meat. Many believe that smoked meat, fish or fowl is better-tasting than the fresh untreated variety.

There are basically two different methods of smoking; hot smoking and cold smoking. Hot smoking is the partial or complete cooking of food as it is smoked while cold smoking is a result of carefully controlling the smoke temperature to prevent its simultaneous cooking.

Some sort of smokehouse or smoke oven has to be at hand. True, if you have the time and the patience you can just place the meat above an open hardwood fire made smoky by the addition of a little damp wood and eventually turn out something that resembles smoked meat. Many amateur cooks do this when they attempt to cook over an open fire. Nevertheless, any old shed can be plugged up tight enough to retain most of the smoke and this will make a usable smokehouse. Some people just use a barrel, or stretch a canvas over a conical frame of poles like a miniature tepee. Old freezers and refrigerators also make good smokehouses. The smokehouse's function is merely to retain enough heat and smoke so the smoking will be complete. A point to remember is that although a smokehouse needs a vent, it shouldn't be directly above the meat since this way the smoke would just rise and move on out the hole, chimney-fashion. This can be avoided by installing baffles or by extending the shelves more than halfway from one side of the structure to form alternate layers preventing the smoke from rising straight up. But usually the wire shelves which supoort the meat or fish will of themselves serve somewhat as baffles and circulate the smoke well enough. Another method of distributing the smoke is to drill holes in the smokehouse roof in a pattern which will insure that the smoke emits from different locations, for instance like a row of holes made in the circumference of a barrel top.

The author developed and has used a smoke box that can be placed over the pipe of a wood stove, thus one can heat his cabin and smoke meat at the same time. Other advantages of this box are its extreme portability and the minimum time and trouble it takes to put it into operation. He learned a long time ago that heat along with the smoke will finish the smoking in a lot less time than by the cold smoking process (below 100 degrees). The finished product is just as good and it will keep just as long.

It is true that all meat and fish can be smoked to preserve it. It is also true that each piece of meat and each fish will require a little different method of smoking and of curing before smoking. Some people keep notes of the heat and times of the actual smoking and the amount of curing or salting before the smoking is started. In this way, when they have made a mistake or done it exactly right they have a record so the correct method can be used the next time.

While heat and smoke will keep and preserve food, most foods will not be properly preserved unless they are first cured in salt. It is desirable to have the salt replace the water in the flesh. A salt content of 5% to 6% will retard the growth of most destructive organisms. Fish can be salted by packing them in dry salt. This will draw out most of the water and form a brine.

It almost goes without saying that common iodized table salt is not the best salt to use. Better and cheaper are the sodium chloride powders sold under the names of rock salt, farm salt, water softener salt, etc. Salt must not be stored in metal containers nor salt brine made in such containers as salt can react with metal to form some mighty lethal toxins.

A saturation brine solution can be measured by adding salt and stirring it into the water until no more will dissolve, which will be indicated by a thin layer lying on the bottom of the container, or it can be indicated by the ability of the solution to float an egg or a peeled potato. Brine can be reused provided that it retains its strength except that it

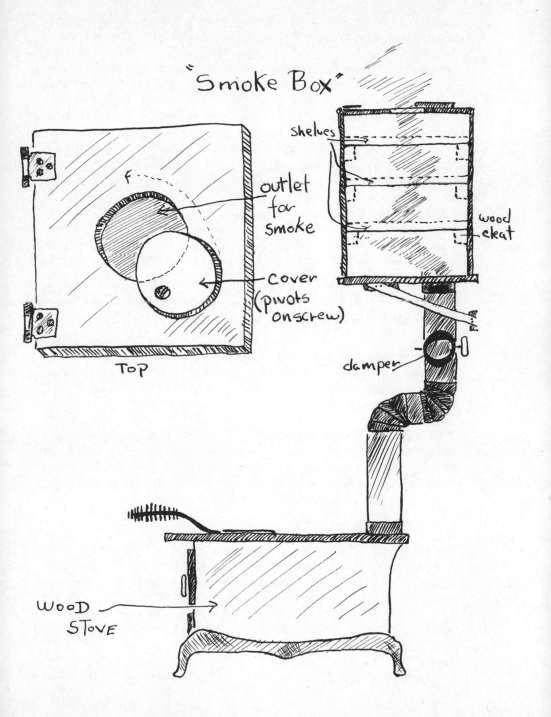

"Smoke Box"

shelves

outlet
for
smoke

wood
cleat

Cover
(pivots
on screw)

Top

damper

WOOD
STOVE

may carry flavors from one type of fish or meat to another. Besides salt, brown sugar or spices may be added to the solution to flavor the meat and retard spoilage.

Some Old Timey additions to salt brine which I have used are wild onion juice, sumac drupe juice, mint and garlic. It is well to keep these additions small. For instance if you like leg of lamb with mint sauce, a cut of tender venison saddle soaked in a saturated salt solution containing a cup of mint tea added per gallon of salt solution, and then smoked with alder or apple wood will deliver somewhat the same flavor. Never use resinous woods for smoking.

Dill and grape leaves also add flavor to smoked fish. Just sprinkle in the dried commodity when you make the brine.

After pieces of meat and fish are taken from the brine they should be thoroughly dried to form a pellicle or shiny tough coating on the outside. This coating helps keep the product tough and together. Fish or meat smoked while it is still wet could fall apart or be so soft that it wouldn't be convenient to handle.

PICKLING MEATS

Pickling is another way of curing meats. To cure meat thoroughly by pickling it must be cut into small enough pieces so the solution will penetrate it well. All meat can be cured by dry-salting it, also, and by pouring off the excess brine as it develops and adding fresh salt. It takes soaking for days to get rid of the excess salt though before it can be used or else it has to be boiled until most of the salt is removed. Salt beef used to be a favorite food to carry on board ship on long expeditions when fresh meat would not be available. Fish can be salted to keep indefinitely by packing them in dry salt. When a brine forms pour it off and add more salt. Fish will absorb salt until about ⅓ of the flesh is salt. At this stage it will keep indefinitely.

YOUR OWN ICE HOUSE

If you construct a fish pond or live near a lake or large river you can construct an ice house which will keep ice from melting all summer and provide a cool place for preserving almost any food. If you don't live near a source of readymade ice it would seem seasonally possible to make or find a form, fill it with water and let it freeze and thus manufacture your own ice blocks, which would not require cutting or transporting.

The chunks are cut when the lake has frozen at least eight inches thick. They are cut in as large a chunk as can be handled since the larger the chunk the slower it will melt. Do the actual cutting by waiting for a very

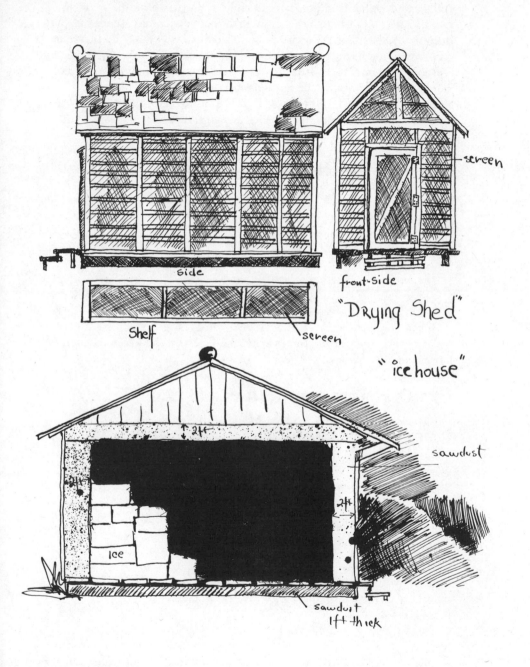

side

Shelf

screen

front-side

screen

"Drying Shed"

"icehouse"

sawdust

2ft

2ft

2ft

Ice

sawdust
1ft thick

cold day. Zero temperature is about right. Sweep or plow the snow off and saw parallel lines through the ice with a chain saw or crosscut saw. These lines should be about 12 inches apart; might as well make them about 20 feet long if you have the space. Saw across one end, cutting out a piece 20 feet long and one foot wide. Now take an ice chisel and chisel off pieces. The first one may have to be pushed under the water to get it out of the way so tongs can be used to lift the rest. Try to make the pieces two feet long. Lift them out, pile them on a low sled or trailer and haul them to the ice house. Try to get about 700 cubic feet if you have four in the family.

The ice house can be made of lumber but ideally it is made of logs. It can be made exactly like a cabin with a good low roof. An unused log cabin with a dirt floor is about as good a building as can be found. First dig a few shallow trenches in the dirt floor so the drainage will be good and then place a one-foot thickness of sawdust on the floor. Pack the ice chunks in as tightly as possible and fill any remaining spaces with snow by shoveling it across the top of the first layer. Next put in the second layer and cover that one with snow and keep on thus until all the ice is packed in. Inside, around the ice house walls, leave a space about two feet wide. Fill this space with tightly packed sawdust. When the top is reached put a two to three-foot layer of sawdust on top of the ice.

When you want ice, shovel off the sawdust, pick out a chunk and cover the ice back up again as soon as possible. Keep an ice box in the cabin for storage of perishables.

RECIPES FOR PRESERVING MEAT AND FISH

SMOKED BEEF, VENISON, MOOSE, GOAT, MUTTON, PORK, FISH

Soak overnight in a saturated brine. Next morning sprinkle pepper on drained pieces.

Slow smoke 48 hours, turning every 8 hours. Check after 30 hours for proper flavor.

Fast smoke at 150° for 12 hours. Check for proper smoking. Smoke longer for stronger flavor. Eat as desired.

JERKY

Cut lean meat into strips ½ inch or less thick. Trim away fat. Boil 3 minutes in a saturated brine. Drain, dry and smoke if desired. Keeps indefinitely. Eat as desired.

SALT MEAT

Cut in strips or small pieces. Place in stone crock or plastic bag. Lay alternate layers of meat and salt. Dump off bloody brine until no more is formed. Keep in glass, wood or plastic containers. Add salt each time brine is dumped off. Slow boil in fresh water for at least 1 hour before eating, or soak in fresh water for 12 to 24 hours.

SALT FISH

Clean fish well, split large fish down the center. Place alternate layers of salt and fish in a stone crock or wooden barrel. Pour off brine and resalt until no more brine is formed. Add small amount of brown sugar if desired. Soak for at least 24 hours in fresh water or boil in fresh water or milk for at least one hour. Keeps indefinitely.

PICKLED FISH

Use any kind of fish fillets. Cut fish into pieces one or two inches long. Pack pieces in a crock. Add ⅝ cup salt for each quart of fish. Cover fish and salt with pure vinegar. Stir thoroughly. Leave in solution for six days minimum. Remove and soak fillets for 12 hours in fresh clean water. Put a slice of lemon and a half slice of onion in each quart glass jar and fill each jar ¾ full of fillets. Then for each quart jar of fish make a solution of:

1 pint vinegar	¼ teaspoon dry mustard
8 whole cloves	¼ teaspoon black pepper
8 bay leaves	½ teaspoon sugar
6 pieces of orange peel	⅛ clove of garlic
½ teaspoon celery seed	½ teaspoon allspice

Place all ingredients in a pan on the stove. Simmer for 30 minutes. Then bring to a boil and pour over the fish. Let stand for 4 days. Refrigerate and eat. Use this solution to pickle meat also except eliminate the sugar if desired.

Books

Hull, Raymond and Sleight, Jack, *Home Book of Smoke-Curing Meat, Fish and Game*. Harrisburg, Pennsylvania: Stackpole, 1971
Angier, Bradford, *How To Live In The Woods On Pennies A Day*. Harrisburg, Pennsylvania: Stackpole, 1971

Suppliers

Luhr Jensen & Sons, Inc.
Hood River, Oregon 97031
"Little Chief" Electric Smoker

13

SPINNING, WEAVING AND KNITTING

UNLESS YOU ARE already an expert at it, probably the best introduction to spinning is to familiarize yourself with this chapter and at least one of the books listed at the end of the chapter. Then go see a demonstration. Even better than this would be to enroll in one of the classes taught at universities or vocational schools. The very best way would be to sit at the feet of an accomplished spinner and learn slowly and easily the few dexterous moves that will turn wild, wooly fleece into soft even threads of yarn.

Some of the materials that a good spinner can work with are sheep wool, Angora goat or Angora rabbit hair, Kashmir goat hair, camel hair, dog hair, cotton or flax. Sheep's wool, though, is most widely used since it is available to almost anyone and indeed many homesteaders keep sheep on their own places.

FLEECE CLEANING

If you're setting out to buy a fleece, as the shorn wool is called, you will look for the cleanest you can get. If shearing your own sheep, try to keep or get them clean beforehand. The old-timers used to stand their sheep under a waterfall to clean them, with the water coming over a gristmill wheel being a favorite place. Most people shear sheep in the cold latitudes just after the weather starts to get warm in the spring. If you pick a warm day to shear, you can wash the sheep down with a garden hose or even a few pails of water. Do this a few hours before he is sheared so the fleece will be free of droplets of water. One good-sized sheep, maybe the one you stake out for use as a lawnmower, will produce all the fleece you might want to spin.

The best for spinning is wool that doesn't have to be washed after having been taken off the animal. In fact many good spinners never wash the wool, preferring to pick the fleece apart and discard the dirty tip of the wool before they card it. This has the advantage of retaining the lanolin which makes it much easier to spin. If the wool is scoured after it is taken from the sheep, some mineral oil or other lubricant has to be sprinkled on the wool or the hands have to be kept greased in spinning.

Washing is necessary if the wool is extremely dirty or if it is to be stored for a long time. Washing is properly done out of doors on a sunny warm day. The first step is to toss the fleece, a small bundle at a time, at an old window screen. You might be surprised at how many leaves, sand particles and pebbles can be shaken out this way. Next fill at least three pails or tubs with the softest water available and let it stand in the sun until it feels warm to the touch. Then take the fleece from the window screen and immerse it in these pails. For added cleaning power grate a bar of homemade general purpose soap or add a little mild detergent to each container of water. Push the fleece under the water and squeeze it several times. This will dislodge more foreign matter. When the water is so dirty that it looks like it couldn't possibly clean anymore take the fleece out and put it in another bucket and repeat the squeezing. When the wool will stay under the water without being held it will probably be clean.

Some very experienced wool washers don't squeeze the wool at all— they simply soak it. They do this by placing the unwashed wool in water that has been warmed to 101° and to which has been added two tablespoons of detergent and one tablespoon of salt. They let it soak for about twelve hours in this solution and then remove it and add two tablespoons of a mild detergent without the salt to the water and let the wool soak for an additional twelve hours. Then it is removed and rinsed.

The best method that we have used is known as the Greentree method. Prerinse the fleece with soap and salt added to the water to remove the coarse dirt. Then immerse the fleece in a pailful of warm water containing a shredded half bar of aged, handmade general purpose soap. Place the container with the fleece in it on top of the stove and heat it to about 150° F. Allow it to steep for about ten minutes; then remove it from the heat and let the fleece stay in the water until it cools. Then have several containers of water at about the same temperature as the now cooled water for rinsing. Rinse it at least three times. It is important to rinse the soap out when the wool is to be dyed because any grease in the wool will cause the dye to run or not work well. In fact you can't dye wool that hasn't been scoured. Once wool has been washed it has to be dried.

Drying wool begins right with squeezing the water out after it has been washed. Squeeze out as much as you can by hand and then run it through the wringer of a washing machine or between the rollers of a hand wringer. If you care to go to the trouble the wool can have moisture wrung out of it by another method. Simply tie the fleece in a bag or cheese cloth or an old onion sack or another large mesh bag. Then grasp the bag by the neck and whirl it around. Do this out of doors, of course, because water will fly all over. When the water is mostly squeezed or whirled out lay it on a sweater drier, if you have one, or on a clean screen. Set the drying rack in front of a window or in a breezy place out of doors but don't let the sun beat on it. Never, never place wet wool near a strong source of artificial heat, nor for that matter in an automatic dryer.

After the wool is dried you are going to have to store it for at least a little while until you make cloth out of it. Wool isn't hard to keep, but don't place it in an airtight container if it hasn't been washed or if there is any suspicion of grease left in it. However, wool that has had the grease washed out of it completely may be placed in airtight jars where it will keep for years. All wool and all-wool garments, unless they have been treated, will have to be stored with mothballs or else severe damage is sure to result. When the wool is thoroughly dried it is ready to be carded.

CARDING

Carding is the process of combing the wool between two hand-held combs or carders. This removes burrs and seeds and straightens the fibers. Wool carders come in different sizes with the larger number carders being used for the finest fleece. A number eight carder is about right for general coarse work. Since the carders fit into each other's teeth they are called right or left. It is a good idea to mark them so the same one is held in the same hand each time. Carders are sometimes available from antique shops, or new ones can be purchased from the addresses given at the end of this chapter. Once obtained, carders should be stored in a warm dry place and, if possible, a lock of greasy fleece should be left on the carder's teeth when it is put away to keep the leather soft and supple.

The first step in carding fleece is to tease it. This means to hold a lock of fleece in one hand and pull it apart, bit by bit, to be held in the other hand. This fluffs the fibers up and whips out still more dirt. The fleece should be held with the cut ends up and it should never be pulled from the ends but rather from the sides, like you would do if you were transferring a clump of straws from one hand to the other, one straw at a time.

After the teasing, the carding can begin. Place a small lock of teased fleece on the left hand carder with the cut ends facing the handle. With the other carder in your right hand, its teeth pointing down and the handle held towards you, very gently stroke it over the carder beneath to straighten the fibers. In stroking, never move the carders in any direction except that of the handles. The idea is to straighten the fibers of the fleece on the bottom carder. It is not necessary to move the bottom carder very much at all and never, never push the carders against each other since this could damage both them and the fleece. Fleece picked up by the righthand carder has to be periodically transferred back to the other one. To do this, reverse the handle of the righthand carder so it points in the same direction as the other one. Then "swoop" the fleece from the righthand carder by gently meshing the teeth of the carders so the fleece is restored to the carder beneath. Then resume the usual carding procedure, continuing until all the wool is carded smooth and clean. Form the carded wool into a batt or rolag by rolling it off the carder with the fingers into a one-inch-thick roll.

This method works well for the short-fiber wools but the long-fiber wools need to be carded by the worsted method, or across the carders. During this process the short fibers have to be picked out and laid aside. Generally it is best to avoid fleece with very long fibers unless a wool carding machine is available. The latter is a simple hand-cranked device that will card long or short wool and do it much faster than anyone can with a hand carder. It quite simply is the ultimate answer to anyone who has a large amount of carding to do. Obtain one of these from the addresses listed at the end of the chapter. Directions for using one accompanies the machine purchased.

SPINNING

After a considerable quantity of rolags have been made up it is time to start spinning.

Spinning twists the fibers of the wool so they form a thread. This is usually done on a spinning wheel but it also can be done merely with a spindle. A spindle is a device shaped like a top which can be spun with a rolag of wool attached to an end, spinning the fibers into thread. A spindle can be handmade by anyone since it is simply a sharpened stick piercing a disk of wood. Make your own by finding a straight, slim oak

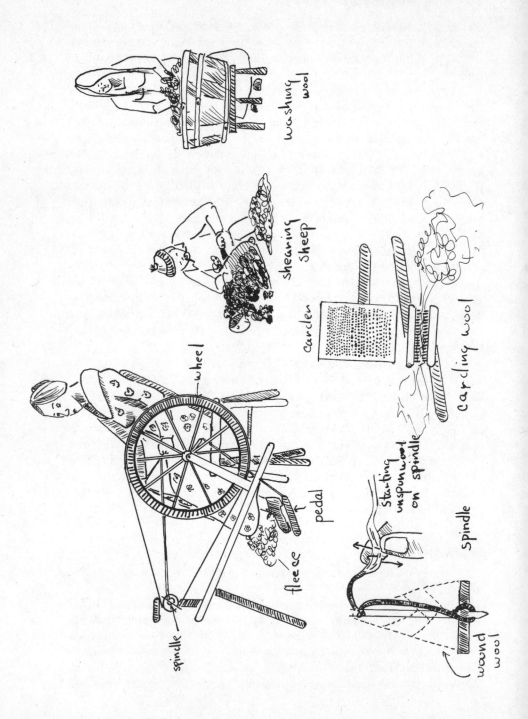

washing wool

shearing sheep

wheel

spindle

fleece

pedal

carder

carding wool

starting unspun wool on spindle

spindle

wound wool

or hickory branch about two feet long and of about ½ inch diameter with the bark scraped off. Taper one end. Then cut a disk or whorl of one-inch board or ½-inch plywood of about four inches diameter. In the exact center of the whorl drill a hole slightly smaller than the branch. Slide the disk on the branch. Place it about seven or eight inches from the sharpened end. This spindle is for spinning heavy wool, if your wool is lighter you can scale down the spindle accordingly. Whatever the size of the spindle it is well to cut a notch about one inch from the top as the yarn must be half-hitched to it.

To start spinning take a three-foot length of yarn already spun and tie it directly above the whorl. Wind the yarn around the spindle three or four times to keep it from slipping, then pass it down over the whorl around the spindle and back up around the whorl and upward to the top of the spindle, taking a half-hitch around the spindle in the notch cut in the top. At least three inches of free end of yarn should protrude for winding on the fleece.

The next step is to take a carded rolag and twist one end between the fingers to start the yarn. Then further twist it into the end of the spun yarn protruding from the spindle. When it is started, lift the spindle from the floor so that it dangles and twirl the spindle clockwise with the left hand while holding the connection between the spun and unspun yarn between the thumb and forefingers of the right hand. When the twist travels up to the right hand, straighten out the fleece fibers with the left hand for a short distance and then move the right hand up to the straightened fibers and let the twist ravel up to them. When the yarn is all twisted up it can be drawn out as fine as you wish by just continuing to draw on it while the spindle is kept turning. When it becomes necessary to attach a new rolag the spindle must be put on the floor to keep it from turning in a counterclockwise direction and untwisting the yarn.

When it becomes desirable to wind the yarn up, stop the spindle from turning, unloop the half-hitch at the top of the spindle and wind it up where it was originally tied to the spindle. Wind it up by spiraling the yarn up the shaft so the turns criss-cross each other, always winding more against the whorl to produce a cone-shaped roll tapering from one turn at its top to a fat roll at the base. This is important to keep the spindle turning smoothly. When you have one length wound on the spindle pass the free length of the yarn under the whorl, make a half-hitch in the top and attach the next rolag and continue to spin. When the spindle is full slide the whorl up the spindle to push the cone of yarn off. Store it on a holder, one you can make yourself by pushing ten penny nails through a foot square section of heavy cardboard.

When you have thoroughly mastered spinning on a spindle you may find yourself wishing for a spinning wheel. Fortunately they are becoming more and more available. In our area they are being sold new at auctions for much less than an antique one would sell for. Also there are several organizations and individuals making them. (For addresses of sources see end of chapter.)

As mentioned before, several good books are available at public libraries and from book stores on spinning and it is recommended that you read at least one of them before purchasing a spinning wheel.

The spinning wheel spindle, the part on which the fibers are spun, is the very same thing, in effect, as the hand spindle. This spindle is connected to the wheel by a band or belt. Turning the wheel rotates the spindle just as the hand spindle is turned by twirling it. The band rides in a groove or grooves on the spindle. The deeper the groove the faster the spindle will be turned and the tighter the wool will be woven. If the band is or becomes loose it will have to be tightened. This is done by turning a tension screw which moves the spinning head away from the wheel. The band should be just tight enough so that it does not slip.

Once the band tension is correct try turning the wheel. If it squeaks or squawks it may need lubrication. Lubricate the axle by removing the wheel, cleaning away all the old grease and dirt, coating it well with axlegrease and reinstalling the wheel. You may have to readjust the tension on the driving band after the lubrication. When the wheel is running smoothly it is ready to start making yarn.

In making yarn the first step is to tie a length of spun yarn about 15 inches long to the spindle. Tie it at the spindle heel and wind it counterclockwise towards the end of the spindle, letting a short length dangle over just as with the hand spindle. Again, as with the hand spindle, a rolag of wool will be twisted on to the dangling end of the spun yarn and held in place with the left hand and the wheel spun clockwise with the right hand. This done, the twisting action "picks up" and starts the yarn. Once well started, the spinner's left hand can be brought to a more comfortable position as the spun yarn is pulled away. The tighter you hold the fleece between the fingers the tighter the thread will wind. Don't overdo this as it causes the thread or yarn to become twisted and kinky. The rolag should be spun to a length of about 20 inches.

When the yarn is spun to the desired thickness, stop the wheel, reverse its direction and unwind the yarn on the spindle as far back as the knot; then, holding the spun yarn between the fingers at right angles to the spindle, rewind to the back of the spindle. Leave the end dangling from the spindle so you can start over with another rolag.

When the spindle is full, slip off the driving band and unwind the yarn onto a "niddy noddy" or other yarn-holding device. The yarn can even be held temporarily by placing a chair face down on the floor with the legs up. Measure the distance around the legs and you will have a good idea how much yarn has been wound on it when the spinning is over.

Fleece that has been so scoured or cleaned that it has lost its natural grease will spin much better if some grease is added to it, maybe by keeping a greased rag handy to pinch once in a while to keep the fingers greasy. Or mineral oil can be mixed with water and sprayed over the fleece the night before spinning. The formula is two parts mineral oil to one part water. But never use grease that can't be washed out unless you don't plan to dye the cloth since the grease will keep the dye from taking.

WOOL DYEING

Dyeing can be done either before or after the cloth is woven. It would seem a sacrilege to use anything but natural dyes on homespun cloth, especially since so many good ones are available. Brown comes from walnut hulls, yellow from goldenrod or onion skins, gray from sumac leaves.

Dyeing with natural dyes is not an exact process and the wool dyer never knows precisely what shade he will get since there are many, many factors influencing this. In all cases, however, if not already done, the yarn must be cleaned well before dyeing. This can be speedily done by immersing it in a kettle of water and gradually bringing it to a temperature of about 190 degrees. Don't boil! If you have an enameled colander, place the wool in that before putting it in water. Then you can lift it out while it is still hot and let water drip from it until it cools down enough to squeeze with the hands. Never wring wool as it will mat and tear the fleece. When most of the water has been squeezed out but while it is still wet and warm, immerse it in the dye pot.

The dye pot has to be readied in advance, of course. The directions given here will be for dyeing with walnut hulls to produce a dark brown color. Chop about one quart of walnut hulls and add them to two gallons of water, letting this stand overnight or longer to soak and soften the hulls. Then boil this mixture for two hours. Cool and strain out the hulls, using cheesecloth or a sieve. Keep the hulls only if you plan to make more dye. Place the dye in an enamel pan, preferably a white pan since colors show up more readily against the white background. Place the washed wool in the pan containing the dye and heat it to the simmering point, then let it simmer for about two hours or until the desired shade is reached, stirring it occasionally but very slowly with a wooden paddle. Heat another pan of clear water to the simmering point, lift the wool out of the dye bath with a colander or small white fish net and immerse it in the rinse water. Rinse at this temperature and then again in a second rinse which is a little cooler, not quite at the simmering point. Keep this up in successive rinses until the water is clear, using cooler water each time. When the water stays fairly clear after the rinse squeeze as much water as possible out of the wool, then wrap it in a towel, squeeze some more moisture out of it, and then spread it on a drying rack or hang it outside but not in the sun until it dries. There are times, however, when dyes turn out brighter if they are sun dried, particularly if mordants are used. A mordant "fixes" a dye solution and makes a dye permanent, affecting its color. Consult the table at chapter end.

THE NAVAJO LOOM

Weaving requires a loom. Looms come in an infinite variety of sizes and capabilities. The following paragraphs describe how to make one simple loom, often called the Navajo Loom. This can be used to weave rugs, blankets or even cloth.

First find four sturdy poles about six inches in diameter. If green wood is all you can find, peel off the bark and treat all rough knots so the poles are perfectly smooth. The side poles should be seven feet long and the cross poles about four feet long. Notch the side poles six inches from each end so that the cross poles will fit the notches. Square the poles up and nail or lash the short poles to the side poles. The ends of the cross poles should be flush with the outside of the side poles. This forms a frame approximately three feet by six feet, inside dimensions.

Directly inside this frame and at each end two smaller poles are needed. They can be about two inches in diameter and they also should be scraped free of bark and knots. One of these poles, called the warp pole, is used to hold the warp thread. The other, or tension pole, is connected to the warp pole and the end of the frame by a series of loops of rawhide. This makes it possible to tighten the warp threads, these being the threads stretched the long way of the frame. Weft threads are the threads woven across the warp threads.

The next part for the loom is a flat stick about four feet three inches long. This flat stick must be about four inches wide and about ½ inch thick. It will have to be sanded very smooth with fine sandpaper or glass. It should be pointed at both ends like a toy boat. This piece is called the shed stick.

The last part which will have to be made is the second shed rod. This is merely a rod or sturdy smooth stick exactly of the same length as the flat shed stick.

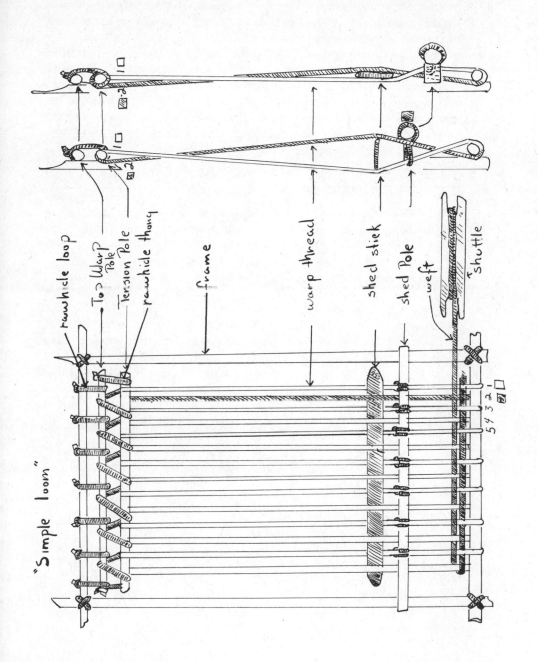

"Simple loom"

rawhide loop

Top Warp Pole

Tension Pole

rawhide thong

frame

warp thread

shed stick

shed Pole

weft

shuttle

5 4 3 2 1

When the frame is made, set it up in a comfortable place or hang it from a tree branch. If you set it up, put blocks under the ends of the lower frame so you can string the warp threads on.

Next, fasten the tension pole to the top cross frame pole. Do this with four separate loops of rawhide or similar material so that some space exists between the poles for stringing the rawhide for the warp pole. Then take a piece of rawhide approximately ten feet long. Tie one end to the warp pole and loop the other end over the tension pole and coil it along the length of both so the warp pole is held. Keep this rawhide very loose since it will need to be tightened to stretch the warp threads.

USING THE NAVAJO LOOM

When the top warp pole is connected to the tension pole it is time to start stringing the warp threads. Tie one end to the extreme left side of the bottom cross pole and carry it up over the (top) warp pole and then back down to the bottom cross pole, around this and back up around the top warp pole. Keep winding the warp thread around and around, keeping it tight until you have covered the distance across the loom or the width that you wish the cloth to be. From time to time while winding, you may have to push the threads against one another to form a tighter weave. For the initial attempt, though, this step can be forgotten. Try not to cross the warp threads over one another. When the warp thread is all strung on, tie it securely to either the top warp pole or the bottom cross pole. Then further tighten the warp thread by untying one end of the ten-foot rawhide piece and pulling on it to move the warp pole closer to the tension pole. When it is as tight as you can get it you are ready to insert the first shed stick.

The first shed stick is inserted under every other warp thread across the loom. Thus, it goes over number one thread, under number two thread, over number three and under number four, repeating across the loom until the shed stick is inserted under every even-numbered thread clear across the loom. Notice that when this flat, first shed stick is turned sideways it will lift the even-numbered threads, forming a hole or "shed."

Now take the second shed pole, lay it across the width of the loom parallel with the first shed stick but about 18 inches above it. Take yarn or thread and tie each odd-numbered thread loosely to the second shed pole. When this is done you will notice that when you raise the second shed rod the odd-numbered threads will be picked up forming a second hole or "shed." Thus by turning the first shed stick sideways we can form a shed by raising the even-numbered threads, and by lifting the second shed pole we can raise the odd-numbered threads to form another shed. Now we are ready to start weaving.

First slide the first shed stick down to the bottom of the loom and turn it sideways. As mentioned, this will form a shed so that yarn passed across the warp thread through the resulting spaces will actually be passing over one thread and under another. This crossways thread is called the weft thread. When the thread is passed completely across the loom it is passed around the side pole and the end brought up to weaving position again. This time, though, the thread will be passed over the even-numbered threads and under the odd. We do this by turning the first shed stick so that it lies flat and lifting the second shed rod so that it pulls the odd-numbered threads up. Do this and pass the yarn across to the opposite side, pass around that pole and then turn the first shed stick sideways and go across again. Keep this up until you have seven or eight weft threads woven in and then insert a comb and push the threads tightly together. Keep this up until the material is done.

When the material is all woven cut the weft threads where they go around the side poles and tie them together. Do this one at a time. Then cut the warp threads, one at a time, where they go around the warp pole at one end and the cross pole at the other and tie them together. Thus each warp thread will be tied to the one next to it. The excess string can be left for a fringe or it can be trimmed off.

Very soon after you start weaving you are going to wish for a stick shuttle. This is used to wind the yarn on as it is passed or "thrown" through the shed. One can easily be made from any scrap piece of thin wood or they can be purchased. See illustration. Another way to make cloth from homespun yarn is by knitting.

KNITTING

Knitting by hand, or weft knitting, is a way of making a cloth or fabric by means of tying yarn in special knots with knitting needles. Knitted clothing is better than woven clothing for some purposes such as sweaters or mittens since knitted material will stretch over the body and still return to its original shape after being worn. Homespun yarn can be knitted into some very useful objects.

All knit pieces are formed by two main stitches called knit and purl. All stitches are variations of these.

The first step in knitting is to obtain the yarn and two knitting needles. If you have your own homespun yarn, you can get by just by purchasing the knitting needles. If purchasing yarn, try to get four-ply wool. Knitting needles could be homemade, of course, but they cost so little that it hardly seems worth the effort. A good size needle is number 7.

Like most other worthwhile skills knitting takes some practice. It is

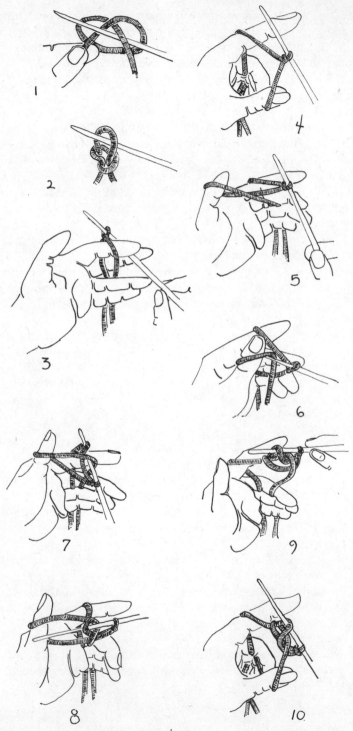

Cast On

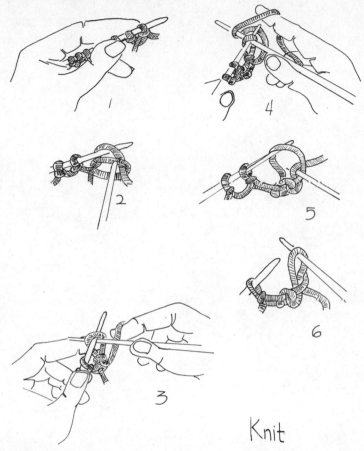

Knit

beyond the scope of this chapter to cover all aspects of knitting, but illustrated here are the methods of casting on (placing stitches on knitting needle for beginning work), the two basic stitches (the knit and the purl), and binding off (decreasing stitches to form an edge); and if a beginner will practice these until they can be done skillfully, he or she will be ready to move on to actually making a pair of mittens or other useful item.

NATURAL DYES CHART

Plant	Part Used	Color	Mordant	Notes
Alder	Bark, leaves	Black, brown	Iron sulphate	
Azalea	Leaves	Brown, red	Slaked lime	Pick leaves in fall
Bayberry	Leaves	Green	Alum	Pick leaves in fall
Blackberry	Shoots	Black	Alum	Iron sulphate will darken color
Black walnut	Green husks	Brown	None	Boil husks for two hours

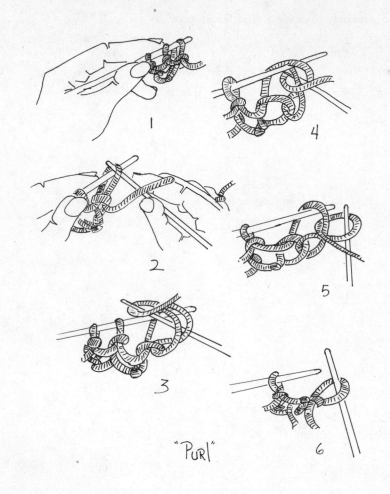

"Purl"

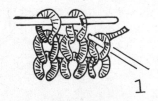

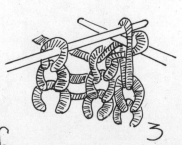

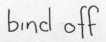

bind off

Blueberry	Berry	Purple	Alum	
Dandelion	Whole plant	Purple	None	
Elderberry	Berry	Lilac	Salt	Crush and boil berries
Elderberry	Leaves	Green	Alum	
Goldenrod	Flower	Gold	Chrome	Pick immature flower
Maple	Bark	Olive	Alum	
Nettle	Entire plant	Greenish yellow	Alum	Wear gloves
Onion	Dried skins	Orange	Alum	
Onion	Dried skins	Brass	Chrome	
Sumac	Berries	Tan	Alum & iron	Pick when ripe
Sumac	Leaves	Dark brown	None	Soak overnight
White birch	Leaves	Yellow	Alum	Longer boiling will produce deeper yellow
White birch	Inner bark	Brown	None	Shred and soak

Magazines

Shuttle, Spindle and Dyepot
Two Northfield Road
Glen Cove, New York 11542

Handweavers and Crafts
220 Fifth Avenue
New York, New York 10001

Books

Coates, Helen, *Weaving For Amateurs*. New York: Viking Press, 1946
Kluger, Marilyn, *The Joy of Spinning*. New York: Simon and Schuster, 1971
Davenport, Elsie, *Your Handspinning*. Pacific Grove, California: Craft And Hobby, 1964
Fannin, Allen, *Handspinning, Art and Technique*. New York: Van Nostrand Reinhold, 1971
Lesch, Alma, *Vegetable Dyeing*. New York: Watson-Guptill, 1970
Taylor, Gertrude, *America's Knitting Book*. New York, Scribner's, 1968

Suppliers

The Spinning Wheel Shop
17521 North Wind Lake Road
Wind Lake, Wisconsin 53185

Mr. and Mrs. R. A. Meisterheim
Route #5, Box 210
Dowaiac, Michigan 49047

Guild of Shaker Crafts
401 Savidge
Spring Lake, Michigan 49459

Handcraft Wools
Box 378
Streetsville, Ontario
Canada

Green Tree Ranch Wools
163 N. Carter Lake Road
Loveland, Colorado 80537

14

SOAPMAKING AND MISCELLANEOUS MATTERS

MANY PEOPLE LOOK askance when soapmaking is mentioned. "Why make something you can buy for a little or nothing?" they ask. Most homesteaders will know the answer to that. It uses up fat and tallow that would commonly be wasted, it doesn't cost anything at all if wood ashes are used for lye and there is a tremendous sense of satisfaction in washing your hands and clothes with soap made by your own hands. Being all organic, homemade soap doesn't pollute either.

LYE MAKING

Usually the first step is obtaining the lye. Wood ashes, especially hardwood ashes, make the best lye. In fact, the ashes of resin woods such as the pines can't be used at all. Simply save the ashes from a wood fire or even create a wood fire of hardwood branches specifically to develop a supply of ashes. Ashes, if they are kept dry, can be stored in any container but once they are moistened they manufacture lye and of course lye will react violently with some metals such as aluminum. A good place for storage is a section of hollowed-out tree trunk, wood or enamel utensil. If you have a cast-iron pot around, that will work too except for a slight rust problem.

When you have a bushel or so of ashes and are ready to start making soap, place the ashes in a wooden trough made by hollowing out a section of tree trunk or by nailing two pieces of lumber together at right angles. Angle the trough slightly so that water will run out and pour water through it slowly, catch it at the bottom and pour it through again. This should be repeated until the lye water is dense enough to float an egg. If you can lay hands on a wooden barrel this is about the best thing around. (A steel barrel will also work.) Set the barrel upright, punch several holes in the bottom. Many barrels have a depression near the center of their bottoms so be sure to punch this out, and place a layer of pebbles about six inches thick in the bottom. If pebbles are at a premium use broken glass, or anything else available that will keep the ashes from plugging the holes or sifting through them; even coarse sand will work if the holes are kept small. Then fill the barrel with wood ashes, make a depression in the top, fill the depression full of water and let it drain down through.

If this is done just right the lye resulting will be strong enough after but one leaching to make soap. If it doesn't pass the egg test run it through the ashes again. Remember to protect the ashes from rainwater.

If smaller amounts of soap are to be made (one bar), the lye can be made by boiling water in a pan filled as much as possible with wood ashes. Boil the water for about a half hour, stop the boiling, let the ashes sink to the bottom, skim the lye water off the top and throw the ashes away. If the lye isn't strong enough at this point just boil the water some more to concentrate it.

Lye can be purchased at any grocery or hardware store if all this leaching and boiling sounds like too much trouble. In fact, some lye manufacturers have directions for making soap accompanying their product.

SELECTING LARD AND TALLOW

The other chief ingredient in making soap is lard (hog fat), beef tallow, mutton tallow or any other kind of fat you may happen to have.

To some extent the kind of fat used will determine the kind of soap made. Lard is good for regular soap but tallow makes the best saddlesoap or soft soap. Soft soap can be made harder by shaving it and boiling it down and cooling it again or by adding salt. A combination of lard and tallow will usually make the best soap. However, most soapmaking homesteaders just save and use whatever fat they happen to have around the place. This means the bacon fryings, the grease from pork chops, the excess tallow from beef roast, rinds left on plates after meals and the cracklings left over from rendering lard, the fat from the intestines of sheep and goats, the same from the geese and ducks and chickens and the fat trimmed off the cuts after butcherings. In short, any kind of animal fat that turns to liquid when it is heated and returns to a solid state when cool. Vegetable fats can also be used to make soap. Olive oil, coconut oil, and cottonseed oil are all used, either pure or in combination with other oils.

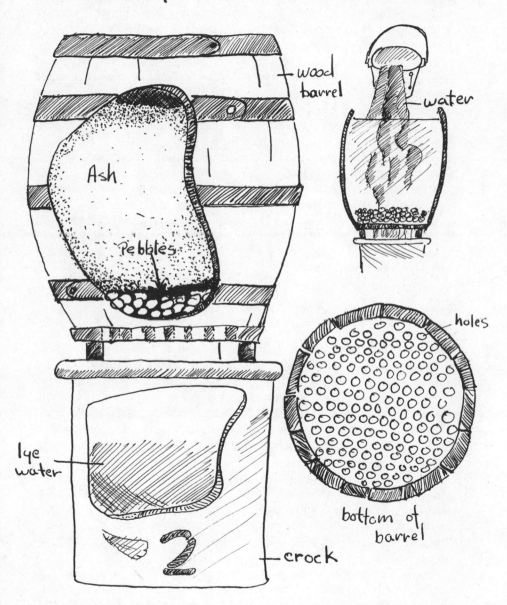

"SOAP MAKING"

wood barrel

Ash

Pebbles

lye water

crock

2

water

holes

bottom of barrel

Fat has to be washed before being used for soap, especially if it is rancid or if it contains large amounts of impurities. "Washing" fat means putting it in boiling water and boiling it until the fat starts to float. At this stage the impurities, bits of meats, etc. will be free from the fat. When the fat is all liquid, stop the boiling and add cold water at the rate of one quart to each gallon of fat boiled. This clears it, causing the solids to sink and the fat to float at the top where it then can be skimmed off. If one boiling isn't enough it can be reboiled. Some don't even bother with this washing process; they just heat the fat and scraps until the liquid separates from the scraps and then they pour off the liquid. If using tallow or large amounts of leaf lard it can be rendered out much faster if it is ground first. Just run it through the meat grinder before heating it, add an equal amount of water and heat it until the fat is all liquid.

Very rancid fats can be made sweeter by adding ¼ teaspoon baking soda and a cup of boiling water before boiling them out.

Cracklings, the stuff left after butchering a pig and rendering out the fat, can be made into soap by covering them to twice their depth with water. Add one teaspoon of lye powder if you have it or one cup of lye made from wood ashes, boil for one hour, remove from the fire and pour in a quart of cold water for every gallon of pressed cracklings. Skim the fat from the top of the water when it solidifies.

MAKING SOAP

The following recipe will make all-purpose soap: 2½ pints lye water, six pounds of clean fat. If using lye crystals, dissolve one 13-ounce can of lye in 2½ pints of cold water. Heat the fat until it is a clear liquid and let it cool at room temperature until it just starts to thicken. Then pour the lye water into the soap in a thin stream, stirring slowly. After the lye is added, if the mixture doesn't start to thicken, keep stirring until it does. When it starts to thicken pour it into a mold. This can be a wooden box that has been soaked in water and lined with a clean, slightly damp cloth. Cover the box with a rug or several layers of newspaper to retain the heat while the soap cures. After 24 hours lift the soap out of the mold by lifting on the cloth which is beneath the soap. When it is out cut the soap with a string or fine wire. A knife blade will work but it tends to crumble new soap. After it is cut place the bars of soap where air but not drafts can get to them. Don't let the soap freeze or even chill too fast for at least the first two weeks.

To make one bar of all-purpose soap add one cup clean fat, one teaspoon borax to five teaspoons of lye and ½ cup of soft water.

If there appears to be liquid either at the top or at the bottom of the new soap when it is inspected after 24 hours, cut the soap into squares and let it stand in the mold until it absorbs the liquid. This might take another 24 hours. Sometimes it will happen that permanent separation occurs. The soapmaker than has a choice of using the soap as is or remelting it and pouring it into the mold again. Remelting the soap will reclaim it perfectly but it must be done according to a definite procedure.

In order to reclaim soap that has separated, save all the liquid. Shave the solid soap into a kettle and add the separated liquid and five pints of water. Remelt the soap over a gentle heat, stirring occasionally. This will have to be continued until the water added has boiled away. This boiling can be continued until the soap will seem to uncoil from a spoon instead of just running off it. When it is cured, pour it into a mold and treat as for the original pour.

Coloring and perfuming soap—some of the reasons why one soap is favored over another—can be done with materials from the fields and forest. Almost any green plant juice will color soap green, onionskin tea will color it yellow, also berry juice will color it blue. Walnut shell tea will color it brown; in fact almost any plant or mineral will easily color it. The coloring material is added to the soap after lye is mixed into it and just before it is poured into the mold.

There is no soap as delightul as soap that has been perfumed by wild flowers and there is hardly anything any easier to do. Just put a good-sized layer of lilac blossoms, mint stalks and leaves that have been bruised, or rose petals or whatever flowers are in season in the box with the soap when it is seasoning and it will absorb the odors very readily. If you wait until a thick glaze forms on the top of the soap the blossoms can be placed right on it. Keep the blossoms with the soap and the odor will get stronger and stronger as the soap gets older, even after you start using it.

The U. S. Department of Agriculture recommends the following dyes: Fluorescein for yellow, Naphthol Green for green and Rhodamine for red. These dyes should be mixed with the soap just before it is poured into the molds.

Many commercial perfumes are also obtainable for perfuming soap but be sure they do not contain alcohol.

I doubt that there is any kind of soap that the homesteader might want that cannot be made at home with less trouble than canning tomatoes. One of these is jelly soap, a lye-hard soap made into jelly soap for convenience in the dishpan or washing machine. Make it by cutting one pound of hard soap into fine shavings and adding it to one gallon of water. Boil it for two minutes and then pour it into a cake pan type of container to cool. This soap will melt in the hot dish water and a little goes a long ways.

Abrasive soap paste is made by melting three pounds of shaved homemade soap in three pints of water. Add three ounces of light mineral oil. When the ingredients are thoroughly blended allow the mixture to cool to a thick mush, and knead or stir in five pounds of pumice stone.

Castile-like soap—add one can of lye to two pints of water, 24 ounces of olive oil, 238 ounces of good tallow, and 24 ounces of coconut oil. The temperature of the lye is 90°F and the fats also 90°F.

For saddlesoap make soap from pure tallow. It is very valuable as a leather cleaner and preserver. The formula is one can of lye, 2¾ pints of water, six pounds of mutton or beef tallow. Temperatures are 90°F for the lye and 130°F for the fat when they are mixed together.

Liquid soap is made by adding one can of lye to seven pints of water, three pints of glycerine, 6½ pints of alcohol, four pounds of cottonseed oil, 1¼ pounds of coconut oil. Dissolve the lye in a mixture of 3½ pints each of alcohol and water, and heat to 125°F. Hold the oils at 150°F and add a few ounces of the lye solution, stirring slowly and evenly. When saponification is about complete add the last of the lye mixture. Saponification is the act of changing an oil to a soap by the addition of alkali.

Adding borax to any soap will quicken the sudsing action. Add it as the soap is being made or use it at the same time as using the soap.

Linseed oil soap is used for washing automobiles and furniture. It is a very soft soap made by adding one can of lye to four pints of water, 5¾ pounds of linseed oil. Temperature for the lye is 80°F, oil 100°F. Add lye in small quantities and stir it well before adding more.

The finest soaps are made by adding lye to the fat when both are at the correct temperatures. (See chart.)

Fat	Temp. Fat Degrees F	Temp. Lye Degrees F
Sweet, rancid fat	97° - 100°	75° - 80°
Sweet lard	80° - 85°	70° - 75°
Half lard and half tallow	100° - 110°	80° - 85°
All tallow	120° - 130°	90° - 95°

Use a dairy or floating thermometer. An outdoor thermometer probably won't work.

TO MAKE BUTTER

Make butter by standing cow's milk in an open crock in a cool place until the cream comes to the top. Skim it off with a spoon. Place it in a fruit jar, put the lid on the jar and shake it by hand or mechanically until the butter "comes." Pour off the buttermilk and press the butter lumps together to form a brick. Add a little salt if you wish. Rinse it with cold water while pressing it. If an electric blender is available, churn the cream into butter with that. Make butter faster than you can buy it.

TO MAKE YOGURT

Make yogurt by pouring milk into a sterilized jar or can. Cover and heat to 110°. Maintain this heat with a light bulb, solar heater, wood stove or keep it close to the ceiling of a heated room. When stable, add a good amount of plain yogurt or yogurt starter. Carefully maintain the temperature between 100° and 120° for about eight hours. Check without shaking it. If it is all curdled, cool and eat. If it isn't, incubate some more. The best yogurt has berries or fruit added to it. Use berry juice or pulp for liquid to mix with dry milk. If it doesn't harden, add gelatin.

TO MAKE SOURDOUGH

Make sourdough by adding a package of dry yeast to a cup of warm water. Add two cups of flour and mix well. Take the mixture to bed with you or at least keep it warm overnight. Next morning, presto, sourdough sponge. Take half and make bread, cake or pancakes. Keep the other half in the cooler. When you desire to use some more mix two cups of flour with it once more and take it to bed again. Then keep half again. If it sours, freshen it out by adding flour or throw it away and start all over again.

HOMEMADE BREAKFAST FOOD

By all means make your own breakfast food. I don't think you can buy any good stuff. Crack wheat or corn in your hand grinder, soak overnight and cook the next morning with fruit. Better than this is combination of fruits, grain and nuts.

Jim Churchill's Breakfast Food For Homesteaders

1 cup hickory nut meats very coarsely ground
1 cup dried June berries—prunes or apricots will work
4 cups wheat germ or fresh cracked wheat (raw)
2 teaspoons honey or to taste, but don't make it gummy
Milk; goat, cow, dried milk, evaporated milk; add to taste
If you don't have any milk, eat it dry. You can snowshoe thirty
miles on a breakfast like this—five, anyway.

TIPS FROM EXPERIENCE

Freeze cooked soybeans and they won't cause so much intestinal commotion.

If you like wild animals, plant food and cover on the place for them. Don't be misled by stocking and No Hunting methods of preserving wild animals. If they have cover and food they can take care of themselves.

Make friends with senior citizens who have lived on the land. They can give more tips in an afternoon than you would learn in a year.

Convert an old corncrib into a drying shed for drying berries, onions, potatoes, fruit, seeds, nuts, etc., but add a series of shelves made of old windowscreen. No old screens? Hang the produce in burlap bags from wires. Keep canvas tacked along the top under the roof overhang. When it rains drop the canvas to keep the food dry. No canvas? Use plastic or cloth. The best drying bins in the world can be made from the metal drawers that commercial chicken hatcheries use. Find a hatchery that is going out of business or updating and offer to take them off their hands.

Use common household bleach to purify water. Add a drop at a time to a pailful. Stop when you can detect the taste of chlorine.

Keep deer out of the garden by tying the family dog in the center of the patch. Make sure Rover is comfortable there with a house and water.

There is no way to acquire money without sacrificing time, individuality or freedom. Therefore let's learn to live without money as much as possible.

Booklet

U. S. Department Of Agriculture
Agriculture Research Service
Southern Marketing And Nutrition
   Research Division
New Orleans, Louisiana 70119
Soap Making At Home
CA - 72 -35

15

FARMING WITH HORSES

THE TYPE OF horse usually used to pull farm implements is the draft or work horse. Purebred draft horses are huge animals sometimes weighing more than a ton. They are in most cases directly descended from the war horses that the knights of yore rode into battle. They are called Belgians, Clydesdales, Percheron, Shire, Suffolk. In addition to the purebreds are numerous crossbreeds which are sometimes combination riding and draft animals.

CARE OF THE DRAFT HORSE

Draft horses are relatively easy to feed and house. A horse will eat mostly hay with timothy and clover hay being desirable kinds. They only need grain when they are working hard. Most horses are pastured in summer and left to take care of themselves. Horses need plenty of good, clean, fresh water every day and a creek or pond in their pasture is desirable. If this can't be arranged, a large tub such as a recycled bathtub can be kept full of water for them. Horses also need a block of salt in their pasture or manger.

When the horse is kept in a building he will do better in a box stall rather than just being tied to a hitch. Box stalls keep the drafts away and a cool draft blowing on a sweaty hot animal can lead to extreme sickness or even death. In addition, where more than one animal is housed together, a box stall keeps them from kicking or biting each other, which also causes very serious injuries.

Kept inside, a horse should be bedded with about three inches of light clean straw or hay and be fed in a manger kept scrupulously clean. The bedding should be changed as soon as it becomes soaked or dirty and the manure should be removed frequently enough so the animal does not have to stand in a damp or wet place. This last is one of the chief causes of foot problems, the biggest single cause of crippled horses. More about it later.

The box stall which should be constructed out of two-inch material, should be as high as the horse, as long as the horse, and have about 18 inches of room on each side of the horse when he is standing.

The manger should extend the full width of the head end of the stall. Since it forms the front of the stall it should be about three feet high to allow the horse to eat easily and yet prevent him from trying to climb over it to get out of the stall. It should be a rectangular box at least 18 inches wide at the bottom with the back wall tapering outward to at least two feet to funnel the hay. Each manger should also have a grain box for feeding oats or hay. Some people simply feed the grain in a pan or some even have a feed bag that they slide up on the animal's nose, which is fairly convenient.

If the horse is tied in the stall the rope should be short enough to keep him from putting his head down to the floor. If he can get his head down that low there is the danger that he would step over the rope and possibly injure himself badly. Horses can be confined in a stall without tying them by putting bars across the back of the stall if the stall is so narrow the horse can't turn around.

HARNESSING UP

The first step in harnessing a horse is to put the collar in place. The collar, hailed by some historians as the greatest invention in history, is a device made of steel-reinforced leather to fit over the horse's neck to allow the shoulder to be used for pulling. Some collars are one-piece and have to be slid over the head while some have a strap at the top to open them so they can be put in place from the bottom. Before the collar is put on the shoulders and neck have to be cleaned of all dirt and inspected for sores or galls. If the collar is equipped with a blanket liner this is put on first and smoothed out well so there won't be any wrinkles under the collar to chafe the horse's neck and shoulders. Then the collar is put in place and buckled to fit tightly over the liner. It should be adjusted until in the proper position since the collar is the most important part of the harness. Then the rest of the harness is put in place. Collars come in a variety of sizes and the measurements of the horse's neck

should be taken before sending for a harness. Some harnessmakers want
to know the horse's height and all about his condition since if he is fat he
may shrink quite a lot with resulting collar looseness. When the collar is
buckled up, slip on the harness.

A draft harness is a rather complicated-looking arrangement of straps
and steel. It is often hung up in reverse order to the steps in which it will be
put on. It is taken off its hook by sliding the right arm under the breech
band, forward under the back straps until the hames can be reached. Then
the righthand hame is grasped in the right hand and the lefthand hame in
the other. Then the harness is carried to and placed on the animal.
Straighten the harness out next and set one hame in place on each side of
the collar, fastening them by the straps that dangle from the bottom of the
hames. Hames have to be put on straight so the harness and load will pull
evenly on the horse's shoulders. Then move back to fasten the bellyband,
which will have a buckle dangling from one side and a strap from the
other. Pull the band up snug but not overly tight. Then fasten the two
straps that extend forward from the breech band to the rings provided on
the bellyband. Harnesses vary somewhat in their makeup but all of them
are held on by the hames, the bellyband and straps to hold the breech band
into place.

After the harness is on the bridle is slipped on and the reins uncoiled
from the hames and strung through their rungs on the hames, then snapped
into the rings on the bit. Placing a bridle on a horse can be easy or hard
depending on whether it will "take the bit" or not. Taking the bit
means the horse's willingness to open his mouth and accept the bit in its
customary place back of the large teeth. Bridling the animal involves
picking up the bridle in the right hand and lifting it up over the horse's
face so that the bit will dangle under the horse's mouth. With the left
hand guide the bit into place in the horse's mouth. A well-broken horse
will open its mouth quite readily. When he takes the bit, slide the bridle
up over the horse's head and fasten it in place.

If he won't open his mouth slide your thumb into his mouth and press
against the upper teeth. When he opens his mouth quickly slide the bit into
place. Some horses will open their mouth also if the upper lip is pressed
tightly against the upper teeth.

After the bit is in place the throat latch is fastened and the forelock adjusted. The throat latch is the strap that goes under the horse's neck; the
forelock is the strap that goes across the forehead.

After the bridle is on the reins are snapped to the rings on each side of
the bit at the bridle. In the case of harnessing two horses or a team they are
usually led outside the barn where the reins are snapped in place. The reins
for a single horse obviously must go back alongside the horse, whereas the

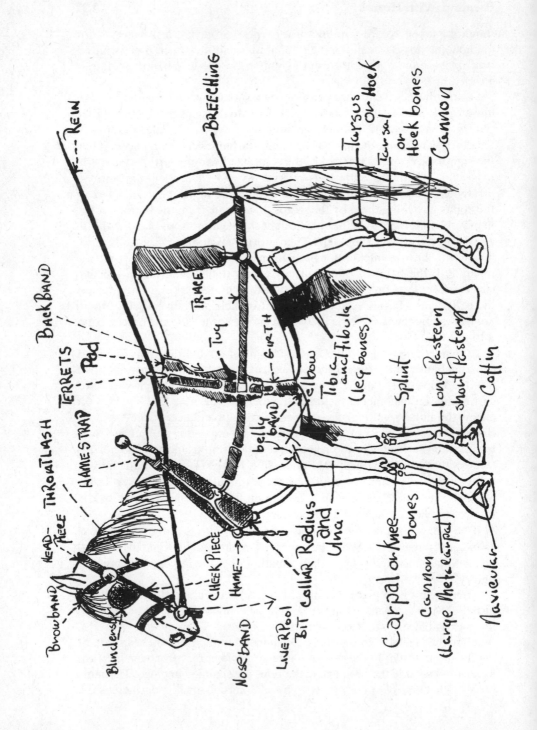

reins for a double horse hookup have a V or wishbone arrangement. One strap goes from the left side of one horse to the left side of the other, with the opposite strap going from right side of one horse to the right side of the other. Thus the lefthand line will pull on the lefthand side of each horse's mouth to turn them both left and vice versa.

When the lines or reins are in place the horse or team can be led or driven over to the load and backed into place. If the implement has a tongue, which most wagons and wheeled implements do, the team is backed to each side of the tongue. When they are in place the tongue is lifted and the neck yoke is buckled into place at the collar. Next the chain links at the ends of the traces are hooked to the whiffletree, these being adjusted so each horse gets an even load. They are always set so the load doesn't pull too close to the horses' hind legs, however, since this can cause them injury or fright. The traces may have to be readjusted to even the horses out once they start pulling since very often one horse will want to pull ahead of the other. This is easily corrected.

PLOWING WITH TEAM AND WALKING PLOW

Plowing with two horses is quite a skilled undertaking, especially if using the single furrow walking plow. First the horses are harnessed and hitched to the plow which has no tongue. The plow is tilted on its side and the horses are driven merely dragging the plow along until they get to the work field. Then the plowman grasps the handles of the plow and sets it upright. Next he ties the reins together and stands back of the plow between the handles in the position he normally will work in and adjusts the reins so they are snug on his back, placing them under his arms and over the handle of the plow. Then, tilting the plow up so the point will enter the ground, he says "giddap" and if all goes well, the plow enters the ground. Then all the plowman has to do is guide it across the field. If the team is well trained for plowing they will walk straight across the field. When he gets to the other end he turns them and takes a comfortable "land" or strip and plows back across the field. Successive furrows are made so the dirt turned up completely fills the adjacent furrow. This means starting the plow one plowshare width over from the previous furrow. Most walking plows are 12 inches wide so succeeding strips will start 12 inches or less over from the previous one. A walking plow can be guided quite a few inches each way by pressing on the right handle to go left or the left one to go right. Once the plowing pattern has been established, the righthand horse will be walking in a furrow.

Using the walking plow, it takes a good team and plowman putting in a good day's work to plow two acres a day. A team of oxen or a mule pulling a plow alone can do only about one acre or less a day.

When horses are worked hard as in plowing they should be offered water about every two hours. At noon the harnesses should be removed or loosened and the animals fed oats. Feeding heavier grain such as corn at noon is not desirable. At the end of the work day and after the harnesses are removed the animals should be allowed to run in a pasture or lot for a while so they can roll in the dust. This is their bath and failure to let them do this may cause sickness and stiff muscles. If they are very sweaty and they are to be kept indoors they should be thoroughly rubbed down with straw to get rid of the moisture.

At the end of the day's work the horse's feet should be inspected for dirt and any dirt between the rim and the frog of the feet should be cleaned out.

There is a tool which you can make yourself that is very effective for cleaning horses' feet. It is called a hoof or foot hook. It is simply an iron rod having a hook on one end which can reach up into a horse's hoof and pry out the mud. An old screwdriver with a fairly blunt tip can be bent to a 90-degree angle at the end and used for this. If a stone has entered the hoof it must be removed or it can cause bad trouble.

THE HORSE'S FOOT AILMENTS

Removing the stone from a hoof is simple with a hoof pick, just get the point under the stone and give it a quick flick. If a piece of gravel is picked up and is not removed it can work its way deeper until the hoof grows over the entry hole. Then the foot can fester and cause inflammation leading to a very lame horse. A stone buried this deep should only be removed by a skilled veterinarian.

Other diseases of the foot are thrush, founder and clubfoot; cracks in the hoof are also quite common. Thrush is a disease which is nurtured in the soft parts of the hoofs. It is almost always caused by unsanitary conditions in the barn or stall. Working the horse in mud and neglecting to shoe the animal properly are contributing factors. Thrush is easily identified by a discharge of dark foul-smelling pus from the center of the hoof. To treat thrush remove the unsanitary conditions, and then the diseased and loose tissue in the frog and sole should be cut away. When this is done bathe the hoof in warm salt water and apply a good disinfectant. There are also commercial preparations which will take care of this condition.

Founder is an inflammation of the sensitive sole and other parts of the internal foot. Founder can be caused by almost anything, including overeating and overexertion. It almost always involves only the front feet. Treatment is to bed the animal well with several inches of clean straw and then bathe the feet three times a day, first with warm water, changing to cold as the condition improves. Keep this up until the swelling goes down.

Clubfoot and cracks can be cured by shoeing the animal properly. Clubfoot is a condition where the animal has to carry most of its weight on the toe, the heels of the hoof being too high. Cracks are actually cracks in the hoof. They can be caused by the hoof being too brittle or by extremely dry working and living conditions. Proper shoeing to correct these conditions will be covered a little later.

Draft horses working in soft ground and kept in a grassy pasture probably will not have to be shod, but horses used for road work, in hard clay or stony fields should be. Horses are called upon to do such work sooner or later; hence it follows that shoeing is important in the care of horses.

HORSESHOEING

In my area of Southeastern Wisconsin the price for shoeing a horse ranges up to $60.00 per animal. How often a horse must be reshod depends on how and where he is used, it could be every three months. Certainly they should be reshod when the toes grow out past the shoe or when the shoes get loose or when one is lost. If you can shoe your own animals you can save money and maybe even pick up some shoeing jobs from your neighbors' horses when work on your own place is slack.

Shoeing a horse does take a few desirable tools. They may cost from $10.00 on up, depending on whether you can get them at an auction or substitute other tools in use around the home. There are, of course, people who say all tools can be substituted. However, use only horseshoe nails; these cost about $1.50 for enough to shoe several horses.

Actually shoeing the horse is simple enough, especially if you have a good relationship with the animal. If you have been lifting his hoof to clean the dirt out of it almost every day then it won't be hard to get him to lift his feet. Horseshoers traditionally start first with the right hind foot. Tie him by a halter short enough so he can't get his head over the rope. Then pet the animal and run your hands down his legs several times to get him accustomed to your hands. Then turn so that your back is to the front of the animal, place your right hand on his hip, slide your left hand down his leg, grasp the hock and pull outward. This should cause the animal to shift his weight to the other side and make it easy to lift the leg. Once the leg is off the ground hold it in your lap. Wear a heavy apron if possible. When you have the hoof in your lap with the leg of the horse extending across your hip and your legs tightly together hold the hoof in place with your left hand. Most horses will stand quietly if this is done slowly and firmly. If the horse tries to jerk his foot away make a sustained effort to hold it since once a horse jerks his foot away it can be even harder to hold it the next time. Some horses can be quieted when they try to jerk away by holding the hoof with both hands and bending the hoof up while the hock is held under the arm. If the horse is very wild it is a job for an experienced shoer using slings to hold the animal.

Once the hoof is in your lap look at the bottom, examining it closely for bruises, stones or foot diseases. A foot that is abnormally hot will almost always indicate a "bad" foot. The foot should also be cleaned well so all portions are visible.

A first step is to remove the old shoe, if the animal is so equipped. Do this by rasping off the clinch of the old horseshoe nails. The clinch is the part that is bent over and is visible outside the hoof. Once all of the nails, and make sure you have them all, are rasped off, pry the old shoe loose starting at the heel. This is properly done with the pincer. Place its jaws on either side of the shoe and press the handles together to move the jaws toward each other so they will come together between the hoof and the shoe. Keep working towards the front, pulling the nails as you go until the shoe is loose.

After the old shoe is off, the hoof can be pared. Excess hoof is the hoof that extends past the normal angle of the hoof. This is cut deep at the toe and tapering out to nothing at the heel. For the first hoof you try, it will be safer if you only cut back about one inch or less from the end and then nip it out to nothing at the heel. Carrying the inch-deep cut all the way around to the heel will result in the heel being too low. After the hoof is trimmed it should be rasped to level it. Rasp across the hoof and keep it level at all times. Never rasp any deeper upon seeing an initial showing of pink at the

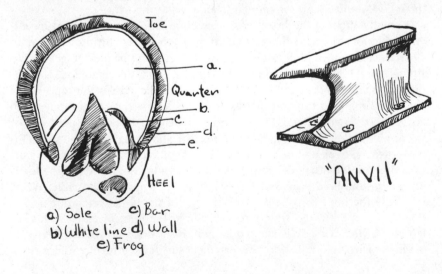

Toe

a.

Quarter

b.

c.

d.

e.

Heel

a) Sole   c) Bar
b) White line d) Wall
        e) Frog

"ANVIL"

hoof. The frog should never be cut down even if it seems to extend past the rest of the foot. If broken or rough ends are showing they can be trimmed off, however.

If it should happen that you do cut too deep the wound should be treated with an antiseptic. Also if you want to be sure you don't lose the animal the veterinarian should be called and advised of the condition.

After the hoof is rasped flat run the rasp around the edge of the foot to take off the burr at the edge.

When this is done fit the horseshoe to the horse. Always select the lightest shoe that can be used without becoming worn out in too short a time. Then proceed to custom-fit each shoe to the foot. Never, never nail a shoe on and then try to fit the foot to it.

Fit the shoe to the foot by laying it up to the foot while it is cold, noting where it has to be bent and then heating it and bending to shape, starting from the toe. With the soft shoes available today many jobs don't even need heat. Just bend the shoe cold over a forge. It might take more than one fitting to get the foot well shod. The next step after the shoe is fitted is to nail it on.

The job of nailing the shoe on a horse's foot is a process which could cause even an octopus to wish for another arm. Properly, the foot is held across the lap, a few horseshoe nails are held in the mouth and a backup supply are kept in the pants' cuff. The shoe and the first nail are held in place with the left hand. Push the nail in one of the front holes with the slanted part of the nail towards the inside of the hoof. Hold the nail forward to keep the shoe from "walking" towards the back of the foot. If this happens, start over. Actually the shoe should walk a little forward since succeeding nails will tend to pull it back. Once the first nail is in place the shoe will hold and it will be a little easier driving the rest of them in. The second nail to drive is the other front one, then work to the back. A good practice for shoeing the first horse is to mark with chalk where the nails should come out of the hoof and drive them at the right slant to be sure they do. The last two nails in the back should be bent slightly so they will emerge from the hoof sooner. They must be kept well away from the "quick." If they don't come out by the time they are halfway driven in, pull them back out and restart them, but don't drive the new nails in old holes.

Horseshoe nails are purposely made too long, so as each one or all of them have been driven through, they should be twisted off with the claws of the shoeing hammer. Just slide the nail into the claws on the hammer and twist. When they are all twisted off rasp the burr away and clinch the nail. Clinching the horseshoe nail is done by placing a metal square or the head of another hammer on the twisted-off end of the nail and flattening it with the shoeing hammer. This makes the nail bend over or even curl back on itself. When the nails are all clinched the foot should be gently put back down on the ground and the clinch tapped into the hoof wall.

The front foot is picked up by gently squeezing the tendon back of the horse's knee or cannon bone. Then catch the pastern and straddle the legs. Then proceed as for shoeing the hind foot.

Cracks in the hoof are usually very painful because tissue bulges into the cracks and then when the horse steps on his feet the crack pinches the flesh. Before such an animal is shoed the swelling should be reduced so the tissue shrinks away from the crack. Then the crack should be grooved out and a new shoe applied. This shoe should have a bar welded across the back to hold the hoof rigid until the hoof grows in to cover the split. Club foot is corrected to some extent by rasping the heel down as far as possible and setting the shoe forward as far as possible. Severe cases may require surgery of the tendon.

Books

Jones, William E., *Horseshoeing*. E. Lansing, Michigan, Caballus, 1972

Government Pamphlets

Write to The Superintendent Of Documents
Government Printing Office
Washington, D. C. 20402

Breeding and Raising Horses, Cat. No. A 1.76:394 S/N 0100-1347
$1.00
Two Stall Horse Barn, Farm Building Plan No. 6082 5¢
Portable Stable for a Horse, Farm Building Plan, Cat. No. 1.38 1188
S/N0100-1149

16

FIRST AID AND HEALTH PROBLEMS

ONE OF THE best ways to avoid doctor fees as well as prepare for emergencies if you are going to be isolated is to take a good first aid course. Contact the local chapter of the Red Cross for information.

Homesteaders are remarkably healthy as a rule but they do cut themselves, break bones, catch cold and have babies, among other things.

CONTROLLING BLEEDING

Since cuts are the most common injury, dealing with them should be general knowledge. As the first thing, the bleeding must be stopped. Almost all bleeding can be controlled by applying pressure to the wound. Nature does most of the work by causing a clot to form. Apply a bandage or cloth folded or wadded into a pad over the wound and hold it tightly for at least five minutes; this will stop almost all bleeding. Don't dab at the wound in an attempt to mop the blood away and don't keep looking at it by removing the pad.

The use of a tourniquet, though highly publicized, is seldom if ever necessary. Frequently tourniquets applied by excitable and untrained persons cause more harm than benefit. The only time one should ever use a tourniquet is for bleeding from an artery and then only if it will not respond to pressure applied directly to the wound. Bleeding from an artery is signified by blood spurting every time the heart beats, whereas bleeding from a vein is continuous. A tourniquet can be a handkerchief with the ends tied together, tightened by pushing a stick between the flesh and the handkerchief and twisting it. But a tourniquet is never necessary to control bleeding on the face or body, only on the arms, legs, hands or feet. Even bleeding from the large veins in the neck will respond if pressure is applied to them as a control measure.

Once bleeding is stopped the wound should be cleaned. This can be done by washing it out with soap and water. If it is possible to boil the water before it is used to wash the wound, do that; however, don't forget to cool it before applying it! Alcohol and all other related antiseptics should not be used for cleaning a wound since they burn and devitalize tissues. If the wound is contaminated with bits of dirt or sticks or any foreign substance, these should be carefully picked out of the wound. Frequently repeated irrigations with cool water will wash all the dirt out. If it becomes necessary to clean the wound with a tool use a pair of tweezers which has been boiled in water for about five minutes. Sometimes the bleeding will start again when the cleaning is commenced. Again it will have to be stopped by applying pressure. Be very careful that the wound is clean before proceeding to the next step of pulling the gaping sides of a cut together.

CLOSING A CUT

Most wounds or cuts will be small and they can be treated by just applying a dressing and a bandage and letting nature take its course, but large wounds must be pulled together with butterfly tape or by suturing. Butterfly tape or butterfly closures are plastic tape which is applied across the wound to pull the sides together. Active members such as a finger or any wound that will not stay closed with tape must be stitched up. It is well to realize that the stitching will cause only temporary pain. It is easier to bear the slight pain than to try to administer novocaine. Be sure to have a complete suture package or two in the first aid kit. In this package the needle and thread are already joined and all that is necessary is to break it open and start sewing.

The curved suturing needle is not handled with the fingers, instead it is manipulated with a hemostat or a scissorslike finger-operated clamp that everyone should have in his first aid kit. The needle is grasped with the hemostat, the point of the curved needle sewed under the skin on one side of the wound, across and up the other. Pull the thread through until about one inch protrudes, loop the length of cord over and tie it to the loose end with two or three knots. Snip the cord off and repeat this knot about ⅛ inch further on. The number of sutures used to close a wound are determined by the size of the wound itself and where it is located. Only use as many as you need to keep the edges of the wound together.

Wounds of the face should be sewn with the finest suture needle and

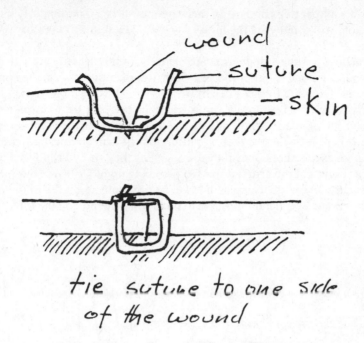

thread since they can cause scars. Do not become alarmed if a little bleeding develops from the sewing. This will cease in a short time. At least one member of an isolated family should practice suturing, maybe on a piece of raw beef or moose meat to get the "feel of it."

FRACTURES

A fracture occurring in the wilderness can be cause for concern. Fracture of the legs particularly below the knee are among the most serious since they are incapacitating and are frequently accompanied by extreme pain. Emergency treatment is usually confined to splinting the limb in place and getting to a doctor as fast as possible. A hip or thigh injury can cause loss of blood and severe shock. Discloations, while not as serious, can be very painful.

Fractures of the ankle or lower leg bone are treatable at home. Just splint the leg to keep it from moving and do not put any weight on it for six weeks. Fractures of the heel bone, if they are not multiple, will heal in six to eight weeks by keeping the patient's foot in a cast. Fractures of the toes and long foot bones also will heal when the foot is kept in a cast for six to eight weeks.

The broken arm is one of the easiest injuries to treat. If the injury occurs below the upper third of the arm the weight of the arm, particularly if it has a cast on, will usually set the injury by itself. Healing will take six to eight weeks.

Fractures of the upper arm are usually treatable only by a trained person if the bone is out of place. If it is not, then the arm can be splinted and kept immobile for six to eight weeks.

An exception on the lower arm is when the bones in the forearm are obviously out of place. The ends of the two bones (there are two in the forearm) are brought together by pulling on the arm and pushing the ends of the bones together. Once they are together they should be held in place with a splint and the arm left unused for six to eight weeks. Hand injuries are usually set by squeezing on a towel or other object placed in the palm. Another way to set hand injuries is to have someone pull on the fingers and

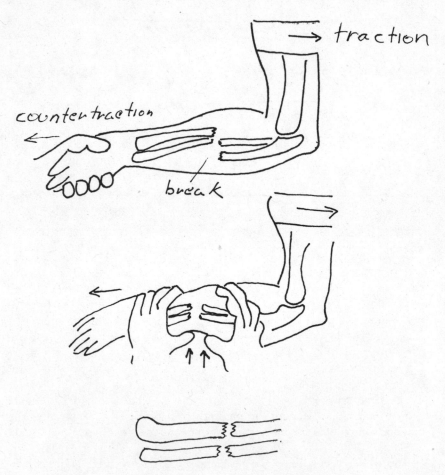

turn them to get the bones into place. A splint can be made by laying a straight smooth stick or board on each side of the fracture and tying firmly in place with several wide ties such as strips of bed sheet. This also should be practiced before an emergency develops.

Broken ribs are not serious and need not be treated unless one end of the rib has penetrated the lung. This will be signified by spitting blood or by the collapse of one lung. This injury can only be treated by a doctor.

All other fractures are treatable by pulling the bone into place and splinting it. More serious are injuries to the head. All deep head wounds or severe blows to the head should be treated as possible concussions and they should be x-rayed as soon as possible.

CHILDBIRTH

Sometimes emergencies are caused by childbirth.

The natural childbirth should be planned for early in pregnancy. The mother should not allow herself to get too fat and of course she should as always have an adequate diet consisting of the right amounts of the different foods.

There has been some interest in the La Maze method of natural childbirth lately and it consists of preparing the mother for birth and the physical acts that are to be expected and overcome. Another one is called the Read method. They have many similarities.

The following information is not meant to prepare a mother for birth, but rather as a discussion of the possibilities of having a baby by the natural method.

First the risks should be discussed. Childbirth without an attendant doctor or trained nurse always is more of a risk than if they weren't there because of the danger of breech births or the mother's excessive bleeding. Some authorities say that in the days before hospital and physician-attended births, one birth in forty resulted in death for the mother. More babies were lost also. No statistics are at hand that compute the number of brain-damaged babies because of difficult births.

However, overprotection of the mother by shooting her full of drugs has also been suspected to cause brain damage since they overrelax the baby and it may not take a breath when it is first born. Also since no birth, even one attended by a skilled obstetrician, is ever completely safe and many babies are stillborn or damaged by drugs some people say we are progressing backwards. It has definitely been proven that the fluids surrounding the baby do not protect it from substances in the mother's blood as was originally thought.

One of the most formidable barriers and the greatest cause for pain and difficult births is the very fear of having a baby. A girl having her first baby knows it is going to "hurt" and hurt it does.

The La Maze method tries to undo this fear and teaches the mother how to work with her body to help the birth instead of fighting against it. Mothers who have been working on a homestead and eating natural organic foods have a lot going for them since diet and exercise has been proven time and time again to be a major factor in health of the new baby and the mother's capacity to deal with the birth.

Generally the La Maze method goes like this. The prospective mother goes to a teacher or trainer who starts the training by teaching her how to breathe. This breathing helps supply adequate oxygen to the baby and gives the brain a countersuggestion to consider when pain comes. This affects the brain somewhat as a conditioning sound or happening.

As she is taught to breathe she is also taught the way the contractions will occur and the way a baby is conceived and grows in the mother's body. Also there is an explanation of the parts of the mother's body and how they interact with each other to bring the fetus to the final development stage and how they expel it from the birth canal.

Next there is a series of exercises consisting mostly of hip and leg movements that will keep the muscles to be used in childbirth elastic and also condition them so they won't cramp during the delivery since this could play havoc with the mother's concentration during delivery.

During the exercise and as an integral part of it the mother practices relaxation. This is not the kind of relaxation that will put her to sleep but rather the kind that causes the muscles to go limp while the brain remains very active. Mostly it consists of concentrating on a muscle until it relaxes and then tensing it and again relaxing it until the process can be done on command. Some say this is the hardest part of the course since it does take some learning. Its importance is that the mother can learn to relax her muscles when they should be relaxed.

Another very important part of the method is that the father is present at all times and he actually takes part in the birth by watching the advance of events and by informing the mother when to push and when to relax. Some say this is the most important part of the method since it allows both parents to participate in what could be the most important moment of their lives.

The mother is taught how to overcome or ignore moments of intense pain by panting very fast. As mentioned, this gives the mother something else to think about and has the bonus value that the baby receives an added supply of oxygen.

The rest of this dissertation concerns conventional childbirth regardless of whether the birth is expected by the La Maze method or whether the baby would decide to come unexpectedly when the parents are far away from help.

If labor pains or contraction develop, carefully time them. The first contractions are about 15 to 20 minutes apart; the more frequent the pains the sooner the birth.

Since there is no way to predict changes in the frequency of pains it might be well to treat any birth as imminent upon the onset of contractions.

The exception could be the first birth for a mother. First children are very seldom emergency births; however, it still could take place within a few hours of the onset of contractions. Have the mother lie down. Supply her with water but a minimum of food is advisable because of the danger of vomiting. As the contractions get closer together, check the vagina for evidence of crowning or bulging. When this occurs birth is imminent. If towels or other coverings are available cover the thighs and abdomen and place a triple thickness of toweling under the hips. Now wait for the appearance of the baby. Tell the mother not to push but to breathe deeply through her mouth and rest between contractions.

The helper then watches for the baby's head to appear. At this stage he should very gently push against the head so that it doesn't suddenly explode from the opening. When the head is clear the attendant should look for the umbilical cord to see if it is wrapped around the baby's neck. If it is, try to gently slip the cord up over the baby's shoulder so that it doesn't strangle him. If it cannot be slipped over his head it will have to be tied off and cut at this time. Do this by tying the cord very tightly in two places two inches apart and then cutting the cord between them. Since this cord will eventually be expelled along with the placenta or afterbirth, that is all that is necessary. The head of the baby emerges with the face down and then it rotates either to the left or right side just before the shoulder is delivered. The upper shoulder is usually born first. If the shoulder appears to have difficulty coming through it can be helped by gently moving the baby's head towards the floor. Remember be very gentle. It is better to do nothing than to use too much force. Similarly, the lower shoulder can be helped out by lifting gently on the head. When the head and shoulders are out the baby should be supported with the hands while the rest of its body is emerging. This is usually very sudden. When the baby is completely out lay it on its side with the head lower than the body. This will allow the mucus and blood to drain out of his nose and mouth. Then take a rubber suction bulb and gently suck the blood and mucus from the baby's nostrils and mouth.

By this time the baby should be breathing spontaneously. If it is not, stimulate it by slapping an index finger against the soles of its feet. If it does not respond to this try mouth to mouth resuscitation. Be very gentle with this but continue it for 15 to 20 minutes before giving up. Sometimes there will be no pulse and sometimes the heart can be stimulated to beat by pushing on the sternum with the index finger. Continue resuscitation and sternum stimulation for 20 minutes before it is abandoned.

Sometimes the "bag of water" will not break and the baby will be born still enclosed in it. Break this bag and carefully remove it from the baby so that it can breathe.

If the umbilical cord has not been cut before be sure to cut the cord now. This is done by tying the cord off in two places with the nearest knot at least two inches away from the baby and then cutting the cord between them. If the cord should become torn without being tied off the baby can bleed to death.

After the baby's airways are cleared and the cord tied off it should be wrapped in a blanket and given to the mother if she desires to hold it. The chief advantage of this is that the baby will nurse immediately and this will stimulate the expulsion of the placenta.

When the afterbirth has been expelled the birth is over and the mother can be fitted with a sanitary napkin and given food or drink as desired. Complicated births, however, are a more serious problem.

One of the most common problems at birth is the breech baby. This means instead of the baby coming head first it is reversed and the buttocks of the baby will be presented first. Physicians watch for signs of this during prenatal care and prevent the problem in many cases by turning the baby around well before time of expected birth. As long as the birth proceeds otherwise as normal there is no complication, even with a breech birth; however, the legs and trunk should be supported as they emerge by placing the palm under the baby's trunk. Usually the head will slip out within three minutes. If it does not you must help since the umbilical cord is compressed by the baby's head and it isn't getting any oxygen.

Helping the baby to breathe when the head is "caught" is necessary to keep it from suffocating. Do this by inserting fingers into the vagina and holding it away from the baby's face so that it can start breathing. Do not pull on the baby but restrain it so that it doesn't pop out. Chances are it will start to slide very soon and the head will slip out.

Occasionally the umbilical cord will be delivered before the baby. This is called a prolapsed cord and it will suffocate the baby, especially if the baby is entrancing, since this will collapse the cord. The only thing to do here is push the baby away from the entrance between contractions and get to a doctor or trained person as fast as possible.

Very, very seldom, but it does sometimes happen, a baby tries to be born with an arm or a leg first. This is called limb presentation and it is one of the most serious problems in childbirth. If trained help is available by all means seek it. If it is not the only chance the baby has is for an attendant to try to straighten it out by turning it in the birth canal. This will have to be done by inserting the hands into the vagina and very gently and very slowly turning it so the head is down. All you can do is try.

Another complication can be bleeding after expelling the placenta. This is usually caused by a small piece still being retained in the vagina. The usual amount of blood loss is about three to five soaked pads. More than that should be suspect and the mother should be taken to a trained person as expeditiously as possible.

After the baby is born silver nitrate drops should be put in the eyes, if possible.

Certainly having a baby is a highly personal event and the mother should be able to choose where and how she will have it. If she decides the usual hospital route is her bag then so be it, but no one should frighten her into using this method when perfectly sane alternatives are available. Many people have babies at home attended perhaps by only the husband or a midwife and everything is all right.

Visiting a doctor during the pregnancy is certainly advisable though and this can be done without charge by going to a clinic which specializes in such care. The address of the one nearest you can be procured by contacting a hospital and asking for the address of the nearest free clinic. Also some doctors will accept "payment later" on examination.

The doctor should be able to tell at the examination whether the physical health of the mother and fetus are normal and whether anything will affect the birth such as an abnormally small pelvic opening. Naturally this wouldn't apply to any but a first birth. Many people are using the La Maze method of birthing these days and others are using the short hospital stay route—in and out the same day. With these days of crowded hospitals, harried doctors and overcrowding of medical facilities many doctors would probably welcome a short visit situation.

A prospective mother can more readily make up her mind about what sort of situation she would relate to by contacting the American Society For Psychoprophylaxis In Obstetrics, whose address is 36 West 96th Street, New York, New York 10025. They have local offices all over the nation.

TOOTH PROBLEMS

Occasionally even though the homesteader is eating whole grain foods and drinking his quota of goat milk he is going to find himself faced with a tooth problem. Probably the only emergency is breaking a tooth, or teeth, from a fall or a blow to the mouth. These can be so painful as to cause the patient to go into shock. The emergency treatment is to apply oil of cloves directly to the tooth with a cotton swab. Usually such teeth mean a trip to the dentist whenever it can be arranged.

Sometimes a filling will be lost and the tooth will start to pain or ache. The filling can be replaced by mixing zinc oxide and Eugenal together and packing it into the cavity.

Infected teeth which cause the classical swollen jaw are potentially dangerous since they can allow infection to get into the circulatory system. The treatment is to apply either moist heat or cold, whichever relieves the pain. Take an antibiotic if possible until cured, and/or have the tooth extracted as soon as possible.

Gingivitis, meaning inflamed gums caused by improper brushing of the teeth, will be cured by taking an antibiotic for three or four days until the inflammation subsides and then resume brushing the teeth three or four times a day. Rinse the mouth with warm salt water or peroxide.

EYE PROBLEMS

Care of the eyes is important to the homesteader since he probably needs his eyes more than most. The usual source of eye irritation is some foreign body entering it. This can be from smoke, wind, water or even dust or a tiny splinter from chopping wood. Usually the foreign body will be found under the upper lid or on the cornea. Most foreign bodies can be found by putting the patient in a good light and examining the upper and lower lid by folding it over a match stick. When the speck is seen, flick it out with the corner of a handkerchief or a cotton-tipped applicator. Sometimes if the object can't be seen it can be washed out or into view by putting the eye in a pan of water and blinking the eye rapidly. If the object can be seen but will not flick out, it is embedded in the cornea. This is not always a serious problem but it does take some knowledge of how to deal with it.

First have the patient lie down on his back. Use an anesthetic in the lower lid and wait five minutes. Then take a sterile pointed instrument such as a scalpel and use the point of it to flick the object out. Needless to say the tip of the scalpel is never pointed down towards the eyeball and likewise this should never be attempted by someone who has hand tremors, who is overtired or nervous.

Conjunctivitis is an eye affliction resulting from infection or irritation. The symptoms are like a foreign body in the eye; indeed a foreign body that has been in the eye will often cause the infection. The treatment is to place three Spectrocin Ophthalmic Ointment drops on the infected eye inside the lower lid. Continue this treatment for three to five days until the eye gets back to normal. Also use a Darvon Compound tablet to combat the pain and nervous reaction.

When treating this or any eye infection carefully observe the pupil. If it is steamy, irregular or red seek professional help immediately. Likewise if an accident should occur in which the eyeball is protruded or otherwise damaged, trained help should be utilized. First aid is to cover the injured eye with the bottom of a paper cup or some object to hold the bandage away from the eyeball and then tape it loosely. Both eyes should be covered so that they don't move.

Sties are familiar to everyone and they need no special treatment since they are generally a pimple under the eyelid which will soon disappear. Only if they keep reoccurring should professional help be sought.

Snowblindness and sunburned eyes such as could be caused by gazing at an eclipse of the sun will usually heal themselves in a few days. All that is necessary is to keep the patient in a dark place until healing is advanced. Relief from discomfort can be obtained by taking aspirin or Darvon. Cold compresses also are beneficial.

USEFUL HERBS

Ever notice that the longer a doctor practices medicine and the more skilled and learned he becomes the less he relies on drugs and chemicals? Ever consider how "primitive people" such as the American Indian without any medical knowledge at all but with a fine regard for the use of plants could heal most of their sick, especially before the advent of white man's diseases?

Come to the same conclusion that I do? The body will try to heal itself or will very seldom get sick if given proper foods, clean air and plenty of exercise. Usually the marvelous organism that our body is will only start to succumb when poisoned by food chemicals, seared by cigaret smoke, polluted air and disoriented by alcohol and narcotics. Thus folks who live on a homestead and who depend on sunsets for their highs, wood chopping for their tranquilizers and natural food for their medicine are living about as healthfully as possible. Which is what most of us knew all the time, right?

Of course from time to time ailments assail even people living close to nature. Fortunately most can be treated by the correct use of a few plants commonly known as herbs. The following is a list of a few common problems and the herb which we treat them with.

1. Colds, flu, mild pneumonia, inflamed lungs.

   Balm Of Gilead (Populus balsamifera). Steep buds in oil and rub on the chest. Add a teaspoonful of bud and oil infusion to a glass of hot water and drink three times a day or more.

Cayenne (Capsicum annuum). Purchase capsules from drug store; take as directed.

Chickweed (Stellaria media). Steep the green leaves in hot water, drink small amounts twice a day.

Rose Hips (Rosa rugosa) (Rosa multiflora) or any native rose. Eat the fresh, dry or powdered hips. Eat all you want, the more the better. Contains massive amounts of Vitamin C. Continue until condition improves. Eat to prevent colds also.

Elderberry (Sambucus). Eat the berries or blossoms. Make tea from the blossoms and peppermint leaves and take at bedtime.

Chestnut (Castania). Make tea from green or dried leaves. Combine with blue cohosh and lobelia for whooping cough.

Golden Seal (Hydrastis canadensis). Make an infusion of powdered root, hot water and honey. Take small amounts three times a day.

Bone Set (Eupatorium perfoliatium). Make a tea, drink small amounts often.

2. Bruises, skin infections, small cuts, burns.

All of the mentioned plants are used by making a poultice of hot water and the green leaves. Apply directly to the wound.

Cleavers (Galium aparine)
Comfrey (Symphtyum officinale)
Shepherd's Purse (Capsella bursa pastoris)
Violet (Clematis virginica)
Yarrow (Achillea millefolium)
Willow (Salix alba)
Aloes (Aloes vera)

Use blossoms of these plants:

Elderberry, violet, vervain *(Verbena hasta)*

As a longtime blood conditioner take fresh green leaves of alfalfa at least three times a week. Drink alfalfa tea also. Heals bruises, promotes blood clotting. Steep burdock root and make into a salve and apply to the wound.

3. Upset stomach.

Aloes (Aloes vera). Chew small pieces of leaves as often as desired.

Colombo (Cocculus palmatus). Chew small pieces of root, make tea, drink warm.

Peppermint (Mentha piperita). Steep whole plant, drink tea.

Spearmint (Mentha viridis). Same as peppermint.

Sweet Flag (Calamus). Chew green or dried root.

Wintergreen (Gaultheria procumbens). Eat leaves, berries. Steep leaves in lukewarm water, drink tea.

The use of herbs for home remedies is a very ancient practice and a much written about subject. Many good books are available which will help a homesteader develop his own home medicines from the plants in his locality. The list at the end of this chapter will aid in finding more information.

The following publications are available through the American Society For Psychoprophylaxis, 36 West 96th Street, New York, New York 10025:
ABC's Of Natural Childbirth
Awake and Aware
Childbirth Without Fear
Husband-Coached Childbirth
Nursing Your Baby
Understand Natural Childbirth
Thank You, Dr. La Maze

Books

Bolton, William *What To Do Until The Doctor Comes.* Chicago, Reilly And Lee, 1971
Kodet, E. Russel and Angier, Bradford *Being Your Own Wilderness Doctor.* Harrisburg, Pennsylvania. Stackpole, 1968
Bethel, May *The Healing Power of Herbs.* N. Hollywood, California, Wilshire, 1971
Gibbons, Euell *Stalking The Healthful Herbs.* New York, McKay, 1970
Doole, Louise Evans *Herbs For Health.* Alhambra, California, Borden, 1971

Suppliers, Herbs

Indiana Botanic Gardens, Inc.
Hammond, Indiana 46325

Northwestern Processing Company
217 North Broadway
Milwaukee, Wisconsin 53202

Dominion Herb Distributor, Inc.
61 St. Catherine Street West
Montreal 129, Quebec, Canada

17

BIG BROTHER WILL HELP

THE FEDERAL GOVERNMENT has so many programs to help the homesteader in his search for land, housing and food that it would require a considerable text just to list them. However, in searching for information one must contact the right agency in the right way and exercise patience.

One of the first agencies with which to interact would be the Superintendent Of Documents. This is the sales agency for the Government Printing Office, which prints and stores most all the publications of the government. Somewhere in their facilities is stored almost all of the knowledge of man! A person desiring information on almost any subject can write to the Superintendent of Documents and ask for their list of available publications dealing with a topic of interest. The address is:

Superintendent Of Documents
U. S. Government Printing Office
Washington, D. C. 20402

The Superintendent of Documents also maintains book stores in many large cities, which should expedite service. If you happen to live near one check the phone books for the address.

Another information agency of particular interest to the homesteader is The National Agricultural Library. This agency has a collection of over 1,212,000 volumes on subjects related to agriculture. It contains books, journals, current periodical reports, films, photos, maps and charts. They will also answer specific questions. Write:

U. S. Department Of Agriculture
National Agricultural Library
Room 1052, South Building
14th St. and Independence Avenue, SW
Washington, D. C. 20251
or
Program Coordination Service
National Agricultural Library
Beltsville, Maryland 20705

Also don't forget every state has an agricultural department which may be able to zero in on your specific question faster than the Federal Government. Maybe the first step is to give the local county agent a try. If he isn't any better than some it is almost a waste of time, but who knows, you may have a good one.

If you have a crop failure don't forget the Food Stamp Program, which is designed specifically to help the needy ones with their food budget. This program is a way to increase the buying power of your food dollar. Food stamps can be purchased from your local county office of General Assistance. If you don't have money for food stamps call at the county office of General Assistance. They will assign a caseworker to your problem who, hopefully, will fill out the necessary forms to make you eligible for surplus food. Once you become eligible you have a few million tons of good food to eat your way through. If you can.

For more information write to:

Food Stamp Division
Consumer And Marketing Service
U. S. Department Of Agriculture
Washington, D. C. 20250

One very benevolent government association that every homesteader should be familiar with is the Farmers Home Administration. This agency will lend money for a farm, livestock, equipment, feed, seed, fertilizer, fish farming and campgrounds. The Farmers Home Administration has offices in most county seat towns. If yours doesn't, write to—

Farmers Home Administration Office
U. S. Department of Agriculture
Washington, D. C. 20250

Don't forget the Manpower Training Act of 1962 when you are living on the homestead. This act makes a farmer with less than $1200.00 net income eligible for free schooling plus mileage and living expenses if he must travel to get to the school. Your local State Employment Service would be familiar with the programs in your area.

Should you wish to start a cottage industry and need capital for a lathe or almost any other equipment don't forget the Small Business Administration. Their reason for existence is starting and promoting small businesses. Make sure you ask for at least a $1000.00 loan since they won't lend smaller amounts. Write—

>   Opportunity Loans P.A. 663
>   Small Business Administration
>   1441 L St. N. W.
>   Washington, D. C. 20416

If you need capital for fixing up an old farmhouse or for putting up a conventional building contact the Federal Housing Administration.

>   Federal Housing Administration
>   451 7th St. S. W.
>   Washington, D. C. 20411

They also have funds for building unconventional buildings and this might cover the solar-heated house or dome you want to build.

Some booklets issued by the Farmers Home Administration are Rural Housing Loans P.A. 476, and Self Help Housing For Low Income Rural Families P.A. 822.

When it is time to build a fish pond, a campground or develop a mineral deposit or tree farm write:

>   U. S. Forest Service
>   U. S. Department of Agriculture
>   Washington, D. C. 20250

Ask for booklets: Forests In Rural Areas P.A. 494, Public Forestry Assistance For Small Woodlands P.A. 401, Loans for Recreation P.A. 723.

Bureau Of Land Management and Geological Survey Offices are listed under Chapter 1.

In addition to its many other programs relating to commercial farming the United States Department Of Agriculture sponsors assistance for developing the wildlife resources on your land. They will make machinery, shrubs and seed available and in some cases supply funds for workmen's wages.

U. S. Forest Service
U. S. Department of Agriculture
Washington, D. C. 20250

If no agency or booklet listed in his chapter will deal with your problem go to any library and ask to see the "Catalog Of Domestic Assistance." The catalog charts almost every program the Federal Government conducts to help low income families.

INDEX

A

Adobe house, 59, 60, 61
Aerating fish ponds, 155
Axes, 29-30

B

Bee trees, 102-103, 151
Beef skinning, 135
Beef tongue, 136
Berries, 110,151
Bleeding, 205, 207
Breeds of horses, 195
Bridging, 37
Bridle, 197
Butchering beef, 134, 136
Butchering equipment, 130
Butchering game animals, 137, 139
Butchering goats, 137
Butchering hogs, 130, 134
Butchering poultry, 140
Butchering rabbits, 139
Butchering sheep, 136-137
Butter making, 192-193

C

Canning, 160, 163
Carders, 172
Carding fleece, 172
Catalog Of Domestic Assistance, 221
Cattail plants, 145, 150
Ceilings, 43
Chicken feeding, 127
Chicken purchasing, 127
Chickens, 126-127
Chicory, 144
Childbirth, 209-213
Chinking, 55
Cistern, 69

Clothing to capture a swarm of bees, 101
Compost, 89
Compost making, 89-90
Conjunctivitis, 214
Cooling fresh meat, 134
Cow. 123-124
Cow breeds, 123
Cow feeding, 123-124
Cow milking, 124
Cracks in the basement, 36
Cranberries, 151
Crayfish, 149

D

Dandelion, 144
Dandelion roots, 144
Digging tools, 34
Drinking water, 18
Drywall, 44
Ducks and geese, 127
Duck eggs, 127

E

Earthworm, 91
Eye problems 214-215

F

Farmers Home Administration, 219
Federal Housing Administration, 220
Feed costs for a cow, 123
Fertilizing the indoor garden, 99
Files, 34
Fixing up an old house, 35
Flat roof repairing, 43
Fleece cleaning, 170

Flies, 124
Floor, 43, 45, 55-56, 59, 61
Flower pot farming, 95
Food Stamp Division, 219
Forage, 34
Foundations
  adobe cabin, 61
  frame buildings, 35-37
  log cabin, 51
  stone cabin, 56
Founder, 200
Fractures, 207-209
Free-for-the-taking-foods, 141
Furring strips, 46

G

Garden seeds, 87-88
Getting your goat, 114-115
Girder, 37
Goat feeding, 115
Goat kidding, 115
Goat meat, 116, 137
Goat prices, 114
Goat shelter, 116
Goat udder, 114
Goats, 113-116
Green box construction, 95-97
Guernsey, Jersey, Aryshire, 123

H

Hammer, ball peen, 27
Hammer, carpenter, 26
Hammer, handle, 26-27
Hand grain mill, 151
Hand injuries, 209
Harnessing the draft horse, 196-199
Heat periods, rabbits, 121
Heat vaporization, 46
Herbs, useful, 214-217
Hog scalding, 126, 132
Homemade breakfast food, 193
Homesteading Act, 11-12
Hole boring tools, 32
Honey and beekeeping, 101-107
Hoof cracks, 204
Hoof paring, 202
Horse collar, 196
Horses, care of, 195
Horses' foot ailments, 200-201
Horseshoeing, 201-204
Horseshoe nail, 203
Horseshoe tools, 201
House jacks, 36

I

Ice chisel, 142
Ice fishing, 142
Ice house, 166, 168
Indoor garden soil, 97-98
Indoor garden without electricity, 100
Insect control, 91-93
Insulation, 46

J

Joists, 37

K

Knitting, 181-183

L

Lady Beetle, 92
Lamp wick watering, 98
Land in Alaska, 23
Land auctions, 12
Land in Canada, 18-19
Land in Canada, where to find, 23-24
Land contracts, 20
Land, Federal, 11-13
Land, Federal, where to find, 22
Land financing, Federal government, 20-21, 25
Land in Hawaii, 17
Land in Hawaii, where to find, 24
Land, mortgages and loans, 19-20
Land, private, 13-16
Land, public domain, 11-12
Land, small tracts, 13
Land value, each state, 21-22
Lard and tallow, 188, 190
Leaf lard, 134
Light needed for indoor plants, 100
Locating a garden, 83-86
Log cabin, 56, 58
Logs, kinds of, 48-49
Logs, notching, 51, 53
Logs, pinning and spiking, 53
Logs, splicing, 53
Longstroth hive, 105
Lye making, 187-188

M

Maple syrup, 107-110, 143
Maple syrup and sugar, 107-110
Mayapples, 151
Milkweed, 146
Mini-garden lighting, 97
Mint, 149
Mulching and weed control, 90-91

N

National Agricultural Library, 218-219
National Climatic Center, 25
Navajo loom, 178-181

O

Opportunity loans, 220
Organic gardening, 83-94

P

Paper mache, 44
Paradise, Hawaii, 17
Pickling
　fish, 169
　meats, 166
　vegetables, 160
Pig feeding, 125
Pig housing, 125-126
Pigs, 125-126
Plant food, 88
Planting, 87-89
Pliers, 33
Plowing with team and walking plow, 199
Plumbing, 45-46
Poles for a tepee, 63
Poles to make a roof, 51, 54-55
Pollinating the indoor plants, 100
Purslane, 147

R

Rabbit bedding, 120
Rabbit breeds, 118
Rabbit diseases, 123
Rabbit feeding, 120-121
Rabbit hunting, 142
Rabbit hutches, 120
Rabbit meat, 123
Rabbits, 118-123
Rabbits, kindling, 122-123
Rainfall, 69
Rainwater, 69-70
Roofing, 42, 54

S

Salt fish, 169
Salt pork, 134
Saws, 27
　crosscut, 28
　reset, 30
　rip, 29
　sharpening, 29
　wood, 28
Screwdrivers, 32-33
Seed flats, 99
Selecting lard and tallow, 188, 190
Sheep feeding, 124
Siding, 46
Silt loam, 97
Smelt, 145
Soap making, 190-192
Sod house, 58-59
Soil judging, 83-84
Soil testing, 85, 99
Sorghum molasses, 110
Sourdough, 193
Sour sap, 108
Spinning, 173-177
Splitting the carcass, 133, 135
Spring water, 70
Sprouting, 152
Sprouting seeds for chickens, 127
Sprouting wild seeds, 152
Squares, 33

Staking goats, 115
Starting and transplanting plants, 98-99
Starting seeds, 100
Stick shuttle, 181
Stone cabin, 56, 58
Subflooring, 43
Sucker, 145
Superintendent Of Documents, 218
Sweets from fruits and berries, 107-110

T

Tepee, 63, 67, 68
Tepee, liner, 67
Tepee, sewing, 63
Thrush, 200
Tilling a garden, 86-87
Tips from experience, 194
Tooth problems, 213-214
Tourniquet, 205
Traces, 199
Transplanting, 98
Turtles, 149

U

Udder attachment, 115
U.S. Forest Service, 220

V

Vegetable storage, 156-157
　cellar storage, 159-160
　storage bin, 157-159

W

Wallpapers, 44
Waste disposal, 77-81
Waste disposal booklets, 82
Watercress, 146
Water purification, 70
Weather, 13, 25
Wells, 71-77
Wells, cleaning, 77
Wells, digging, 72-75
Wells, geology, 72
Wells, point, 74
　cleaning, 76
　pulling, 75
What to plant in the garden, 93-94
Whip-sawn lumber, 55
Wild onions, 145
Wild strawberry, 147
Windows and doors, 40-42, 55
Wiring, 44
Wool dyeing, 177-178

Y

Yogurt, 193
Your own fish pond, 153-155